Letting Go of the Status Quo

A Playbook for Transforming State Government

William D. Eggers
Robert N. Campbell III
Tiffany Dovey Fishman

Foreword by Governors Tom Ridge and Thomas R. Carper

Deloitte.

About the Deloitte Public Leadership Institute

The Deloitte Public Leadership Institute, a part of Deloitte Touche Tohmatsu's (DTT) public sector industry group, identifies, analyzes and explains the major issues facing governments today. The focus of the Institute is to help public leaders tackle their most complex policy and management challenges. Through the Institute, Deloitte member firms deliver cutting edge thought leadership, innovative solutions to issues facing governments and strategic policy development. With offices in Washington, DC, London, Ottawa and Sydney, the Institute delivers practical insights governments can use to improve their operations and deliver better value to their citizens. The Institute realizes these objectives through four major programs:

Thought leadership. In conjunction with Deloitte Research, a part of Deloitte Services LP in the United States, Institute staff and Fellows produce provocative books, studies and commentaries on the most pressing issues facing public leaders.

Public leaders dialogues. The Institute regularly brings together distinguished current and former senior public officials, management experts and academics to discuss topical issues and share best practices.

Benchmarking. The Institute regularly surveys government executives to better understand the magnitude of 21st century challenges across government agencies. Survey data are then used to develop a clearer picture of the areas of greatest weakness and to help discern best practices that can be more widely disseminated.

Academic partnerships. The Institute works closely with the world's leading graduate schools of public policy and administration to co-sponsor forums and co-produce books and studies.

Letting Go of the Status Quo: A Playbook for Transforming State Government

William D. Eggers
Robert N. Campbell III
Tiffany Dovey Fishman

Foreword by Governors Tom Ridge and Thomas R. Carper

ISBN 0-9790611-2-1

ISBN 13 978-0-9790611-2-7

About Deloitte Research

Deloitte Research, a part of Deloitte Services LP, identifies, analyzes, and explains the major issues driving today's business dynamics and shaping tomorrow's global marketplace. From provocative points of view about strategy and organizational change to straight talk about economics, regulation and technology, Deloitte Research delivers innovative, practical insights companies can use to improve their bottom-line performance. Operating through a network of dedicated research professionals, senior consulting practitioners of the various member firms of Deloitte Touche Tohmatsu, academics and technology specialists, Deloitte Research exhibits deep industry knowledge, functional understanding, and commitment to thought leadership. In boardrooms and business journals, Deloitte Research is known for bringing new perspective to real-world concerns.

About Deloitte

Deloitte refers to one or more of Deloitte Touche Tohmatsu Limited, a UK private company limited by guarantee, and its network of member firms, each of which is a legally separate and independent entity. Please see www.deloitte.com/about for a detailed description of the legal structure of Deloitte Touche Tohmatsu Limited and its member firms. Please see www.deloitte.com/us/about for a detailed description of the legal structure of Deloitte LLP and its subsidiaries.

Deloitte.

Member of Deloitte Touche Tohmatsu Limited

Printed by Printcrafters, Winnipeg, MB, Canada

Contents

PART VII: OVERHAULING STATE OPERATIONS

PART V: GETTING IT DONE

APPENDIX

Foreword

~ by Governors Tom Ridge and Thomas R. Carper

Governors hold the best political jobs in the nation. State leaders today wield unrivaled potential for improving Americans' lives and implementing positive change. Perhaps uniquely to U.S. politics, your state programs directly impact huge segments of society — and in many cases, they shape national policies. You enjoy wide latitude to innovate and have enough influence over state operations to translate your ideas into reality.

The 2010 elections produced one of the largest classes of new governors ever. Voters have placed immense responsibility in your hands. Your constituents are looking for leaders who will make tough choices, but who also have an eye on the long-term decisions that will affect them, their children and their grandchildren. It's a great opportunity to demonstrate leadership in tough times. It's easy to cut ribbons; there's no challenge there. Much harder is dealing with a fiscal crisis and applying proven business principles — examining every program and making sure that from this time forward, people don't think just because a calendar flips you're entitled to another five, six, seven percent increase.

Letting Go of the Status Quo: A Playbook for Transforming State Government delivers insights into solving some of the most vexing challenges facing new governors and other state government leaders, including issues that already top your own to-do lists. Now's the time to look at innovative public-private financing models. Now's the time to look at legacy pension costs and transform the way you provide them. Think anew, act anew, imbed technology, and try to figure out different ways to achieve desirable outcomes.

Letting Go of the Status Quo focuses on both the immediate and practical, while also delving more deeply into medium- and long-term issues that state leaders must grapple with. The book is filled with useful advice for how to tackle day one issues from the state fiscal crisis to health care reform. It then goes a step further to lay out some new approaches for renewing prosperity after the recent global economic meltdown. You'll find innovative approaches for jump-starting your economies and setting your state on a path of sustained economic growth. The Playbook's final chapter is packed with solid advice on how to convert your big policy ideas into great successes.

For newly elected state officials, the book offers advice that can help your administration get off to a quick and effective start. *Letting Go of the Status Quo* will help you to face head-on the challenges of state governance — which soon will be landing on your desk at an overwhelming and intimidating pace. For those returning to office, these pages contain fresh ideas for implementing reforms that deliver lasting improvement. There is no simple recipe for transformation. We recommend that you consider the concepts presented here and apply them in ways that fit the unique requirements of your state.

Our nation is starved for problem solvers. Citizens are ready for leadership. They know the problems are complex. They know the solutions are not easy.

Today's state policymakers will take office during one of the worst state fiscal crises in decades. While there are some signs that state revenues are beginning to rebound, states are nevertheless on an unsustainable long-term fiscal path. Both in Washington, DC and state capitals, fundamental structural issues facing the states must be reckoned with. This also makes it a good time for change, a good time for state leaders to bring their governments into the 21st century.

As you go about transforming state government, we urge you to make a real — not just a perceived — effort to find common ground with the other side of the aisle to get things done.

All of you — governors, cabinet secretaries, senior staff members and state legislators — face awesome responsibility, and yet you also have unlimited opportunity. It's all part of what makes your jobs among the most challenging and rewarding positions anywhere on Earth. Clearly, implementing meaningful changes carries significant risk, and it demands courage. Be confident. Think big. Much of this nation's history was written by state leaders. Now, this opportunity is yours.

The Honorable Tom Ridge
Independent Senior Advisor
Deloitte LLP
First Secretary of the U.S. Department of Homeland Security
Former Governor of Pennsylvania

The Honorable Thomas R. Carper
United States Senator
Former Governor of Delaware
Former Chairman of The National Governors Association

Introduction

The November elections signaled a widespread frustration with the status quo. With high unemployment and deep economic uncertainty for a backdrop, voters sent a crystal clear message. Focus on the basics, especially jobs and economic prosperity. Keep your promises. Citizens want government to be smaller, more modest in its ambitions and more competent in its implementation.

To accomplish all this, the voters have placed a group of newcomers in charge of state government. A majority of the states are seeing new governors take office — the largest freshman class since 1936. Moreover, twenty legislative bodies will change hands. Most of the new governors and legislators, regardless of party, campaigned on pledges to reduce costs, make government more efficient and effective, boost economic vitality and uproot the status quo. These were stirring promises, and governors — and their legislative partners — can position their states to thrive in the years ahead, but only if they can deliver on these promises.

To achieve their goals, these new governors — and those who kept their seat in the corner office — will have to pursue five broad avenues of change. The first, starting from day one, is to cut costs, reshape expectations for state services, and rebuild public faith in their abilities. The second is to generate jobs now and lay the groundwork for deep improvements in state competitiveness. Third is to transform two policy areas that weigh heavily on state budgets: health care and human services. Fourth — the one that will make all the others possible — is to plunge deep into state government operations and make them more innovative, more technologically proficient and more attuned to emerging needs. Lastly, part V outlines how to effectively execute a bold state government reform program.

I – WHERE TO START ON DAY ONE: CUT COSTS, RESTORE TRUST

Reduce the cost, size and scope of government

Governors face a cumulative state fiscal gap that the Center on Budget and Policy Priorities forecasts could reach $125 billion by the end of FY 2011.[1] Making matters worse, the federal government is no longer in a position to help through bailouts; the economy remains uncertain; programs, staff and benefits have already been cut; rainy day funds are depleted; and polls find voters opposed to tax increases.

Governors and other policymakers have no choice but to rip up the old fiscal playbook. The tricks of the past — borrowing against anticipated revenues or underfunding pensions — have run into the brick wall of reality.

For most governors, no issue will be more important in the near future than cutting costs and streamlining state government to live within its means. Some have already begun. In Indiana,

> "You need to build a culture that challenges each and every need to do this or not. You have to try to convert thousands thing to do."
>
> ~ MITCH DANIELS, GOVERNOR OF INDIANA

Governor Mitch Daniels has been reining in spending since he took over in 2005, forcing agencies and local governments to look far more carefully at what they do and how they do it. State newsletters settled for black-and-white printing; unused state cars were decommissioned; costs associated with administration and buildings were controlled. Pushing cost control measures gave the state a healthy $1.3 billion surplus before the recession hit. Daniels says more cost reductions are needed given the fiscal outlook ahead.[2]

In Michigan, Governor Jennifer Granholm has cut the number of state departments by a quarter, eliminated nearly 300 state boards and commissions, and consolidated the state's 10 public finance authorities into a single entity.

New Jersey's Chris Christie's first budget was $3 billion smaller than the previous year's. In September 2010, this "take-no-prisoners" governor called for major reforms to the state pension system, including raising the retirement age, changing the formula for pensions, requiring state workers to contribute 30 percent of their health care premiums and increasing their co-pays.

Big moves like these will need to become the norm, not the exception. This will require honesty about the true condition of state finances, a rigorous process of setting the state's priorities and a politically realistic approach to winding down unsustainable state activities.

Controlling costs won't be easy. With rare exceptions, states have struggled to assess their roles, tie programs to outcomes and appraise those outcomes based on the funding they require. Yet, reining in costs will require governors and their staffs to define appropriate services, measure their value and keep only those programs that deliver real public value.

While controlling spending will bolster the financial outlook, this process can also help incoming administrations advance one of their most pressing tasks: regaining public confidence.

Rebuild public trust

In October 2010, The Pew Center on the States and the Public Policy Institute of California issued a joint report on polls in five states delving into residents' views on fiscal conditions and trust in government. In three of the states — California, Illinois and New York — less than 20 percent of respondents trusted their state governments. In Florida and Arizona, the figure was higher, though hardly reassuring, coming in at about one-third.[3] "Across all five states," the report noted, "two-thirds or more of respondents report that they either never trust state government to do what is right, or trust it only some of the time. Residents overwhelmingly believe their state should pursue major reforms to their budget processes, and pursue them now."[4]

No issue captures this challenge more dramatically or with greater symbolic importance than reforming state retirement benefits. As the Pew

xpenditure and thinks critically about whether we really f people into thinking this way and believing it's the right

Center on the States points out, over half the states had fully funded pension systems in 2000; by 2008, the number had fallen to only four. Countless stories over the past year bemoan public pension arrangements that seem outlandishly generous to many voters. Tackling the issue will be vital to new governors — not just because a tide of red ink threatens to drown them, but because there is no better way to demonstrate the state's intention to set its fiscal house in order.

For states trying to rebuild public trust, methods will matter as much as results. Leading governments are recognizing that they need to fundamentally change the way they relate to citizens. A series of early initiatives, such as the Texas Comptroller's financial transparency site, is making public data available to the masses in an effort to foster collaboration with citizens, businesses, nonprofits and others. For state governments, a culture of collaboration and transparency between governments and citizens offers the chance to navigate tangled fiscal issues and make government smarter, more innovative, more responsive — and more trusted.

Transparency will be essential to building trust. But governments will have to go beyond simply opening their data vaults and actually make that information useful. That's what Washington, DC did with its "Apps for Democracy" program. The city spent $50,000 to generate $2.3 million worth of citizen-generated applications using government data, including a biking guide; a historic tours mashup; and a location-aware iPhone tool alerting users to crime reports, new building permits and other location-specific news.

"Two-thirds or more of respondents report that they either never trust state government to do what is right, or trust it only some of the time. Residents overwhelmingly believe their state should pursue major reforms to their budget processes, and pursue them now."

~ The Pew Center on the States and the Public Policy Institute of California

"You have to look at the state's overall cost structure an world for investment and business activity. Companies can tur people to places that are closer to their customers and whe

~ Deborah Wince-Smith, CEO, Council on Competitiveness

II – IMPROVE STATE COMPETITIVENESS

Competitiveness is critical to every state's long-term future. States today compete not only against each other for jobs and talent but also against China, India, Brazil and other countries. For states determined to move beyond their hard times and recharge their vitality, they'll need to focus on competitiveness boosters like revitalizing infrastructure, pursuing radical education reform and reinventing economic development.

Economic development and infrastructure

It seems obvious, but it can't be stressed enough: The fiscal future of the states depends on getting their economies back on track. Thriving companies and jobs form the underpinnings of prosperity and, therefore, of state government coffers and ambitions.

But just as the recession has stripped away the illusion that governments could indefinitely live beyond their means, it has also made clear that old economic development habits must go. When state governments are being forced to cut deeply into education, social welfare budgets and employee benefits, offering massive incentive packages to corporations seems hard to justify.

The traditional approach to economic development rests on the notion that states must woo specific businesses with tax breaks and other expensive incentives. But this flies squarely in the face of the underlying trends reshaping the economy. A general business-friendly environment — including low taxes, reasonable regulations and an educated workforce — will attract business even in the absence of large, targeted incentives. Access to knowledge, the skills of workers, the ability to innovate and the facility to collaborate with regional, national and international partners are the emerging building blocks of business competitiveness and, hence, of smart economic development.

usiness environment . . . States now compete against the whole n a dime and decide they're going to move operations and he overall business environment is more favorable.”

One key strategy: increasing student interest in math and science to satisfy workforce demands. A promising example is the Manufacturing Institute's partnership with Discovery Communications to help nurture a new generation of engineers and technologists through more real-world learning and programs like "Inventors Workshop."

Invigorating the economy should start with a significant investment in the state's infrastructure: roads, bridges, rail lines, sewer lines, electric grid, ports and, crucially, broadband. A well designed infrastructure program would not only create badly needed jobs in the near term, but would lay the groundwork for future economic growth. Businesses relying on crumbling roads, aging tracks, erratic electricity and slow broadband speeds start with a disadvantage that no amount of subsidy can make up.

But states also need to go beyond the obvious. Strategic purchasing decisions can boost the information and technology services industry within their borders. Collaboration among public agencies, research institutions and businesses with an eye toward nurturing innovation can produce big payoffs, as South Carolina has discovered with its International Center for Automotive Research at Clemson University.

New economic development strategies may take various forms. Reshaping economic development efforts so that they move "at the speed of business, not the speed of government," as Indiana Governor Mitch Daniels put it when he replaced his state's commerce department with a nonprofit corporation, will let states react to opportunities before they've slipped away. Boosting the attractiveness of cities and designing initiatives to keep university graduates in the state will give states an edge in building their talent pools. Aligning state economic strengths with future industry needs — the BioBusiness Alliance of Minnesota's 20-year strategic plan for life sciences is a good model — can be another differentiator. And a regional approach to economic development — such as linking the Great Lakes states' universities and corporate research facilities to explore clean energy development — would seed innovation in important regional industries and sectors.

All of this will require hard political work. It means breaking down funding and other silos, investing money wisely at a time of scarce resources, and inducing state agencies and higher education institutions to move more quickly, more openly and more collaboratively. Yet, the result will be a state government that understands both its potential and its limits as a catalyst for economic development.

Education

A strong economic development program is meaningless if a state doesn't have the workforce it needs to thrive in the 21st century. American high school students aren't competitive in math and science

"Twelve percent of the high schools produce 50 percent o[f]
highest need — the worst performing schools and the school[s]
impact. We've found that if you can reach 25 percent of th[e]
kids who are likely to drop out."

~ Michael Brown, CEO, City Year

scores. U.S. students constitute just 14 percent of the world's population of college students these days, down from 30 percent three decades ago.[5]

There is a direct link between the quality of our education system and our economic competitiveness. The supply of highly skilled workers coming out of our colleges and universities simply does not meet the private sector's needs. This is a national problem but not necessarily a federal problem. It is the states and local school districts that are going to have to create the solutions.

The window is currently open. The universe of for-profit and nonprofit organizations pushing innovative solutions — from Green Dot schools to the Bill and Melinda Gates Foundation — has grown exponentially in recent decades. Education reform is one of the rare issues on which many legislators from both sides of the aisle can find common ground. And perhaps most importantly, a reform-minded president and secretary of education are overseeing a drive for education innovation.

The reform movement is everywhere, and it is both powerful and winning broad acceptance. You can see it in New Orleans' post-Katrina system of charter schools, and in New York City, where former schools chancellor Joel Klein raised $75 million in private funds to create the largest training program for principals in the country. You can see it in innovative nonprofits like College Summit and City Year, which are helping to lower school dropout rates and develop college-going cultures in underrepresented areas.

The first task for governors, then, will be to find ways of amplifying the school reform movement within their own systems. Some states are already putting in place aggressive reforms aimed at improving the bottom 5 percent of schools in the country. They're channeling U.S. Department of

---

U.S. students constitute just 14 percent of the world's population of college students, down from 30 percent three decades ago.

he dropouts in the country. If you can serve in the places of
hat feed into them — you're going to have a disproportionate
chools in most urban centers, you can reach 50 percent of the

Education dollars to refocus resources on them; letting school districts close them or turn them into charters; and bringing in Green Dot, City Year and other organizations whose mission is to help turn them around. Most states are considering plans to reform tenure, boost pay for the best teachers, implement pay-for-performance and pursue other means of ratcheting up teachers' effectiveness.

School districts are also ripe for technological innovation, as California is trying to prove with its effort to shift to online textbooks in hopes of slashing the $350 million it spends annually on the paper kind. Georgia and Virginia, meanwhile, are providing every student access to online advanced placement courses.

Math and science education needs special attention. Some states are trying to address the supply side of this dilemma by using alternative teacher certification to boost the numbers of qualified math and science teachers; in Texas, for instance, over 55 percent of the teachers in the field are arriving in schools through alternative certification programs. The real challenge, though, will be finding ways to boost demand — that is, students' interest in math and science.

One of the greatest needs in school systems is to spend more money where it counts the most: the classroom. In part, this will depend on lowering costs elsewhere. So cooperative purchasing arrangements between school districts and other players hold out the hope of reducing costs associated with utilities, equipment and services. Pennsylvania's Common Cents Shared Services Initiative has 49 of 501 school districts throughout the state combining their resources, spending power and business operations to save money.

Implementing the federal health care law will try with its complexity. Medicaid administrators expanded role under the law, which will bring

III – TRANSFORM HEALTH AND HUMAN SERVICES

Each new governor will have his or her own agenda, but given the budgetary implications and the huge changes they face thanks to the federal health care legislation, two areas need particular attention: health care and human services.

Health care

States occupy the center of one of the most significant transformations in decades in our health care system. And despite the continuing machinations in Washington and the courts over the Patient Protection and Affordable Care Act of 2010, no state can afford to stand by waiting to see what happens to it. They must move forward now.

At a bare minimum, they will have to join with others at the table — providers, payers, regulators and consumers — to lower costs. But that's just the ante; their real challenge will be to replace old models, structures and barriers to change with innovative approaches to a host of issues, including medical management, Medicaid costs, public-private collaboration, health system redesign, insurance regulation and creation of health exchanges. No responsible governor will allow his or her state to get sidetracked by partisan wrangling on this front.

While health care reform offers states the chance to make meaningful reforms they've been waiting years to see, implementing the federal law will try the patience of even the state's best and brightest with its complexity. Medicaid administrators are already fretting over how to cope with their expanded role under the law, which will bring in many new enrollees beginning in 2014. States are already under pressure to design and implement health exchanges and integrate them seamlessly with the Medicaid eligibility system, not to mention overseeing new regulations on the insurance industry, upgrading workforce training in the field and overseeing integration of public health programs with local delivery systems.

That's not all. They will also have to find funding for the expanded Medicaid population at a time of ongoing budget shortfalls. They must implement the mandatory technology changes defined by the HIPAA 5010 standards for the electronic transmission of health care transactions and the international ICD-10

he patience of even the state's best and brightest re already fretting over how to cope with their n many new enrollees beginning in 2014.

codes for reporting diagnoses and procedures. Lastly, they must immediately develop an infrastructure and process for managing provider incentive payments for electronic health records adoption.

For incoming administrations, the first step will be to assess the legislation's impact on state government and set priorities for projects. In the course of this, states will also need to investigate federal funding opportunities that can support investment in technology and other infrastructure changes required to make the reforms work. And given their budget constraints, they will also need to explore existing technology — such as self-service portals developed by state health departments, and the Medicaid Management Information System.

Governors and their state Medicaid director will also have to come to grips with two other challenges. The first is that state-administered Medicaid has become the nation's primary funding source for long-term care for those in need — a burden that will grow to immense proportions as the population ages. States are already innovating in this field. The State of Washington uses an automated assessment tool to gauge the most appropriate setting for care and to monitor services; Vermont is allowing consumers to hire caregivers in order to promote community-based care; other states are looking at ways of improving the management of chronic diseases. Not every state has been actively experimenting with ways to cut costs, however — and all will need to before long.

Similarly, in many states, Medicaid is the single largest expense category in the budget. Unless states can learn how to deliver the right care to the right enrollee the first time they try, they will be swamped by rising costs. In particular, they will need to develop patient management systems that allow them to prevent, diagnose and treat illness effectively. Blue Cross and Blue Shield of Tennessee, for instance, uses "predictive modeling" to identify gaps in care and develop plans for treating patients whose health can be improved with the right early interventions. Meanwhile, several states have developed "single point of entry" systems to give Medicaid enrollees access to all administrative functions, with the goal of boosting their engagement in caring for themselves.

Human services

The next few years will be especially challenging for state human services departments. Facing increased demand for services while federal stimulus aid dries up and budgets are at great risk, human services organizations must find a way to redesign and modernize delivery — quickly.

This will mean changing the way they work. Streamlining bureaucracy, eliminating duplication and deploying resources to the front lines as efficiently as possible will be crucial to addressing new demands. To achieve this, states will need to focus on four major areas.

> "When I came here there were 29,000 adult household are now fewer than 3,000 ... I attribute it to the value w the work."
>
> ~ B.J. Walker, Commissioner, Georgia Department of Human Services

First, states need to change their methods on the front line. A combination of mobile technology, social media and data analytics, for instance, can give front-line social workers access to information at the moment they need it — helping them make good decisions on the spot and solicit insights from colleagues with experience in similar circumstances. The State of Florida, for example, outfitted more than 2,300 caseworkers with smart phones and laptops, allowing them to collaborate with each other and upload critical data in real time. Alameda County, California's use of mobile devices, advanced analytics and real-time reporting allows social workers to find the immediate status of any child, as well as their colleagues and any support services and programs connected with that child.

Second, state human services agencies need to transform the ways they interact with the citizens they serve. Families and individuals should be able to connect to all the resources they need, both inside and outside government, through a single point of entry. This means redesigning systems to create simple portals, like Pennsylvania's COMPASS and Massachusetts' Virtual Gateway, which allow clients to be screened for eligibility, apply for benefits and track their accounts. In addition, involving clients in service delivery — clarifying needed services and using social networking to become smarter, more self-sufficient consumers — can radically change existing service models.

Third, states should look for ways to implement services across agencies and departments — so that the state serves a family rather than a set of "needs." For example, states can designate categorical pools of funding that serve families and establish "human service banks," which can make loans that require specific outcomes rather than interest.

Lastly, there is the issue of how human services are financed. Their funding today is highly fragmented. This results in extra administrative expenses that rob money from workers and clients. Moreover, financial models have tended to give short shrift to long-term effectiveness, service quality and outcomes. They have focused on programs rather than the individuals and families served by the system.

Finding ways to redesign the flow of money through the system, then, is a basic step in revamping human services to make them both more targeted and more effective. In 2007, when the Commonwealth of Virginia reversed the perverse incentives in how it funded children and family services, it saved $100 million over two years and improved outcomes for kids.

n TANF (Temporary Assistance for Needy Families). There
xplicitly drove into how we ask the workforce to approach

IV – OVERHAUL STATE OPERATIONS

States are poised for a period of significant innovation — fundamentally reforming governments' structures and systems with daring policy experiments. The fiscal situation leaves them no choice. States today have a unique opportunity to regain public trust by tackling some of the tough policy issues that have stymied a generation of political leaders, while also addressing the new challenges of the 21st century.

To do this, however, state governments will need to change. Nearly a decade into the 21st century, states are still struggling with public structures and programs designed to meet the needs of the 20th century with funding programs that, in many cases, exist simply because they existed the year before.

Innovation

If ever state government needed to be daring and innovative, it's now. The status quo is untenable. Without a mindset that prizes innovation, it will be next to impossible to make progress on the concrete policy initiatives that states so desperately need to realize.

In most governments, innovation has been piecemeal. It arises from a leader's determination to establish a legacy in one policy arena, a response to a crisis, or from a desperate call for "good ideas." Once a crisis subsides, a term ends or a good idea inevitably stumbles, public organizations are left without the capacity for sustained innovation.

In a rapidly changing world — one in which only the fleet-footed can garner success — this is not enough. Sustained innovation needs to be part and parcel of how state governments work. "Sloughing off the past," as management guru Peter Drucker phrases it, is as crucial to government as it is to

> "I continually challenged my Cabinet to find innovative ways to do business. Governors can set the expectation for innovation, and they can encourage creativity and risk-taking, empowering employees to make decisions."
>
> ~ Jennifer Granholm, Governor of Michigan

business. In fact, just as the business world talks about "disruptive innovation" that can fundamentally change a market, radically new ways of delivering services — virtual charter schools, for instance — carry the potential for improving public service.

How exactly can states become serial innovators?

One of the most important steps is to open up the innovation process and seek ideas from all quarters: from within state organizations, from business and academia, and from citizens and "consumers" of their services. This implies using Web 2.0 technologies to elicit cutting-edge thinking from employees, partners in the business community, networks of academics and the public at large. Consider the way Apple cultivated an immense community of developers to build hundreds of thousands of apps for the iPhone and you get the idea. Just as important as the links to external ideas is the process of sustaining and deepening them over the long term so that collaboration becomes part of how state agencies do business.

In Massachusetts, Governor Deval Patrick launched a new Life Sciences Initiative in 2007 that joins state government, industry, research hospitals, and colleges and universities. Its goal is not just to spur new research, but to put money in the hands of researchers in the state with promising ideas who are not able to get funding from the National Institutes of Health.

Technology

Four technology trends, in particular, have the potential to undergird the ability to innovate and redesign states. Given past experiences with cost overruns, failed IT projects and flawed implementations that don't deliver promised benefits, governors and legislators ought, in fact, to remain cautious. But this caution should spur them to thoughtful, attentive use of new technology — not cause them to disdain it altogether.

The first trend is "cloud computing," which gives state governments a way of cutting IT costs and taking advantage of vastly greater computing resources than any agency could afford on its own. This is why New York City just struck a deal to give 100,000 city workers access to Microsoft's Web-based cloud computing services, which may save some $50 million over five years. Moreover, the "cloud" is evolving rapidly, offering states the possibility of reshaping their processes as they shed the costs associated with in-house applications. New cloud capabilities offer states the chance to do business in new ways, as well. Michigan, for example, is pursuing plans to build a data center that will offer cloud

> "We need to shorten project development cycles and make development more agile and responsive to new technologies, leveraging new services as they become available."
>
> ~ Dave Fletcher, Chief Technology Officer, State of Utah

computing services to state agencies, cities, counties, school districts and the private sector.

The second trend is social media, which can improve communication among state employees and citizens and improve the delivery of government services. The potential for recipients of social services to network with social service workers and with one another, for instance, gives state agencies new ways to boost their self-sufficiency and react to emerging economic or social trends.

However, states will have a hard time fully capitalizing on social media without the third trend: consolidating piecemeal and redundant IT systems that have been allowed to evolve within state government. These inefficient networks, with their inconsistencies and inability to allow ready communication, are an obstacle not just to efficiency, but to states' abilities to meet their challenges.

This brings up the final trend: data analytics. As government leaders recognize that unlocking public data can bring new insight into problems, new approaches to solving them and new levels of performance, they are trying to make data more broadly and meaningfully available. This alone, however, is not enough. The true benefits will come when state agencies understand how to use the tools available — mashups, crowdsourcing, data mining and the like — not only to enhance their own capabilities, but to capitalize on the resourcefulness of citizens and entrepreneurs. One bright spot: The State of California makes raw state data widely available to citizens and organizations that want to incorporate it in their own applications. The state's Web site also provides a link to a variety of tools that allow users to query state agency databases and download raw data.

Used correctly, technology can help transform the way governments do business. It doesn't just enable government to work faster and cheaper, it allows policymakers to re-envision everything from what the bureaucracy looks like to what services it should provide.

Redesign state government

Many states find themselves shackled by the old ways of governing. A redesign is urgently needed because as state governments struggle to respond to the imperatives for change, many find themselves hampered by their dated practices: hierarchical, siloed organizations; obsolete pension systems; service models driven by bureaucracy instead of citizen needs; budgets that ignore results; and tax systems designed around yesterday's economy.

The exorbitantly high costs embedded in our education system, for example, are a product of old business models and archaic laws. In many states, at least 40 cents of every dollar spent on schools never makes it into the classroom, and teachers make up a little more than half of all school district staff. One culprit? Thousands of tiny school districts, each operating its own transportation, human resources,

Many states find themselves shackled by the old ways of governing. A redesign is urgently needed because as state governments struggle to respond to the imperatives for change, many find themselves hampered by their dated practices.

food services, information technology, building maintenance, administration and other support functions.

The same kind of huge administrative inefficiencies can be observed in the duplication and overlap between many county and city governments and special districts in states across the country. In some cases, the answer is intergovernmental service sharing. But a more fundamental question must be asked of many of these units: Are they simply relics of a different era?

Legacy thinking also permeates the ways many states still hire, fire, pay and promote their employees. Survey after survey demonstrates that many highly skilled job candidates who say they would like to work in public service end up not working in government. Why? One reason is state pensions. With their 10-year vesting, assumption of lifetime employment and lack of portability, they offer little appeal to today's "free agent" Generation X and Y workers. Outmoded hiring practices, which often require multiple levels of clearances and approvals, likewise hold no attraction. To become a choice employer among the emerging workforce, the public sector must appeal to these young workers' expectation of a social, flexible, purposeful and technologically modern work environment.

New technologies are already calling into question some long-established ways of delivering services and organizing workforces. If a state can make advanced placement courses available online, it may not need AP teachers in every high school. The shift to cloud computing hosted by a single company does away with the need for contract specialists to oversee the dozens of separate licensing agreements (New York had 40) and their associated service contracts.

Given the huge gap between past practices and current and future needs, incremental change won't be enough. Century-old systems need to be replaced with new models that better address the needs of the 21st century. This transformation will require new ways of doing business for every aspect of government, from organizational structures and operating practices to personnel systems and service delivery models. These changes won't be easy, but they are necessary. Moreover, they are now possible — states have new tools and, for the time being, an environment that's conducive to change.

V – GETTING IT DONE: FROM BIG IDEAS TO BIG RESULTS

There are lots of ways one of your initiatives can fail, but to succeed the following must occur: You need a good idea, a well-designed piece of legislation, political support and strong implementation. Ultimately, every big initiative will be judged on the results it produces.

The successful initiatives we examined managed to get the process right. Proponents took the time to listen to opposing viewpoints and often incorporated this into the program's design. Lawmakers saw themselves as crafting a design that needed to work in the real world, so sponsors allowed for thoughtful debate rather than ramming their bill through.

Once the bill was passed, a political champion recruited a strong manager to lead the implementation, one chosen for their managerial ability rather than their politics.

The successful implementers we studied took the possibility of failure seriously. They established a dedicated unit to manage the launch and often tested the program design in smaller pilots before rolling it out more broadly.

The stakes are high. If 2010's large crop of new governors and state legislators are to be successful, they first will have to take the process of getting big things done in state government very seriously.

"It is not the strongest of the species that survives,
Nor the most intelligent that survives.
It is the one that is the *most adaptable to change.*"

~ Charles Darwin

PART I: COST REDUCTION

Introduction

Addressing the continuing state fiscal crisis will be the dominant issue of 2011

Dealing with the state fiscal crisis will be the most essential and pressing issue facing every governor who arrives in office in January 2011. Veteran or rookie, all governors will take the oath of office facing an era of high unemployment, a housing market that remains on its knees and a veritable Gulf oil spill of red ink splashed across their budgets.

Facing one of the worst economic recessions in U.S. history, state governments have already cut programs, services and staff; sold surplus state property; and shut down everything from DMVs to parks. They've tried every budget gimmick in the playbook, from underfunding pensions and other post-employment benefits (OPEBs) to "monetizing" future revenues, all of which merely amount to kicking the fiscal can down the road.

The overall economy may have improved moderately, and there are signs of recovery in some state revenues, but the news remains very, very bad — and it's likely to get worse. Of the 44 states that had closed their FY 2010 books by the time of the latest Rockefeller Institute report on state revenue collections, only 10 had seen some modest increase in tax receipts.[6] This means that almost three dozen — well more than half the states in the nation — saw continued declines in overall tax collections for the year.

So the picture is bleak, indeed. Fiscal 2012 budgets will face a projected collective shortfall of $112 billion according to the Center on Budget and Policy Priorities.[7] Meanwhile, estimates of states' unfunded pension and health care obligations currently hover at just below $3 trillion, a number that many experts view as overly optimistic and destined to keep growing.[8]

In short, states face a massive imbalance between expected revenues and promised expenditures. This underlying threat can be termed "the Gap."

The Gap is a twofold problem consisting of a fiscal gap (the deficit) between revenue and expenditures, and a performance shortfall between the realities state government faces and the way it operates.

The fiscal deficit has both a cyclical and a structural component. Its cyclical guise emerges in response to variation in economic output over time. This happened in previous recessions, and it will happen in future ones.

The structural component of the deficit, while exacerbated by the cyclical downturn, is more fundamental. Many states have over-committed current and future resources. Steadily rising costs for public pensions, retirees' health care and Medicaid costs, together with significant demographic shifts, mean that incremental changes or reductions in "waste, fraud, and abuse" won't even come close to solving the problem — though it remains important to run an efficient, effective state government.

1-1. State shortfalls after use of ARRA funds, largest state budget shortfalls on record

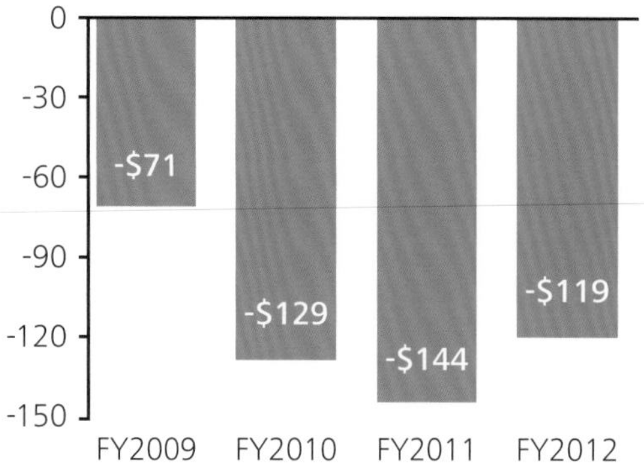

Source: Center on Budget and Policy Priorities, June 2010

At first glance, closing the Gap appears to be an economic problem, a financial puzzle that can be solved by simply making some short-term budget cuts and waiting for the economy to get better. This time, that strategy won't work.

Systemic structural changes will be needed to bend the cost curve of state government down (the likelihood that any state will be in a political position to raise taxes significantly any time soon is highly dubious right now). Getting from here to there requires navigating two phases that comprise a long, grinding journey to state fiscal sustainability: The blueprint phase and the transformation phase.

1-2. Percent change in state appropriations (FY 2010 appropriations compared with FY 2009 spending)

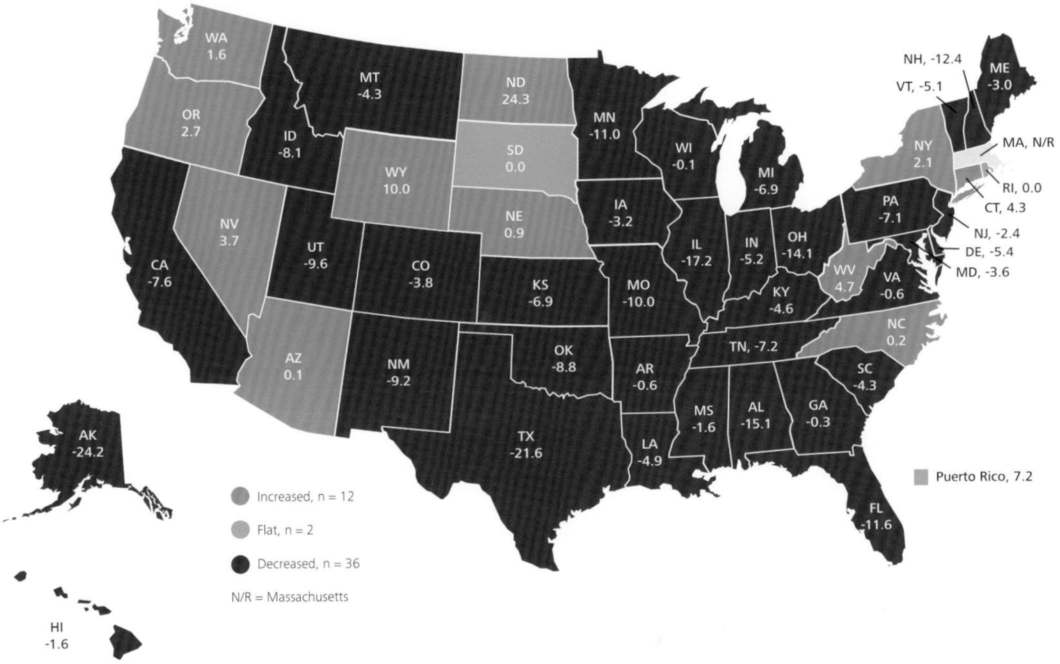

Source: NCSL survey of state legislative fiscal offices, 2009

The blueprint phase

Designing a workable political roadmap for taking the hard steps

the journey to fiscally sustainable government

The first step to addressing the Gap is to develop a political roadmap for the journey to fiscal sustainability. This requires overcoming several realities that make progress daunting:

- Special interest politics work against dealing with the Gap.
- Elected officials at every level have a political incentive to serve their current constituents over future taxpayers. Politically, the best time to deal with the Gap will always be "soon."
- In general, any party out of power has an incentive to exploit for political gain the hard choices the ruling party might make toward closing the Gap.
- In general, any party in power has an incentive to move incrementally rather than get blamed for the pain associated with moving boldly to close the Gap.

No one knows better just how treacherous the politics of downsizing can be than California Governor Arnold Schwarzenegger, who took office in 2003 dedicated to reining in out-of-control state spending. In his first state-of-the-state address, he called the state government "a mastodon frozen in time" with "multiple departments with overlapping responsibilities" and pledged to "blow up the boxes" of state government. He launched a major reform initiative that proposed some of the most sweeping and radical reorganization changes ever proposed in the state. He even sponsored four major ballot initiatives, including one to limit expenditures.

All the while, Schwarzenegger warned Californians of the consequences of sticking with the status quo: a future of mounting budget deficits and a state government that would become virtually ungovernable.

The result? The legislative initiatives backed by the governor lost at the polls, the reform initiative generated little change, and the status quo prevailed in the legislature. More importantly, the grim future predicted for California has come to pass. Despite massive federal subsidies, the state was reduced to issuing IOUs, and despite large tax hikes and deep service reductions, it still faces massive budget deficits and a staggering debt.

ACTION PLAN FOR NAVIGATING THE BLUEPRINT PHASE

Crafting the political journey to fiscally sustainable government is a daunting and complex task. The following strategies can help governors and state legislative leaders to accomplish that task:

Achieve consensus on the magnitude of the problem

To build the political consensus for the changes that will have to take place first requires state leaders to reach agreement on the magnitude of

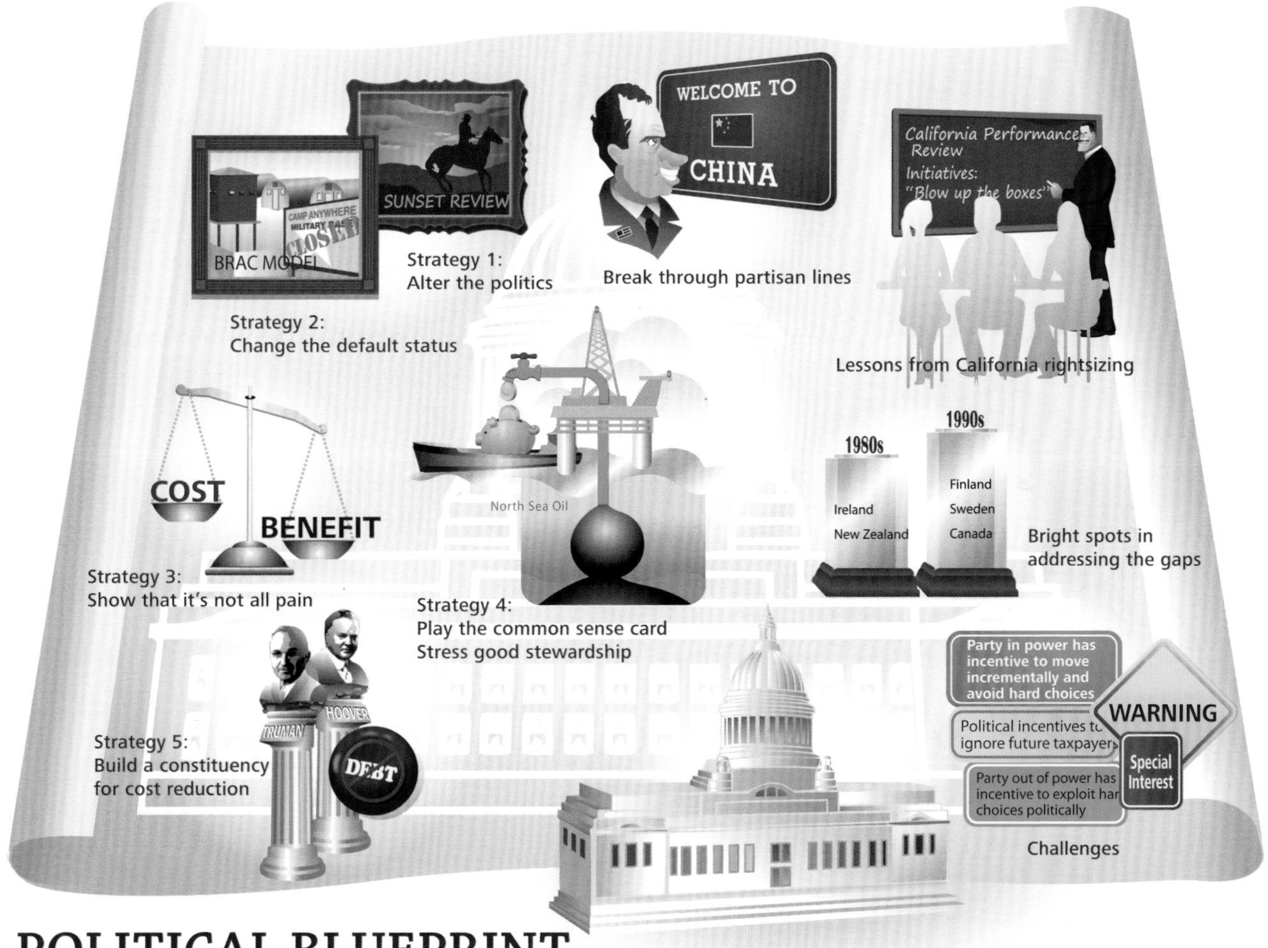

POLITICAL BLUEPRINT

Source: Deloitte Research

the problem. This requires widespread popular acceptance of several "realities," annoyingly persistent facts that cannot be wished away.

- The Gap is real and large.
- The Gap cannot be closed by merely cutting waste, fraud and abuse, or by eliminating some unneeded programs.
- The Gap cannot be closed by merely raising taxes.
- The Gap, in many states, is structural and will not go away when the economy finally recovers.
- The Gap is based, in part, on a failure to put away sufficient funds to pay for promised benefits, including to retired public employees who contributed to and expect these benefits.

Widespread acceptance of these truths is an important step in coming to terms with the difficult choices ahead. That's why, for example, New Jersey's Governor Chris Christie took pains to warn constituents about the painful cuts required to close the $11 billion budget gap the state faced for the 2011 fiscal year. "We don't have the money, so you need to prepare for what's coming down the line," Christie told the audience at the New Jersey League of Municipalities' 18th Annual Mayor's Legislative Day in February 2010. "You all know the state can't continue to spend money it doesn't have. And you all know that the appetite for tax increases among our constituents has come to an end." Christie's promise to implement pension, benefit and arbitration reforms that would save cities money drew loud cheers from the mayors.[9]

Alter the politics

One way to alter the politics of budget balancing is to design political mechanisms that allow the hard choices to be made jointly, with shared blame and credit. One such strategy is the Base Realignment and Closure Model (BRAC), which helped depoliticize a necessary defense retrenchment in the 1990s. Congress had to vote up or down on a package of proposals within 45 days. This process helped to overcome parochial political interests in Congress. Similar thinking could be applied to state governments.

What works: The Commission for a New Georgia

When Georgia Governor Sonny Perdue took office in 2003 he was naturally curious about the state of the state he'd just been elected to govern. How well was it functioning? Was it optimizing spending? Did it actually need to be doing all the jobs that it had taken on? Was it running efficiently? To answer these questions, Perdue created The Commission for a New Georgia, made up of an enlivening mix of Republicans and Democrats, business people, public servants, NGOs and other appropriate experts, with an administrative staff to do research and propose action. Besides its eclectic makeup and the staff assistance, one other thing made the commission different from similar efforts elsewhere: It didn't produce fat reports, but rather, it made recommendations as it found things to fix.

The commission is credited with finding savings and new revenues totaling upwards of $200 million. Based on the commission's findings, the state's fleet of vehicles was downsized by almost 10 percent; surplus real estate was sold for over $22 million; leases were renegotiated to save almost $9 million; and energy rates were adjusted, saving the state another $6 million. The state now auctions retired cars and equipment on the Internet, increasing sales revenue by 30 percent.[10] (One of the more celebrated eBay auctions was for a Lear Jet that the state hadn't even realized it owned — courtesy of a major drug bust.) Meanwhile, the state procurement office, which contracts over $5.7 billion in purchases a year, saved the state $101 million in one year by renegotiating all contracts.

Numerous states in recent years, including Arizona, Georgia, Louisiana, Minnesota, New Jersey and Virginia, have created government reform and cost reduction commissions as another way of changing the politics. Typically bipartisan in nature, they can take some of the partisanship out of cost reduction discussions. "The Virginia Government Reform Commission served as an ideas laboratory to vet big and potentially contentious concepts publicly," explains Commission Director Mike Reynold. "This, in turn, allowed Governor Bob McDonnell to propose better legislation to cut costs, eliminate inefficiencies and improve service delivery."

Change the default status

Another approach is to create a sunset process: an action-forcing mechanism to encourage elimination, reform and merger. Under sunset, a review of the agency must be done by an independent agency, and the legislature has to pass a new law to save the entity. In the language of choice architecture, it shifts the default status to "terminate."

The Texas Sunset Commission, the most successful sunset process in the United States, has abolished 54 agencies and consolidated 12 others. For every dollar invested in the sunset program, the state has earned a return of $31, resulting in $784.5 million in estimated savings between 1982 and 2007.

The legislators who sit on the Texas Sunset Commission are proud of their independent viewpoint. "We're not constrained by convention," explains Representative Carl Isett, the 2008 chairman of the Sunset Commission. "We don't come in with any preconceived ideas. We don't care how they've done things in the past. We come in with ideas as reformers."[11]

Shift the focus to results

Another option for limiting the political gamesmanship in tough budgetary decisions is to shift the focus squarely to results. Numerous states claim to be using data on results to inform budgeting. In fact, only a handful have made good use of data as part of the budgeting process. In Maryland, Governor Martin O'Malley has aggressively pursued a results-informed approach to state government. Early on, this meant closing down the state's expensive and ineffective maximum security prison, signaling right away that the new governor would be bringing the same data-driven approach to Maryland that he'd honed as mayor of Baltimore. One key to a data-driven approach to governance, says O'Malley, is that numbers should never be used as a bludgeon. "You have to go about this with real openness and transparency," says the governor. "And everyone wants to be seen as doing a good job; nobody wants to be singled out as not performing. We might lean hard on a department, but it's never a matter of giving a department head a blindfold and a cigarette and putting them up against the wall."[12]

The legislative branch of government is traditionally considered to be the least tuned-in to using program results to allocate resources. In Connecticut, however, a small group of crusading legislators has begun to put teeth into the legislature's "Results-Based Accountability" approach to spending. Agencies that can't accurately answer their questions are now starting to see their budgets cut, which has led the rest to begin taking the exercise seriously.

The transformation phase

Delivering the cost reduction program

Once public and political support have been achieved for what ought to be done, the next step is implementation. Actually altering a government's structure to deliver on a reform plan is a considerable challenge.

Closing the performance gap in government requires a public culture that embraces a relentless pursuit of innovation — a commitment to adopting new, more efficient ways of creating public value. Reexamining both mission and methods will be essential for governments seeking to become sustainable in an era of retrenchment.

Such a shift will not come easily. The bureaucratic barriers to change in the public sector greatly exceed those in the private sector — due not to bad intent, but to a culture of risk aversion and program protection, and as a systemic consequence of the way government has been organized since the early 20th century. Navigating the transformation phase is about overcoming these barriers.

Much of the work during this stage needs to happen concurrently with the previous stage. Much of the efficiency savings, for example, will need to be mined before all the difficult political issues are resolved that allow for the really hard choices to be made.

> "We ask every agency three basic questions: How much did you do? How well did you do it? And is anyone better off?"
>
> ~ Connecticut Representative Diana Urban[13]

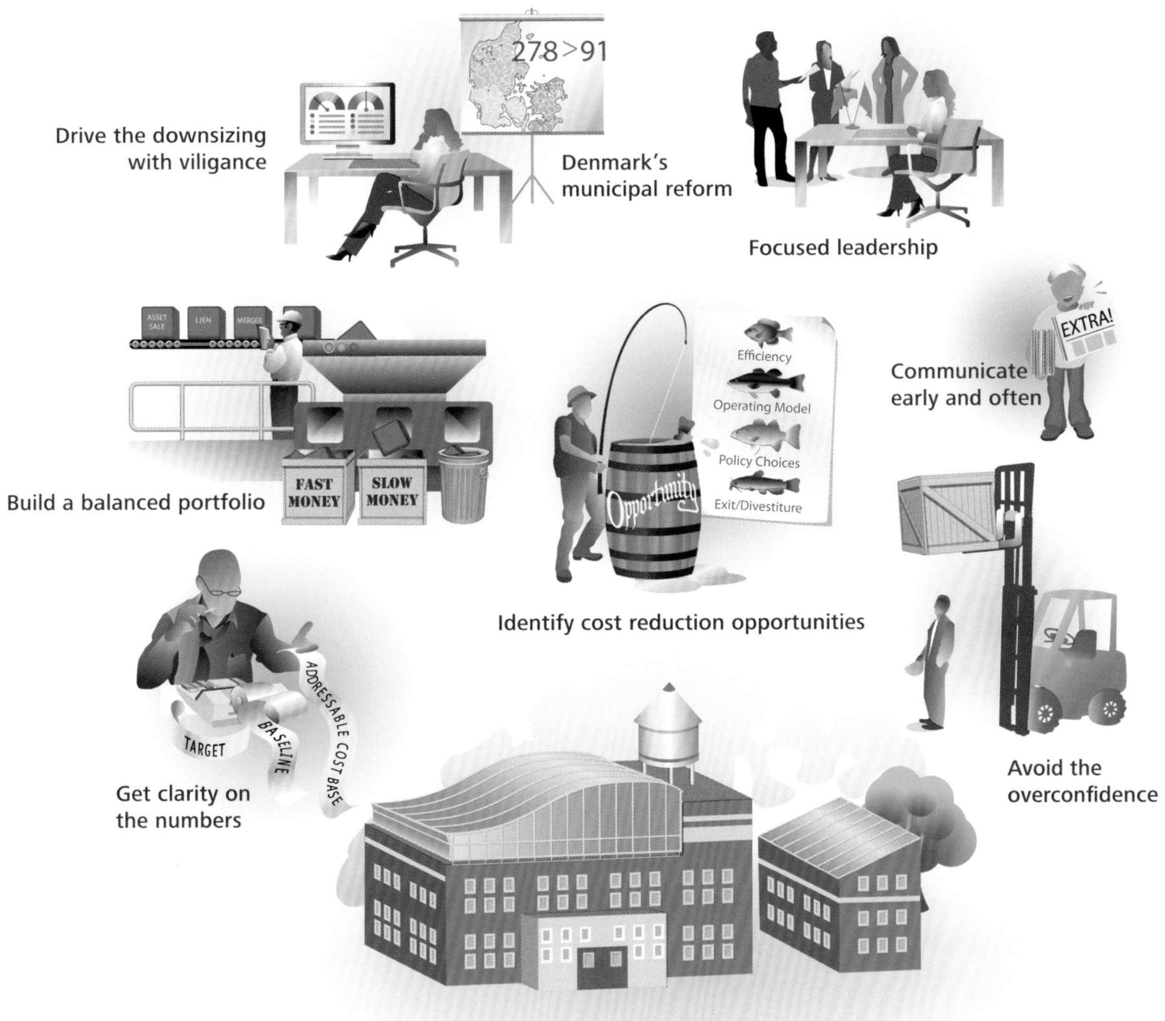

TRANSFORMATION PHASE

Source: Deloitte Research

Management guru Peter Drucker contends tha
nature and purpose of everything they do by asking:
If the answer is yes, they ask the follow-up question

ACTION PLAN FOR NAVIGATING THE TRANSFORMATION PHASE

1. Identify cost reduction opportunities

There are hundreds of different ways to reduce costs.[14] These opportunities generally fall within seven broad categories:

Drive meaningful short-term change and savings:

- **Stop spending** – Freeze budgets, stop hiring, cut capital budgets
- **Sow the seeds wide to change culture** – the small items add up, encourage hundreds of small projects
- **Reduce wastage** – eliminate fraud and waste, buy better

Overhaul operations and rethink policies and structures:

- **Reengineer processes** – make model for delivering current services more efficient
- **Change the operating model** – deliver services in a different and more cost effective way
- **Transformational** – drive fundamental change, cost control culture
- **Change and/or exit the services** – review policy options and the service portfolio, challenge everything, ask whether government should be involved at all

This last approach gets to the root of one of the toughest challenges for the public sector — stopping unneeded activities and rethinking policies that were enacted for a different time. This gets at a simple but profound truth: In some cases, what is being done no longer makes sense. In other cases, how it is being done no longer makes sense.

2. Build a balanced portfolio

The biggest transformation traps include taking on too many initiatives at once and constructing a cost reduction portfolio that lacks balance and coherence. This can lead to one initiative diluting the benefits of another and possibly a wider failure of confidence in the whole program.

A "funnel" approach may be the best way to identify worthwhile initiatives as well as to weigh political considerations. Not all cost-cutting ideas will, or should, make the cut. Develop a score sheet that places political risks, other risks, complexity and implementation time on a scale. How fast do you need the savings? How much heat are you willing to endure? Compare cost savings to where an opportunity falls on those other scales, and weigh options against one another.

3. Use your business case

A well-documented and easily understood business case is needed at the start of the transformation to communicate the need for change. Equally important, the business case should be updated

uccessful organizations periodically reexamine the *If we were not already doing this, would we now go into it?" If we were to start doing this today, how would we do it?"*[15]

periodically throughout the effort to track performance, measure results and adjust expectations based on new facts and circumstances that arise during the course of the transformation.

4. Avoid paralysis by analysis

Over-analysis can paralyze transformation efforts, causing them to lose critical support and momentum. At the same time, the history of government transformation is littered with failed projects that were started without sufficient forethought, coalition building and project management structure. Work to strike a balance between study and action.

5. Celebrate quick wins

Set up a formal process for capturing results from cost reduction and revenue enhancement reforms that can be instituted quickly — those that deliver measurable improvement within 12 months. Sharing credible results from quick wins with stakeholders builds support for longer-term transformation projects. Quick wins improve the initiative's credibility, expand support within the state government and create positive momentum for the overall effort.

Quick wins also help the new chief executive to make early, visible progress in cutting the underlying cost base and changing the culture to one of spending restraint. "If you're trying to come out

What works: Minnesota's "Drive To Excellence"

In 2005, Minnesota Governor Tim Pawlenty initiated the Drive to Excellence. The goal was to retool, reform and improve government to reinvigorate the quality of life in the State of Minnesota.

Within this broad mandate, the Drive had three primary objectives: 1) Identify and implement long-term solutions to challenges facing the state; 2) Refocus state government to serve citizens as one enterprise rather than a collection of semi-autonomous agencies and boards; and 3) Serve citizens better through increased quality, improved customer service and at reduced cost.

The Drive to Excellence teams involved more than 2,000 individuals representing more than 75 state agencies, boards and commissions. They are involved in 14 major statewide projects; eight have been completed (including strategic sourcing and statewide e-licensing) and six more are underway. Savings have so far totaled more than $350 million.

> "You have to relentlessly tear down fiefdoms...We centralized certain functions — procurement, personnel, information technology. Enormous savings come from taking these steps."
>
> ~ Indiana Governor Mitch Daniels

of a fiscal hole as deep as most governments are looking at now, you have to attack spending on every front," explains Indiana Governor Mitch Daniels. "We did a number of things that were very large, that brought very large savings immediately, but you also have to do literally hundreds of lesser things that add up. You need to build a culture that challenges every expenditure."

6. Communicate early and often

Cost reduction programs often involve eliminating sacred cows, shifting resources and eliminating jobs — each extremely controversial in its own right. Communication therefore needs to be focused on gathering support, developing trust and increasing transparency. This entails creating a messaging campaign to tell citizens about what you're doing and why. Employees should clearly understand the implications of the efforts for their jobs and benefits. A cost management dashboard, which publicly indicates the level of cost savings and achievements to date, increases transparency.

The political champion needs to convey the same messages communicated elsewhere. That individual should be given regular updates on the progress of different activities.

7. Focus on implementation

The transformation phase requires strong leadership. Unfortunately, politicians have historically focused on policy and politics rather than implementation. The new roadway, the new program, the legislative strategy, and signing a bill into law — these are interesting and politically valuable. On the other hand, overseeing a portfolio of efficiency measures and grappling with bureaucratic challenges are neither inherently pleasurable nor politically beneficial. They are crucial to long-term success, however. A governor must focus relentlessly on more efficient, streamlined government.

Look for transformation ideas through multiple lenses:

- **Top-down:** Cabinet members, policy staff, legislators.
- **Bottom-up:** Managers, line-level employees and unions.
- **Inside-out:** Leading practices from other governments and the private sector.
- **Outside-in:** What do our customers and citizens want from government services?

Too many governments?

It's more a notion than a movement. But some state policy leaders who are taking a broad look at the overall cost of government are beginning to ask hard questions not just about how services are provided, but who is providing them. Some, like New York's Governor-elect Andrew Cuomo, argue that significant administrative inefficiencies exist in the duplication and overlap of services and responsibilities among many counties, cities and towns, not to mention the thousands of special districts that have mushroomed over the last three decades nationwide. Overall, more than 90,000 units of local government exist in the United States.

The most obvious answer would seem to be to encourage local governments to coordinate and share services. But a more fundamental question is also now being asked: Are many of these smaller jurisdictions and special districts simply relics of a different era and no longer needed? That's the argument being made by Rich Pahls, a Nebraska state senator from Omaha, who has proposed merging many of his state's 93 counties — the vast majority of which contain fewer than 20,000 residents.[16] The jurisdictions were designed for the days of the horse and buggy, he pointed out to *The New York Times* this year after his bill died in the legislature, not an era when "people will drive 100 miles to the grocery store."

Or consider a place like New Jersey, which has some of the highest property taxes in the country thanks in part to 567 municipalities — a third of them with fewer than 5,000 residents — along with 611 school districts and 486 local authorities and special districts. Bergen County alone has 70 school districts and 76 superintendents.

There are two initial tasks for anyone hoping to get a handle on whether dissolving or merging local governmental units makes sense. The first is to understand where the opportunities are for eliminating duplication, inefficiency, excess administration, fragmented accountability and glacial decision making. The second is to lay the groundwork for public understanding and acceptance of the need for change because merging and eliminating even the smallest units of government has proven politically daunting wherever it has been tried.

Key to both of these goals is gathering hard data on what every unit of government does, how much it spends and what it gets for its money — and then making that information readily available to the public. This is not an easy task; government is complicated and, with many states possessing thousands of jurisdictions, the sheer breadth of the data collection task is enormous. But without the ability to shine a light on just what is taking place under the status quo, driving change will continue to prove difficult.

Addressing the pension crisis

The special problem of state pensions

While states can work the annual budget and operations side of the equation, there is one looming fiscal issue that will dominate — and could devastate — state budgets into the future.

According to the Pew Center on the States, state pension and health care funds are underfunded by a whopping $2.73 trillion, a figure the report itself describes as "conservative" (other analyses put the number at well over $3 trillion).

The report, *The Trillion Dollar Gap: Underfunded State Retirement Systems and the Road to Reform*, released earlier this year, calculates what states have committed themselves to by way of pension payments and "other post-employment benefits" — mostly health care coverage — to the tens of thousands of once and future state government retirees who will be counting on the cash and coverage to carry them into a comfortable old age.[17]

While not everyone agrees with the dire picture painted by the Pew report — organized labor disputes that the long-range fiscal picture is that terrible — the overwhelming consensus is that this is a ticking time bomb under state budgets. A recent report by The Center for Retirement Research at Boston College predicts that state and local pension plans are headed for continued tough times, projecting that collectively they'll be 72 percent funded in 2013 — 8 percent below what is considered minimally healthy.[18]

Estimates suggest that the situation has worsened since the financial crisis. The Illinois Retirement System had a funded ratio of 54.3 percent, with assets of $64.7 billion and liabilities of $119 billion as of fiscal year 2008. Massachusetts has funded only 63 percent of its pension bill. Its liabilities grew 85 percent between 1999 and 2008, outpacing its assets, which grew only 34 percent in the same period. If a healthy system is at least 80 percent funded, then 16 states are showing cause for serious concern.[19]

If there is debate over just how dire the retirement funding situation is, many states, at least, appear to be getting the message. The spring of 2010 saw a flurry of legislative action aimed at closing retirement fund shortfalls.

ACTION PLAN FOR FIXING THE STATE PENSION PROBLEM

Governors and state legislators must face up to the problem of huge unfunded pension and retiree health care obligations. The following basket of reforms can help to address an urgent fiscal issue and rebuild public trust.

1-3. State pension funding levels 2008

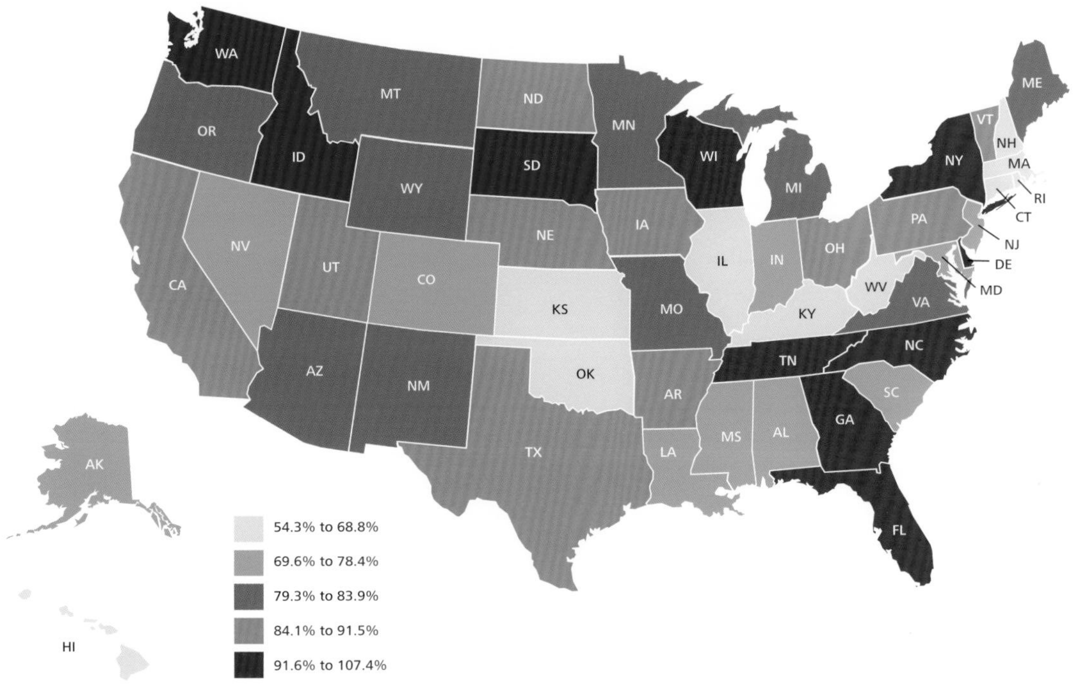

Source: The Pew Center on the States

Stop — or at least slow — the bleeding

The first thing states need to do is make sure that current contributions at least cover current liabilities. There are generally no requirements forcing public retirement plans to fund their pension liabilities. As a result, these plans are funded to varying degrees, including some that are completely unfunded and operate on a "pay-as-you-go" basis. Over the last few years, the faltering economy crimped general government revenues, leading jurisdictions to divert retirement fund contributions to other priorities. Paying less than the actuarially determined contribution each year is only making a bad situation worse.

Close loopholes

Two options for closing loopholes are: 1) Tighten the practice of granting large pay raises in the years immediately before retirement, which can allow employees to spike final earnings amounts; and 2) Narrow the eligibility for high-cost public-safety pension benefits. To prevent spiking, the California Association of Highway Patrolmen will now base its retirement benefits on the highest three years of earnings rather than the single highest year. In exchange, the organization is going to increase its monthly contribution to 10 percent from the original 8 percent.[20]

Introduce two-tier retirement programs

Extremely common in the private sector, these programs reduce retirement and health benefits for employees hired after a specific date, while maintaining agreed-upon benefit packages for existing workers. Several states have recently taken this route, including Kansas, Arkansas, Colorado, Louisiana, Mississippi, North Dakota, Rhode Island, New York and Texas, which have all created new classes of employees who, in some combination, will receive less generous pensions; take longer to be vested; have to work longer to get benefits and be older to receive them; and contribute more of their salary to their plans.

Phase in retirement

This strategy is designed to keep older employees in the workforce longer and therefore delay the onset of full pension benefits. North Carolina kicked off a program in 2006 under which state employees can start receiving partial pension benefits at age 59 while they continue working flexible hours.

Increase minimum retirement age

Some states have increased their minimum retirement ages. Mississippi is considering this after already requiring more years of service for benefits. Iowa, Minnesota, Vermont and Colorado are enacting similar measures.

In Illinois, legislation sailed through Springfield requiring new hires to work longer for benefits and limiting the size of pensions. The new law also increased the retirement age from 62 (or lower for some classes of employees) to 67, which officials estimate will save the system more than $40 billion over the next several decades.

Trim down past promises

Colorado lowered its cost-of-living increase, and South Dakota and Minnesota have taken similar measures to limit payouts over time. Other states, such as California and New Jersey, are changing benefits packages already promised to current employees and future retirees.

Put a circuit breaker on benefits increases

In 2007, Hawaii passed legislation barring any boost in benefits between 2008 and 2011 if such increases add to unfunded pension liabilities.

That same year, Missouri enacted legislation that prevents increases in any benefits where the relevant retirement fund is less than 80 percent funded.

Share risks through hybrid systems

A few states, reports the Pew Center on the States, are "sharing more of the risk of investment loss with employees by introducing benefit systems that combine elements of defined benefit and defined contribution plans. These hybrid systems generally offer a lower guaranteed benefit, while a portion of the contribution — usually the employees' share — goes into an account that is similar to a private sector 401(k)."

Georgia and Nebraska have adopted such hybrid plans for new employees, while Alaska and Michigan have adopted 401(k) plans for new workers.

What works: Growing union cooperation

Vermont hammered out a deal with its teachers' union that requires teachers to work longer before they're eligible for retirement and to make larger contributions to their pensions. Vermont, in fact, may be a harbinger of a new and more cooperative attitude on the part of organized labor when it comes to long-range pension and health care costs. Minnesota's largest public employee union recently signed off on a reduction in annual cost of living increases. In Kentucky, teachers decided to step up and begin contributing more to their future health care costs.

State retiree health care: Another ticking time bomb?

On the health care side — where only six states are on track to be fully funded, according to the Pew report — the most basic strategy being pursued by conscientious states has been to create dedicated, irrevocable trust funds to pay for retiree health care. According to the National Conference of State Legislatures, more than a dozen states have adopted this approach since 2007, although the amounts of money they are depositing in those trusts vary.[21]

Other options for dealing with long-term health care costs range from cutting coverage to requiring higher health care contributions and co-pays. Utah is asking retirees in essence to fund their own post-employment health care using the value of leftover sick leave, which is invested in a 401(k) account. (The 2006 law was challenged by the Utah Public Employees Association, which took its challenge all the way to the state supreme court, where the new plans were upheld.)

1-4. Number of states with fully funded pension programs

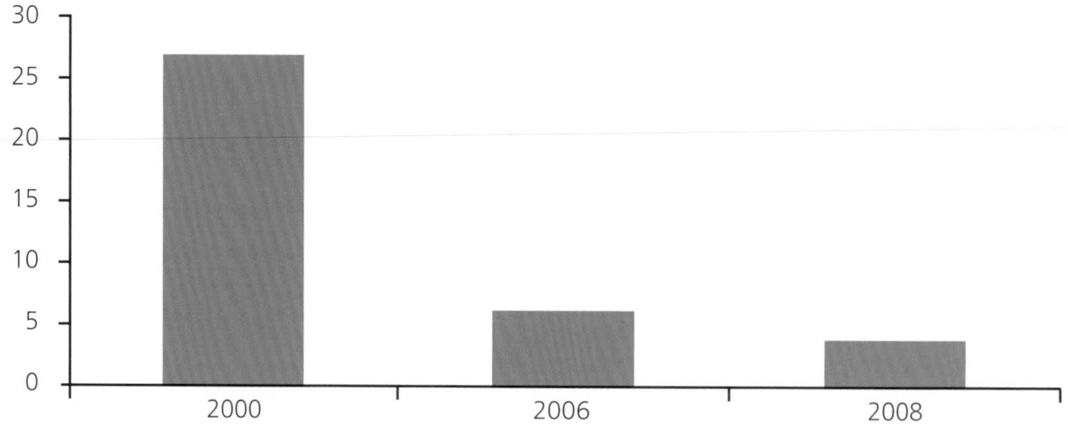

Source: The Pew Center on the States

In March, New Jersey passed a package of three bills that among other things, allows employees with fewer than 10 years of service to switch to 401(k) plans (making them portable if an employee wants to leave state service); bans future part-time workers from the pension system and requires any part-time worker making more than $5,000 a year to join a 401(k)-style plan; and requires all public employees to contribute 1.5 percent of their salaries to health care.

Reduce administrative costs

Another area of potential pension savings — one that won't even come close to solving the pension crisis, but is worth working on — is cutting plan administrative overhead. The biggest opportunity lies with consolidating multiple pension plans. There are more than 2,600 public employee retirement systems nationwide, according to the U.S. Census Bureau. In Texas, for example, dozens of state and local public retirement plans cover government workers, teachers, police and firefighters. Similarly, the State of Illinois has five separate retirement boards, each with its own workforce and infrastructure.

Roadblocks to overcome

Difficulty of modifying retirement plans

Retirement benefits are often the product of collective bargaining agreements, and these benefits are fiercely guarded by employee groups. Politics also plays a large part in the decision-making process. Public pension rights typically are considered part of a contract between the employer and employee. That makes it much harder to modify a public pension plan's terms. Furthermore, public employee pension benefits, once approved, have constitutional protection in some states.

Attractiveness of defined benefit programs

Unlike the private sector today, the vast majority of government retirement systems still offer defined benefit plans, which guarantee retirees a predetermined benefit amount based on the number of years they work and their final or highest average compensation amount. Public employees typically contribute a fixed portion of their paychecks into a pension fund, which is invested to produce revenue to pay for a portion of their retirement benefits. Because retirees are guaranteed a certain benefit amount, the government must make up any shortfall resulting from actual investment returns that are less than anticipated. While more expensive, defined benefit plans afford retirees greater security.[22]

Failure of political will and fuzzy math

Not even budget hawks are immune to the temptation to underfund state pension systems. Pew's Susan Uhran notes, "For far too long states have sort of ignored this issue, increasing benefits when times were good, but making no accommodation for paying for that." Meanwhile, governors and legislatures alike have been too willing to shuffle the problem off to the future. "The attitude has been, 'We'll worry about it next year,'" she says.

Interview with Mitch Daniels

Governor of Indiana

the journey to fiscally sustainable government

Q...Are we moving into an era of permanent fiscal crisis in the states? Might states need to think about how to do less with less?

Most states until recently haven't done anything significant to curtail spending. It was growing grotesquely in many places, so there's a lot of room to shrink. It will be a fundamentally different trajectory going forward. Let's hope the economy revives to the point that state revenues do show some growth year-to-year, but they're not going to catch up to the trendline they had been on.

Q...Indiana has emerged as the poster child for fiscal sanity during this time of fiscal crisis. How do you turn a deep budget deficit into a surplus without closing DMVs and slashing school spending?

You limit the growth of state spending to something less than revenue. When we came in, Indiana was technically bankrupt. We simply insisted that we have the tightest budget in 55 years and found that in state government, the fruit hangs very low.

People ask me often, "What were the biggest surprises in office?" One of them was how easy it was to find excess, duplication and unnecessary spending. Once we capped spending at what theretofore would have been an extraordinarily low level, human ingenuity started to assert itself. We heard the usual lamentations about how hard and painful it would all be, but it wasn't, not at all.

Q...In 2006, you leased the Indiana toll road for $3.8 billion to a private Spanish/Australian consortium. When it occurred it was quite controversial and cost you a lot of political support. Now it looks to be extraordinarily successful. What are some lessons?

If you have an underperforming asset from which someone else believes they can extract more value, you ought to consider monetizing it, then investing the money in something you get a better return out of. That's what we did in the case of the toll road and also in many lesser things. We've shed thousands of state vehicles, two-thirds of the state aircraft and redeployed those proceeds into things that we think are more useful for our citizens.

The results are spectacular. We will now deliver to the next generation billions of dollars worth of new public infrastructure that this state never would have had otherwise without a dime of new taxes or a dime of borrowing.

Q…How important is it to establish a central cost-saving group rather than just asking all your department heads to cut costs?

You have to relentlessly tear down fiefdoms. In most of life I've taken a sort of libertarian outlook on things, but when it comes to things like IT and procurement, I'm for dictatorship.

We centralized certain functions — procurement, personnel, information technology. Enormous savings come from taking these steps. We also launched into volume purchasing right away. You can't have every department running around with their own credit card and buying things in small quantities from who knows whom.

We also moved to a pay-for-performance system across the state government, moving away from the old industrial model where the best worker in a group at the end of the year got treated exactly the same as the worst loafer in the group.

Q…Some might argue that, given the magnitude of the fiscal crisis, it's not worth spending much time on micro-savings. Instead, just go where the big money is. You didn't do that.

If you're trying to come out of a fiscal hole as deep as most states are looking at now, you have to attack spending on every front. We did a number of things that were very large, that brought very large savings immediately, but you also have to do literally hundreds of lesser things that add up.

You need to build a culture that challenges every expenditure and thinks critically about whether we really need to do this or not. If we do, what is the least expensive way to get the job done? By working relentlessly on that for six years, I hope we're getting there. You have to, over the course of time, try to convert thousands of people into thinking this way and believing it's the right thing to do.

Q…You had a proposal to rationalize the number of local government units. It failed to pass the Indiana legislature. Can you talk a little bit about that issue?

The inertia is bipartisan. Folks are wed either sentimentally or for patronage purposes to these old, outmoded, duplicative structures.

There are two ways it can happen. One is by thoughtful reform legislation that just simply looks at the changed environment and takes the necessary steps to consolidate or rationalize these local government units.

The other way is if circumstances will compel it. The days of easy money that led to growth are over. Here in Indiana, we put a cap on property taxes after we cut them. Initially this isn't going to be impossible for localities to deal with. But going forward, it will mean that they are going to have to have a hard look at doing some of the things that we've been doing in state government.

Here's a small example: The Fort Wayne school district, our state's second-largest, didn't have all the money they wanted for the current school year. After much debate they took the radical, brilliant, breakthrough step of outsourcing custodial services. Every business I know did this about 20 years ago. They saved $4.5 million dollars a year, which is equivalent to about 80 teachers. So why didn't they do it 20 years ago? The answer is: they didn't have to.

Q…If you were given a clean sheet of paper to redesign state government to meet today's realities, what are some of the ways it might look different?

The question is what pieces of today's state bureaucracy might best be delivered in some other way? How small can the core of state government be? You could pay the people in state government dramatically more than you do now if they're project managers, contract supervisors and auditors. The goal would be to ensure that the taxpayer was getting a great result at a good price and that everybody was following the rules. The exception, not the rule, would be taxpayers pay for a building and we fill it up with thousands of permanent or full-time permanent state employees.

PART II: IMPROVING STATE COMPETITIVENESS

Introduction

Improving economic competitiveness

A few years back, The Gallup Organization launched its "world poll," designed to gather more than mere opinions. It set out to collect insight about what people all over the world are thinking *about*. When it released the results of the first poll in 2007, Gallup minced no words. "[W]e may have already found the single most searing, clarifying, helpful, world-altering fact," it said. "At the very least, it needs to be considered in every policy, every law and every social initiative. ... What the whole world wants is a good job."

In an age of instant and ever-expanding communications, unfettered capital flows and footloose talent, this puts enormous pressure on policymakers and political leaders. After all, if *you're* not thinking constantly about how to improve economic competitiveness and job prospects within your borders, the leaders of the next state over certainly are — along with those in the next country over and the next continent over. And the people who lead companies, as well as the workforce whose skills and knowledge are becoming increasingly important in highly competitive markets, are paying close attention.

The ground under policymakers' feet is shifting. Emerging from the recent recession will not be a return to the status quo or easing economic and competitive pressure. In fact, it will be quite the opposite. Ongoing shifts in the foundations of economic life are displacing and reshuffling the traditional building blocks of economic competitiveness. The result is that whatever state economic development efforts looked like a few years ago, they won't resemble what is needed a few years from now.

State leaders would do well to wonder what this means for them. For instance, companies' need for a skilled, knowledgeable and innovative workforce has implications for state education policy. The ballooning importance of the digital infrastructure provides clear opportunities for high-tech growth strategies. A company's ability to profit from knowledge flows is just as crucial as a state government's ability to access ample knowledge infrastructure.

States that remain economically competitive will share several characteristics. First, urban economic development strategies will make cities attractive to firms and their workers. Second, state economic strategies will build on long-term sectoral strengths and devote the resources necessary to buttress universities, research institutions and other organizations that can underpin those sectors. Finally, they will adopt organizational changes that allow them to adapt to the changing marketplace as nimbly as their private sector counterparts.

The shift to an innovation economy

Redesigning state economic development for the new economic realities

Formidable as it remains, the recession is not the most difficult economic challenge confronting governors and state policymakers. They also face deeply rooted changes that have been gaining strength for decades — changes that are dramatically reshaping the global business environment, which many states have yet to reckon with.

Three basic forces are at work. The first is a long-term trend toward economic liberalization, which has removed barriers to the movement of ideas, capital, products and people. The second is the exponential improvement in performance of the basic infrastructure of technological capacity: bandwidth, digital storage and computing power. The third is the ever-expanding penetration of new technology throughout the business world and society as a whole — that is, both the adoption of innovative products and the changing practices and protocols that allow business to use the growing power of digital technology.[23] The confluence of these three forces has been dubbed "The Big Shift" (see figure 2-1).

The fundamental changes outlined in The Big Shift have ramped up the competitive pressure on American firms. The "topple rate" at which big companies lose their leadership positions has nearly doubled over the last 40 years.[24] The average lifetime for companies on the S&P 500 has fallen dramatically. Perhaps most strikingly, U.S. companies' return on assets has fallen to almost one-quarter of their 1965 level, even as labor productivity has improved.[25] "Given these long-term trends," write John Hagel, John Seely Brown and Lang Davison, "we cannot reasonably expect to see a significant easing of performance pressure as the current economic downturn begins to dissipate — on the contrary, all long-term trends point to a continued erosion of performance.[26]

The way out depends on companies' ability to transform the challenges presented by the changing competitive landscape into opportunities. Even while the initial wave of forces has proven exceedingly disruptive, it has also seeded a second wave that is reshaping the ingredients crucial to company performance. In other words, economic liberalization and the evolution of the digital infrastructure may put new pressures on businesses, but they also encourage the flows of knowledge, talent and capital that allow companies to innovate, boost productivity and create jobs. But first, businesses need to figure out how to turn these pressures into opportunities.

Where companies once gained competitive advantage through building and then safeguarding stocks of proprietary knowledge, they now survive by taking

2-1. The Big Shift Index

The Shift Index consists of 25 indicators within three indices that quantify the three waves of The Big Shift — the Foundation Index, Flow Index and Impact Index

Index	Category	Indicators
Impact Index	Markets	**Competitive Intensity:** Herfindahl-Hirschman Index **Labor Productivity:** Index of labor productivity as defined by the Bureau of Labor Statistics **Stock Price Volatility:** Average standard deviation of daily stock price returns over one year
	Firms	**Asset Profitability:** Total ROA for all US firms **ROA Performance Gap:** Gap in ROA between firms in the top and the bottom quartiles **Firm Topple Rate:** Annual rank shuffling among US firms **Shareholder Value Gap:** Gap in the TRS[1] between firms in the top and bottom quartiles
	People	**Consumer Power:** Index of 6 consumer power measures **Brand Disloyalty:** Index of 6 consumer disloyalty measures **Returns-to-Talent:** Compensation gap between more and less creative occupational groupings[2] **Executive Turnover:** Number of Top Management terminated, retired or otherwise leaving companies
Flow Index	Virtual flows	**Inter-firm Knowledge Flows:** Extent of employee participation in knowledge flows across firms **Wireless Activity:** Total annual volume of mobile minutes and SMS messages **Internet Activity:** Internet traffic between top 20 US cities with the most domestic bandwidth
	Physical flows	**Migration of People to Creative Cities:** Population gap between top and bottom creative cities[3] **Travel Volume:** Total volume of local commuter transit and passenger air transportation[4] **Movement of Capital:** Value of US Foreign Direct Investment inflows and outflows
	Amplifiers	**Worker Passion:** Percentage of employees most passionate about their jobs **Social Media Activity:** Time spend on social media as a percentage of total Internet time
Foundation Index	Technology performance	**Computing:** Computing power per unit of cost **Digital Storage:** Digital storage capacity per unit of cost **Bandwidth:** Bandwidth capacity per unit of cost
	Infrastructure penetration	**Internet Users:** Number of people actively using the Internet as compared to the US population **Wireless Subscriptions:** Percentage of active wireless subscriptions as compared to the US population
	Public policy	**Economic Freedom:** Index of 10 freedom companies as defined by the Heritage Foundation

1. TRS - Total Return to Shareholders
2. Creative Occupations and Cities are defined by Dr. Richard Florida, "The Rise of the Creative Class", 2004
3. Ibid
4. Measured by the Bureau of Transportation Services Index

To assemble the list of 25 shift index metrics, we carefully analyzed more than 70 potential metrics, using a process detailed in Exhibit 90 of the 2009 Shift Index

Source: Deloitte Center for the Edge

advantage of other avenues. Knowledge flows; ideas for process-improvement conversations between people within and outside a company; and the problem-solving prowess of connected individuals with diverse experiences, perspectives and expertise are powerful tools for creating competitive advantage.

For businesses, success in today's changing economy hinges on three key capabilities: a) to position themselves to participate as fully as possible in knowledge flows; b) to learn from those flows and be able to scale what they learn; and c) to attract, retain, motivate and unleash people with the skills and talent that can help them thrive.

ACTION PLAN FOR RESHAPING STATE ECONOMIC DEVELOPMENT

What will pull firms toward success in the 21st century is their ability to find, attract and nurture talent, and to give workers at all levels — not just the most educated or skilled — the right environment in which to learn, innovate and solve problems.

A reshaped state economic development strategy would use all the levers state government possesses to nurture these capabilities, helping companies position themselves to take advantage of knowledge flows and turning states and their cities and regions into places that draw the talent companies need. The following actions could form the core of this new approach:

Operate at the speed of business, not government

Soon after coming into office, Indiana Governor Mitch Daniels abolished the state's Department of Commerce and replaced it with a nonprofit called the Indiana Economic Development Corporation. "By being a nonprofit corporation, we're able to raise outside money," says Governor Daniels. "We hire real business people. We operate at the speed of business, not the speed of government. Employees told me of occasions when by the time they got a clearance to buy an airplane ticket to go somewhere, some other state had the business already."[27]

Catalyze innovation

There are several ways state governments can help grow their capacity to innovate. To begin, a smart government will pay close attention to the market structure for information and communications technology services — the companies doing business, the degree of competition, the opportunities for a strategic nudge to spur innovation — and then use its role as a major customer for these services to spur innovation and competition where needed. It can identify and then eliminate barriers to entry for new service providers, offer incentives to companies that try to expand their knowledge networks and provide access to its information infrastructure where shared access makes sense.

Similarly, training programs to develop the information technology and Internet skills of entrepreneurs, business executives and the general population can stoke demand and help businesses understand how to take advantage of emerging innovations. Rhode Island's Innovation Providence Implementation Council (IPIC) includes leaders from the region's business community, academia and hospitals, civic organizations, and state and local governments. IPIC's charge is to boost the state's knowledge economy. It does so by developing training and development opportunities to retain young talent and strengthening connections among entrepreneurs, universities, government and select grant recipients.

Build on strengths

Every city and state cannot be the biomedical capital. Each city and urban area is distinct, and the more state policies take account of their strengths — as opposed to forcing them to follow the herd — the stronger they will become as magnets both for businesses and the employees who will help them thrive.

Instead of going after whatever happens to be the hottest industry of the moment, states, cities and regions should map their existing assets and build upon those strengths. As Portland, Oregon-based

What works: BioBusiness Alliance of Minnesota

The BioBusiness Alliance of Minnesota produced Destination 2025, a 20–year strategic plan and roadmap for Minnesota in the six life science markets in which the state participates: medical devices, biologics and biopharmaceuticals, animal health, food, renewable energy and renewable materials. The process involved over 600 people from around the world who work in and with the industry and who are experts in their area of focus. One outcome was a roadmap that examined the overlap between the six industries and made a series of recommendations for the state to advance its position in the life science industry and beyond. Stakeholders then used the roadmap to align the recommendations with existing assets within their regions.

> "Human and economic activity will cluster in areas where people expect to find jobs and opportunity, where innovation, ideas and freedom are welcomed, incubated and encouraged."
>
> ~ *Back from the Brink*

economist Joseph Cortright and graduate student Heike Meyer have written, "Contrary to common wisdom, high technology varies dramatically from place to place. Different metropolitan areas tend to specialize in certain technologies and have major concentrations of firms and employment in relatively few product categories. A region that is strong in one area, say medical devices, doesn't necessarily have a competitive advantage in another area, like telecommunications, or semiconductors or software."[28]

The question at hand is a twofold one: "What do we have, and what can we do to strengthen those industries?" The Piedmont triad area of North Carolina looked at its furniture industry and surmised that it had a real future in the region and developed that base. Milwaukee 7, with its focus on the water industry, and the California Space Authority in Southern California have also done a commendable job building on their existing ecosystems.

Spur collaboration

States can also support research institutions and public-private collaborations that explore and stimulate opportunities for new businesses. Spurring collaboration between academia, industry and government is key to fostering innovation and developing the clusters that will drive economic growth. As the World Economic Forum's *Global Information Technology Report 2009/10* noted, "The recent development history of some of the most networked economies in the world, be they Estonia, Israel, Korea, or Singapore, shows that the alliance between a farsighted government and an actively engaged private sector on the definition and implementation of a common [information and communication technologies] vision has been extremely powerful."[29]

What works: Georgia Research Alliance

Stung by losing its bid in the 1980s to host the headquarters of a cutting-edge semiconductor consortium, Georgia responded in 1990 by creating the Georgia Research Alliance (http://www.gra.org). Its goal was to bring business leaders, the state government and Georgia's research universities together to find ways of using innovative research to fuel the state's high-tech development. Funded by the state legislature, the GRA wooed a series of high-profile researchers to Georgia's universities — often to the chagrin of universities in neighboring states — and helped those institutions invest in the infrastructure and technology needed to support high-end work. The GRA helped to establish more than 150 companies capable of commercializing the research it funded.

Recognize that metropolitan areas drive competitiveness

State legislatures are notorious for their urban-suburban-rural tussles over money and other state resources. These are political disputes that states simply cannot afford.

In the world's more developed regions, some three-quarters of the population already lives in urban areas, a figure that is projected to increase to 81 percent by 2030.[30] "Human and economic activity will cluster in areas where people expect to find jobs and opportunity, where innovation, ideas and freedom are welcomed, incubated and encouraged," writes Greg Pellegrino in *Back from the Brink.*[31] Certainly that has been true in this country, where, as *BusinessWeek* noted at the height of the dot-com boom, "Today, big cities are developing into idea factories — tightly integrated combines that generate the information, the conversations, and the spontaneous innovations that are the lifeblood of a knowledge-based economy."[32]

State policies, therefore, need to recognize that helping metropolitan regions resolve issues with infrastructure, traffic flow, provision of basic services, central-city public education and the like is not a matter of "the rest of the state subsidizing the city," but a crucial piece of the state's competitive posture in an economy where knowledge and talent pools are fundamental drivers.

Roadblocks to overcome

Legacy efforts

Every new gubernatorial administration must confront the legacy left by previous economic development efforts. There may be a plethora of public and quasi-public organizations, each focused on one small part of the picture, operating with no common direction. They may lack the connections or ability to catalyze strategic partnerships with the broad range of players (the private sector, community colleges, utilities and so on) that affect a state's competitive profile. Often, a state either lacks a clear economic development strategy or just focuses broadly on business retention and attraction without industry- or sector-specific approaches, defined metrics and measurable progress.

Funding

Efforts might also be hampered by vastly curtailed budgets or funding sources for economic development that were raided over the years to help the general fund. A state's regulatory environment may hinder competitiveness and increase business costs, and its infrastructure may need dramatic upgrades.

Boosting manufacturing competitiveness

Not your grandfather's manufacturing

We are not suggesting that the future of economic competitiveness lies solely with high-tech industries. Rather, a firm's ability to compete will rest, in part, on the extent to which it can use technology and knowledge networks and from them maintain an edge over its competitors, regardless of the sector it inhabits.

To understand this better, it's useful to look at one specific economic arena — manufacturing — and to consider how states can best help manufacturers thrive in this shifting economy. For most states, the competitiveness of its manufacturing sector is critical to its long-term economic prosperity and growth. It creates good jobs — not just within the sector but in financial services, infrastructure development and maintenance, customer support, logistics, information systems, health care, education and training, and real estate. A strong manufacturing sector also boosts a state's intellectual capital and penchant for innovation by underwriting research and development, pushing the technological envelope, and driving the growth in demand for highly skilled workers and scientists.

However, manufacturing has been one of the industries hardest hit by the recession. The United States has lost two million manufacturing jobs as a direct result of the recession. States that used to compete with one another for new factories and manufacturing jobs are now going head-to-head with countries all over the world. These countries are creating aggressive tax and trade policies and negotiating trade agreements to position themselves to win in the new global economy.

Despite the recent troubles, a survey of the American public's opinions on the manufacturing industry and its future show a nation that is surprisingly bullish on the skills and abilities of our workforce in the face of global competition.[33] Moreover, Americans ranked manufacturing second in its importance to a strong national economy, behind only the energy industry, but ahead of technology, financial services, health care, communications and retail (see figure 2-2).

2-2. Ranking of industries by respondents as most important to maintain a strong national economy in the US

Industry	Rank
Energy	1
Manufacturing	2
Technology	3
Financial services	4
Health care	5
Communications	6
Retail	7

(Aggregate ranking of sectors by all respondents)

Source: 2010 annual index, Deloitte and the Manufacturing Institute.

> At the height of the global recession, 32 percent of surveyed companies reported moderate to serious skills shortages in the hiring pool.
>
> ~ THE MANUFACTURING INSTITUTE

While bullish on U.S. manufacturing, Americans are very concerned about U.S. government policies and leadership in this area. Respondents singled out state and federal government leadership, tax rates on individuals and government business policies as their top three areas of concern (see figure 2-3).

With manufacturing playing such a vital role in a state's economic health, state policymakers must take seriously their role in creating an environment in which manufacturing can thrive. Especially today, when the landscape of manufacturing dominance is shifting, synchronizing government policy with the investment decisions of manufacturing executives is critical for a state to remain competitive and create a positive cycle of prosperity.

Policymakers must look to the mid-term future of manufacturing competitiveness — as little as a five-year window — to enable a thoughtful dialogue between policymakers and business leaders. State governments that fail to understand the barriers that prevent manufacturing investment may find themselves missing the window of opportunity to create a better business climate for investment.

ACTION PLAN FOR BOLSTERING STATE MANUFACTURING COMPETITIVENESS

For policymakers, the implication is clear: Take action before the proverbial train has left the station. An action-oriented blueprint for boosting manufacturing competitiveness would include these seven strategies:

Enhance talent pools

Talent, specifically talent that drives innovation, trumps all when it comes to competitiveness at manufacturing companies — well ahead of factors that have more traditionally been associated with competitive manufac-

2-3. Attributes behind U.S. competitiveness as ranked by survey respondents

Most important attributes to U.S. competitiveness	Attributes providing U.S. with biggest advantage	Attributes causing the most concern
Work ethic	Technology use & availability	State & federal leadership
Skilled workforce	Skilled workforce	Tax rates on individuals
Productivity	R & D capabilities	Government business policies

Source: Deloitte and The Manufacturing Institute

turing. Having a steady supply of highly skilled workers, scientists, researchers and engineers is seen as the top driver of manufacturing competitiveness. Having a capacity for innovation driven by a plentiful and talented workforce at all levels is what will ultimately differentiate the long-term winners in this race.

Create a low-cost economic environment

Cost still matters when it comes to where a company locates a manufacturing plant. "I can tell you definitively that it costs $1 billion more per factory for me to build, equip, and operate a semiconductor manufacturing facility in the United States," says Intel CEO Paul Otellini.[34] According to Otellini, 90 percent of that additional cost of a $4 billion factory is not labor; it's the cost to comply with taxes and regulations that other nations don't impose. States can increase competitiveness with tax policy, research grants and regulations that indirectly promote manufacturing and innovation.

What works: Edison Welding Institute in Ohio

The ability to join two materials together is crucial to manufacturing. Yet, as manufacturers strive to remain competitive, it's difficult to invest resources in staying abreast of the latest technology — let alone obtain that technology for themselves. The Edison Welding Institute, a nonprofit corporation based in Columbus, Ohio, fills that gap.

It was founded in 1984, the result of a collaborative effort among Ohio State University, the Battelle Memorial Institute, England's The Welding Institute, and then-Governor Dick Celeste, who established a program of "technology excellence centers" around Ohio, including one for research into welding techniques. With 150 employees, EWI works with some 350 companies to pursue innovations in materials joining, study and resolve process and production problems in specific factories, design manufacturing processes, build prototypes at its own lab and then help clients make the transition to manufacturing and test new ideas. Funding comes from the State of Ohio, federal grants and its customer base.

There are 39 regional economies across the United States, according to the Council on Competitiveness

Connect the dots

Huge amounts of federal money for applied research and economic development flow through the states, but the funding is delivered through silos. Almost none of it is connected. To fix this, states need to create intersections between universities and institutes that deal with processes and research facilities for advanced computing and manufacturers. One way is to build greater access to talent and facilities. Modeling and simulation, for example, are an increasingly important part of high performance manufacturing, but 90 percent of small manufacturers cannot access this asset. Moreover, most are not trained to use these computational assets. Aligning postsecondary education and connecting small manufacturers to high-performance computing constitutes one powerful strategy for connecting the dots.

Boost manufacturing innovation networks

The old thinking about how manufacturing works — that it relies on linear, one-step-after-another supply chains and "R & D pipelines" — is outmoded.[35] Networks of parts and materials suppliers, sub-assembly plants, design and logistics suppliers, financial advisers and the like allow participants to learn from one another and to innovate faster. The more robust the network, the better its members can reinforce one another. Public policy related to workforce development and training, financial incentives, public services aimed at small manufacturers and cross-state cooperation all need to take into account the networks that a given industry or cluster relies upon.

Build a virtual "one-stop-shop" shared services system

Linking existing manufacturing innovation networks to premiere shared services providers and networks — such as state workforce development organizations, economic development leaders, and management consultancy groups such as the various state manufacturing extension partnerships (MEPs) — will enhance the ability of manufacturers to promote growth and strengthen a state's economy. Start by piloting small and focused programs. These can be used as a stepping stone for flexible and sustainable programs.

Engage regionally

States should explore a regional approach to economic development around a key emerging industry. For example, linking Great Lakes states together could create a regional center for clean energy production. Regional engagement requires moving from competition to collaboration with neighboring states and then creating a connected system of manufacturers, educational institutions and training. The Transformative Regional Engagement Network, for example, connects universities, government, businesses and nonprofit organizations in efforts to innovate around key industries on a regional basis.

Drivers of manufacturing competitiveness

In 2009, Deloitte and the Council on Competitiveness gathered data from more than 400 CEOs and senior manufacturing business unit leaders worldwide.[36] The manufacturers identified the ten most important drivers of competition. All ten drivers reflect the critical interplay between market and government forces (see figure 2–4).

2-4. Drivers of manufacturing competitiveness

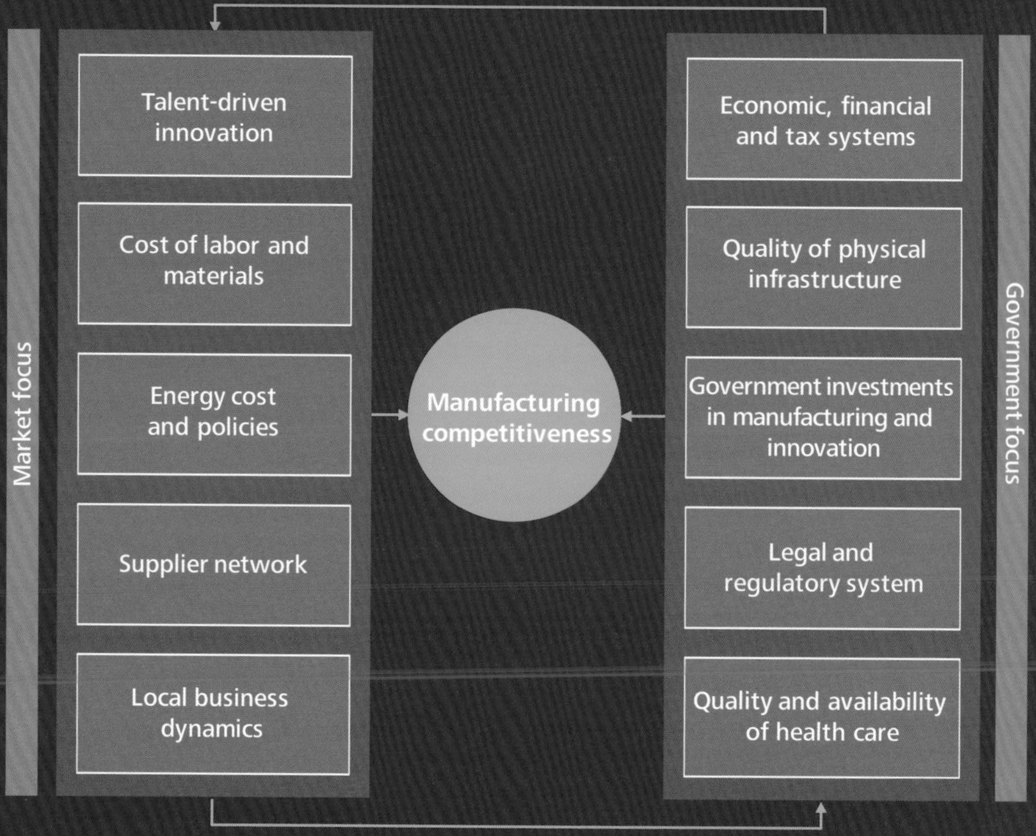

Source: Deloitte and the Council on Competitiveness

The drivers were also ranked in terms of importance by the manufacturing executives who participated in the study (see figure 2-5). Overall, the classic factors of production — labor, materials and energy — constitute three of the four most important drivers of manufacturing competitiveness, as identified by the U.S. and Canadian senior manufacturing leaders who participated in this study. These are all primarily driven by market forces, even though they can be greatly influenced by government policy.

While this result should not be surprising, it is crucial to note the qualitative difference between the classic view of production and these findings. Namely, how the availability of talented people — scientists, researchers, engineers and production workers — now heavily drives manufacturing innovation and influences manufacturing's overall competitiveness.

Align educational and career pathways in postsecondary education

"Education leaders should be aligning educational pathways in degree programs to portable, industry-recognized skills credentials, creating more 'on and off' ramps," says Emily Stover DeRocco, president of The Manufacturing Institute. This, in turn, will help close the gap between the high-tech skills that manufacturers need and those that recent graduates have upon entering the workforce.

The Clemson University International Center for Automotive Research (ICAR) in Greenville, South Carolina forms a bridge between academic research and practical applications in the automotive industry. It connects university researchers with research by companies involved in automotives, so all the testing can be done in one place. BMW and the university worked together to develop the curriculum. BMW, along with Michelin, IBM and Microsoft collaborated on an information technology research center.

Over the years, other firms have set up shop at the Center. Proterra, a company that builds drive and energy storage systems for buses and other heavy vehicles, is building a new R&D and manufacturing facility there.

The research center collaborates with researchers from the other parts of Clemson University, such as those with expertise in textiles and advanced materials. Building off ICAR's presence, Clemson also recently decided to create a graduate level department of automotive engineering.

2-5. Drivers relative importance to manufacturing competitiveness

USA and Canada	
Drivers	**Driver score (10=High; 1=Low)**
Talent-driven innovation	8.72
Cost of labor and materials	7.81
Economic, financial and tax systems	7.50
Energy cost and policies	6.79
Legal and regulatory system	6.68
Quality of physical infrastructure	6.43
Government investments in manufacturing and innovation	6.18
Supplier network	5.65
Local business dynamics	3.61
Quality and availability of health care	1.15

Source: Deloitte and the Council on Competitiveness

Interview with

Deborah Wince-Smith

CEO, Council on Competitiveness

Q...We lost two million manufacturing jobs during this recession. Are they ever coming back?

It is naïve to think we will reclaim these jobs. However, if we do things right, we're going to develop, retain and grow higher-value manufacturing jobs. We lost a lot of manufacturing jobs to automation, the rise of Asia, the rise of the emerging economies and to the commoditization of many of these products. A good example is the PC where we still play a role in design and a lot of the higher value functions, but the actual fabrication has migrated to lower cost countries.

Q...What would be an example of a higher value manufacturing job that we might grow?

Manufacturing has a very deep embedded use of computational capabilities and very advanced automation. Having a skill set that enables workers on the factory floor to understand and operate highly complex automation is one area where the game has changed. Add to that the use of modeling and simulation for design work. In the future, we'll be moving to self-assembly of materials. That will demand a whole different skill set and capability than existed in the past.

Q...Certainly not your grandfather's manufacturing. Won't all the automation mean fewer jobs for people?

We are going to have to move away from the more classic early- to mid-20th century assembly line type of jobs. The real challenge here is not that there aren't going to be enough jobs, it's that the jobs will change and be different. And that's where our skill base comes in.

Q...What can states do to be more economically competitive?

We have a very untenable, unsustainable federal and state regulatory environment for a 21st century innovation economy. Let's just look through the energy lens. If an entity wants to move on some of the new clean energy technologies — whether it's wind, or solar, or let alone try to move forward on nuclear energy — the permitting, the regulatory hurdles you have to go through are punitive not just in cost but in time. There's just no rationality on the regulatory front.

Then, there is the issue of the role of states versus the federal government. An example is product liability laws where each state has its own system, its own interpretation. You see class action suits that are just the bane of existence for U.S. companies versus their competitors. Trial lawyers take suits to specific jurisdictions where there is a better opportunity to extract awards for damages. This is a tremendous burden, not just on cost but also on corporate decision making about where high-value investments are made. A conservative number is that the United States spends more than 2 percent of our GDP on torts. The closest number to ours is in the UK, where it is .08 percent. There's no other country in the world that has this tremendous burden placed on it from product liability and tort laws.

Q...What other recommendations would you make to a new governor about competitiveness?

The first thing to do is identify what assets you have in your state. Do you have world-class universities? Do you have a network of community colleges? Do you have the capacity now and in the future to develop the human capital, the skilled workforce that's needed in a rapidly changing economy and that will make your state an attractive place to do business? And if you don't, what do you need to do to develop that capacity?

Second, you have to look at the state's overall cost structure and business environment. The old model that we would compete on wages within our own country, where manufacturing would move out of the northeast and go down into the south, that model has played itself out. That's not the way to attract investment and grow economic activity. States now compete against the whole world for investment and business activity. Companies can turn on a dime and decide they're going to move operations and people to places that are closer to their customers and where the overall business environment is more favorable.

If you have a total 40 percent cost penalty to manufacture here versus China, then a company's boards of directors will say go to China.

Q...Do regional approaches to economic development hold any promise?

Let's look at the north Midwest, the heartland of our industrial might: the rubber industry, the auto industry, the production slicing of all of those capabilities that existed. And many still do in Ohio, Michigan, Indiana and Illinois. Our country is poised to be a huge player in clean energy and to revitalize our auto industry if those states come together as a region and integrate their tremendous industrial capabilities. If the governors in these states pulled together and brought all the private sector players together, they could do something very powerful in the region.

Q...What about small manufacturers? How can they be more competitive on the world stage, and what is the role of the states in enabling this?

How you knit together the small, sometimes fragile, but critical supplier base to larger business enterprises is very important. First, states can inventory the regulations that are really hurting their small manufacturers, and then outline how to alleviate the burden. States could then go forward as a group to Congress with a reform package.

Second, high performance computing is really changing the game for this country. We need to get the power of supercomputing into the hands of the supplier base of small manufacturers in this country. If we can do this, it will be revolutionary.

Introduction

Educating the workforce of tomorrow

Providing a high-quality education to America's youth is essential to our nation's economic competitiveness. In a global market predicated on knowledge and innovation, a poor education is a ticket to the economic margins of society.

To sustain its competitive position among world economies, America will need to radically improve its educational prowess. American high school seniors today rank near the bottom in the Western world in math and science scores.[37] Moreover, U.S. college students today constitute only 14 percent of the total world population of college students, as compared with 30 percent three decades ago.

One consequence of this decline is the growing chasm between the business demand for high-skilled labor and the supply coming out of our colleges and universities. The shortage of students pursuing math and science careers, as well as outdated teaching methods, threaten America's competitive advantage. With India and China enrolling almost one and a half times the number of students in tertiary education, the United States needs to graduate more students to retain its position in the global marketplace.[38]

Few experts doubt that this will require wholesale changes in our education system.

In particular, the United States needs to drive much greater innovation and competition into education. Simply giving students more of the same — more hours per day and more weeks per year following status quo educational strategies — won't produce the necessary change. If the United States is to rekindle its competitive edge, its schools will have to discover some entirely fresh approaches (see figure 3-1).

The number of students pursuing careers in math and science must increase in order to accommodate the needs of industries that hinge on these skills. The jobs with the fastest growth rates are in the science and technology fields.[39] The United States ranks 16th out of 17 nations in the proportion of 24-year-olds earning degrees in natural science or engineering.

The United States ranks 16th out of 17 nations in the proportion of 24-year-olds earning degrees in natural science or engineering.

To satisfy this demand, America will need to increase student interest in math and science. It can do this by improving teacher recruitment and training, engaging students earlier and educating the public about the importance of nurturing more science and engineering professionals.

Implementing reform programs for schools can be expensive, and states and school districts are feeling increasing pressure to reduce education costs. Thirty-four states have cut services for FY2011 in K–12 and early education, and all but eight have done the same for higher education.[40] New Jersey's state budget, for example, slashed $1 billion in state aid to local districts.

In such tight fiscal times, states and school districts need to explore every avenue for squeezing efficiencies out of the current system. The State of California has explored digital textbooks as a way to cut costs while simultaneously encouraging the use of technology. Indiana, Pennsylvania, New Jersey and other states have created incentives for schools to reduce costs through sharing services. While economics weighs heavily on school reform, the consequences of not implementing effective reforms will be far more perilous.

Transforming education

Mounting momentum for radical change

Education reform has been a national priority for four decades. During the Reagan administration, Bill Bennett's Department of Education released "A Nation At Risk" and even equated the crisis in our educational system to a hostile takeover by an enemy. What have decades of urgent pleas for education reform produced? Unfortunately, most key education indicators have worsened.

More than 30 percent of American students never graduate from high school.[41] SAT scores have fallen every year since 2004.[42] Of those who make it to college, 60 percent of incoming community college students and 30 percent of freshmen at four-year colleges need remedial reading and math courses, indicating that many high schools fail to prepare students for college.[43] Only half of those students who enroll in college end up with a bachelor's degree.[44]

Rising against this backdrop of despair is an education reform movement that is more determined, more bipartisan and more powerful than anything seen in this country in decades. It can be seen in Washington D.C., where test scores rose after a series of reforms were enacted.

In New Orleans, after Katrina struck in August 2005, the state legislature swept 107 of the city's 128 public schools (most of them already closed because of the hurricane) into the Recovery School District. At these 107 schools, the move instantly wiped away all existing school leadership, teachers, contracts, processes, procedures, forms, rules and policies, along with oversight from the Orleans Parish School Board. The schools were given a clean slate.

Education reform is also alive in New York City, where former schools chancellor Joel Klein raised $75 million in private funds to create the largest training program for principals in the country and where the city's School of One uses personalization to improve learning.[45] Teachers collect data based on the results of classroom and virtual instruction as well as one-on-one tutoring to develop individual plans tailored to each pupil.

Likewise in high schools across the country, the Bill and Melinda Gates Foundation has invested more than $250 million in grants to divide large, underperforming high schools into smaller schools through its "schools-within-a-school model."[46]

Supporting most of these efforts, either financially or rhetorically, is a reform-minded president and education secretary in our nation's capital. President Obama's Race to the Top initiative is committed to reforming schools by investing in education innovation. The Department of Education has also placed leadership in its top priorities, choosing schools to receive Race to the Top funds partly based on the effectiveness of their principals and insisting on better communication among state and federal education leaders.[47]

ACTION PLAN FOR REFORMING EDUCATION

Preparing young people to meet the demands of economic competition in the 21st century will require a broad range of new solutions. These five strategies should top the list for school reformers:

Enhance the effectiveness of teachers

Teacher quality is almost universally considered the most important variable determining how well students do in school. A study of more than 7,000 eighth graders and their science and math teachers, conducted by Harold Wenglinsky of the Educational Testing Service, agreed with this claim. Students outperformed their peers by a significant margin if their teachers majored in the subjects they taught or conducted hands-on learning activities, if their science teachers received professional development in laboratory skills or if their math teachers emphasized higher-order thinking skills.[48]

Unfortunately, teacher quality today is uneven. Improving teacher effectiveness starts with measuring current outcomes to establish benchmarks. Some 46 states have outlined plans or passed legislation to enact fundamental changes, such as reforming tenure, boosting pay for the best teachers, implementing pay-for-performance, weeding out ineffective teachers and offering just-in-time professional development. Florida's winning Race to the Top application focused on the need for highly effective teachers, which it will get by changing the culture of the teaching profession; reforming the way teachers are paid, evaluated and promoted; and using student achievement on tests as a factor in measuring teacher performance.[49]

Use metrics to drive high school reform

High school is where American students experience the largest drop in competitiveness compared

3-1. Ten shifts that change everything about learning

Factor	From	To	To
Responsibility	Parents	State	Individuals/parents
Expectations	Social reproduction	Success for all	Individual choice
Aspirations	Practical skills	Disciplinary knowledge	Learning how to learn
Content	Books	Textbook	Learning objects
Pedagogy	Observation	Testing	Embedded assessment
Assessment	Apprenticeship	Didacticism	Interaction
Grouping	Mixed-age	Age cohorts	Individual progress
Location	Home	School	Anywhere
Culture	Adult culture	Peer culture	Mixed-age culture
Relationship	Personal bonds	Authority figures	Social networks

Source: Tom Vander Ark, edReformer (Adapted from *Rethinking Education in the Age of Technology*, Collins and Halverson)

The "bridge year" — the first year of schooling after high school — is the make-or-break year for many students' college careers. About 30 percent of students who start college do not return for a second year.[50]

to their peers in other Western, industrialized countries. A student drops out of a high school in America every 26 seconds.[51] The two factors most at fault for the falling rate of graduation from U.S. colleges are the high school dropout rate and the inability of many high schools to adequately prepare students for higher education.

To get high schools to focus more on college readiness, states could begin comparing, school by school, the percentage of students who go to college to those who drop out. The Center for American Progress suggests that measuring the rate of "college proficiency" — how quickly a high school's students finish one year of college-level work and how well those students perform later on in their college careers — gives educators key data they can use when deciding how to improve high schools.[52] Successfully tracking the college proficiency of high schools can better prepare students for college and increase the number of graduates.

Improve the lowest performing schools

Some states are implementing aggressive reforms aimed at the lowest-performing 5 percent of schools in the country. The U.S. Department of Education is spending billions of dollars to refocus resources and attention on the worst-performing schools. Many low-performing schools are being closed or turned into charters. Others are experiencing a much-needed uptick. The Green Dot program, for example, is transforming low-performing schools in Los Angeles and the Bronx.[53]

Possibly the most powerful example of turning around low-performing schools is in New Orleans. Roughly two-thirds of the schools are run by independent charter operators, up from less than 2 percent prior to Hurricane Katrina. The improvements in student performance have been encouraging. Sixty-four percent of the city's schools were considered academically unacceptable before Katrina; by 2009, that number had fallen to 42 percent. Also, the number of seniors who graduated from the Recovery School District increased from 50 percent in 2007 to 90 percent in 2010. The number of New Orleans students who scored at or above the basic level in English increased from 37 percent in 2007 to 52 percent in 2010.[54]

Encourage education innovation

Paul Vallas, the individual recruited to lead the Recovery School District in New Orelans, is a veteran education reformer, having been superintendent in Chicago and Philadelphia. In both Chicago and Philadelphia, Vallas had to take over an existing system and try to reform it. In New Orleans, he has been able to start virtually from scratch, freed of the pretzel logic that dominates so many urban school bureaucracies. The ability to start anew is part of what attracted Vallas to New Orleans. "Without question, this is the easier job," says Vallas. "You can come and, with no restraint on who you hire and no institutional obstacles blocking you, change the whole curriculum, the length of the school day, length of the school year."[55] Vallas did all that and more in his first two years.

Over the last 40 years, public education reforms have historically focused on trying to make the system work, rather than reexamining the system itself. Many reformers remain anchored to the existing structures and desperately yearn for a way to get different results from the same system. Results have been meager. No doubt, transformative change — a clean slate approach like New Orleans — is painful, but isn't it more painful to watch generation after generation of children robbed of an education? Disruptive changes like virtual charter schools, competition, choice, blended learning and for-profit schools can all play a role in bringing about new approaches to education.

> There are more than 173 virtual charter schools in 18 states serving 92,235 students.

Promote online and personalized learning

Online learning is growing 30 percent annually in K–12 education and currently shows no signs of slowing.[56] The advent of low-cost computing technologies, such as netbooks and broadband, presents opportunities for states to save money. Textbooks cost the State of California $350 million annually.[57] By transitioning to online textbooks, the state hopes to encourage students' participation in virtual learning while reducing textbook costs.

Schools are beginning to break free from traditional assembly-line education models, integrating personalized learning into students' curricula. New York City's School of One uses special algorithms to recommend activities and lessons that maximize student engagement and improve learning. Its technologies offer virtual tutoring and one-on-one teacher/student modalities, simultaneously requiring teachers to track metrics of student performance to ensure continued progress.

3-2. States that have established state-led and virtual charter programs

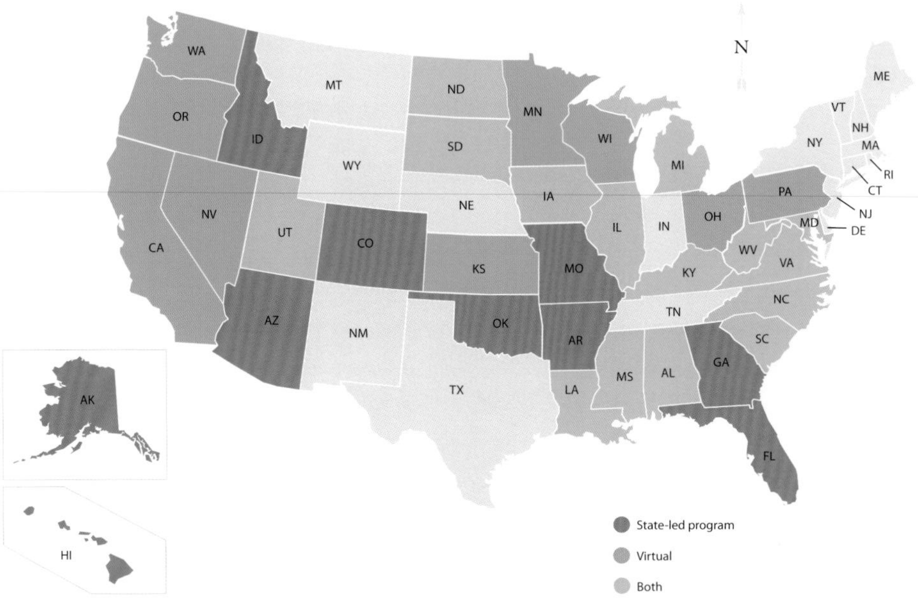

Source: Technology Counts 2008 STEM, *Education Week* and Editorial Projects in Education Research Center, Watson, J., & Ryan, J. (2007). *Keeping Pace with K-12 Online Learning: A Review of State-Level Policy and Practice*.

Expanding focus on science, technology, engineering and mathematics

Promoting STEM is key to our nation's competitiveness

Economists don't agree on much. One area of little debate, however, is that future American competitiveness will depend on producing a skilled workforce with significant abilities in math and science. American colleges and universities are not graduating enough scientists and engineers to meet the expected needs of our future economic growth.

Reports such as the National Academies' *Rising Above the Gathering Storm* argue that unless America vastly improves K–12 mathematics and science education, it will not be able to compete in the future in scientific and technological areas. Compared with the growth in industries related to math and science, the number of students

3-3. U.S. competitiveness and education

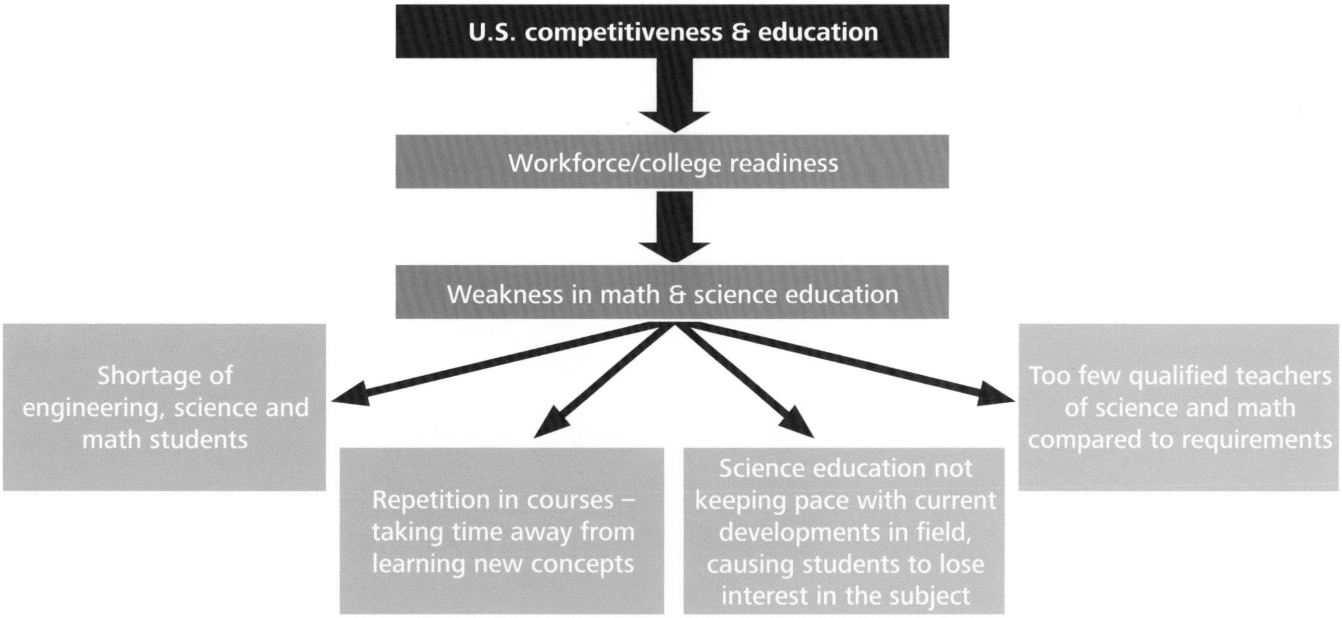

Source: Deloitte Research

pursuing careers in those areas is small, leaving a growing gap in the workforce. Making matters worse, school curricula haven't been updated to reflect the needs of the 21st century, and repetitive courses take up time that students might otherwise spend learning new concepts.

To date, most efforts to address the shortage of math and science students have focused on the supply side of the issue. For example, they have focused on enhancing rigor in the math and science curricula and required coursework. Other strategies have included better and earlier assessment tools to measure student progress and improved teacher recruitment and training.

But what of the demand side? Governments need to adopt new approaches to increase student

What works: FIRST, building competitive spirit

For Inspiration and Recognition of Science and Technology (FIRST) designs accessible, innovative programs for elementary and high school students. The goals are to build an interest in science and technology and to help students develop self-confidence, leadership and life skills. FIRST signature programs include a robotics competition, the tech challenge and the LEGO league; all of these give students a chance to compete against teams from across the U.S. and around the world. Now in its 18th year, the program has over 130,000 participating students with 60,000 volunteers. FIRST has shown that students who participate in its challenges are more than twice as likely as other students to pursue a career in science and technology. FIRST's many corporate supporters include Delphi, General Motors, Motorola, Xerox, Abbott and FedEx.

engagement in math and science. The Science, Technology, Engineering and Mathematics (STEM) Education Coalition has developed a learner-centered philosophy. It emphasizes a 24x7 learning culture that encourages questions, creativity and possibilities through concepts such as "after school must become school." Another essential element of this kind of new approach is to engage businesses and the community in providing each young person with the best education possible.

ACTION PLAN FOR INCREASING STEM GRADUATION RATES

Getting all the key education, government and business stakeholders to focus on improving the demand side of STEM won't be easy. These five strategies can form the foundation for such a change:

Forge public-private partnerships

The National Science Foundation's Math and Science Partnership program awards competitive, merit-based grants to teams comprised of institutions of higher education, local K–12 school systems and their supporting partners. Partnerships develop and implement new ways to advance math and science education by bringing innovation, inspiration, support and resources to educators and students in local schools, colleges and universities. Such programs can help schools to provide challenging curricula for all students and encourage more students to succeed in advanced courses in math and the sciences.

Intel works with governments and educators to improve teaching and learning in more than 50 countries, offering programs in formal and informal K–12 education. Also, to expand elementary and secondary students' knowledge of and enthusiasm for science, mathematics and engineering, Intel sponsors a number of competitions, including the Intel International Science and Engineering Fair and the Intel Science Talent Search. The

What works: College Summit

Not-for-profit College Summit aims to create lasting change by helping high schools and their surrounding communities develop college-going cultures in underrepresented areas. The program worked so well in Brooklyn that it has been replicated at hundreds of high schools across the country. College Summit combines teacher training, community outreach, coaching and counseling, and robust data tracking that facilitates accountability in high schools. Workshops serve 12,000 students, 79 percent of whom end up enrolling in college.[58]

Almost 30 percent of high school mathematics students an
who either did not major in the subject in college or are nc

aim of these competitions is to recognize the accomplishments of students and to recognize their schools for promoting math and science.

Introduce mentors and role models

Local school districts can partner with businesses to establish programs that provide scientists and engineers as role models and resources for schools. These forums should facilitate direct contact between teachers and scientists and engineers and, as appropriate, direct contact between scientists and students. Such an initiative would also engage the popular media in teaching children about famous and semi-famous people who use (or have used) math and science extensively to achieve their success.

The Futures Channel uses new media technologies to promote a bond between today's scientists, engineers, explorers and visionaries and the next generation. The Futures Channel creates movies in which science and technology professionals talk about their work. Educators can obtain these movies, plus related classroom activities, through the organization's Web site, or by purchasing DVDs.

Target underrepresented students

Some of America's brightest students are not receiving an adequate education.[59] Low-income students who score in the top 25 percent on tests apply to college about as frequently as upper-income students in the bottom 25 percent of test-takers.[60] This problem is frequently caused by socioeconomic issues, lack of guidance in schools and lack of information about college. Improving access to education, particularly to programs that teach high-demand skills, may help close gaps in the labor market.[61]

Programs that have proven effective in promoting high achievement among traditionally underrepresented groups of students in K–12 STEM courses should be replicated. Governments must redouble their efforts to support traditionally underrepresented undergraduate students in the STEM pipeline.

Tie math and science to the real world

States can engage businesses to provide financial and logistical support to extracurricular math and science activities, as well as the time and talents of their employees, to enrich students' learning

50 percent of those enrolled in physical science have teachers certified to teach it.

experiences. Educators could organize student groups to participate in such activities, if they do not already exist, and work to integrate business support into these programs. Such community-based learning initiatives could also include a significant technology component, using a blend of low-cost, Web-enabled applications to engage students and mobilize community-based projects.

One promising model is the partnership between The Manufacturing Institute and Discovery Communications to help nurture a new generation of manufacturing engineers and technologists through experience-based learning. The initiative will use multiple platforms in programs designed to excite students and build competency through project-based learning. Components of the program include: "How To Week," a series on Discovery's Science Channel that spotlights the latest in science and engineering in manufacturing; "Inventor's Workshop," a national program to celebrate young inventors; "Head Rush," a STEM curriculum that integrates on-air, online and in-class learning; and "Dream It! Do It!," a video competition in which students solve real-world STEM puzzles.

Engage students through new learning technologies such as gaming

Gaming technologies can be used to develop higher-order thinking skills such as strategic thinking, interpretative analysis, problem solving, plan formulation and execution, and adaptation to rapid change. Gaming can enhance personalized learning and help bridge the growing attention gap that seems to be contributing to the dropout rate. A University of Wisconsin study shows that gaming, in some cases, increases cognitive learning and literacy.[62] Downtown High School in Columbus, Ohio has improved student test scores through collaborative e-Learning software.[63]

One of the most successful education game initiatives underway today is Carnegie Mellon University's Alice program, currently in use at a couple hundred colleges and some high schools. Alice focuses tightly on sparking greater interest among young women in computer science. Because Carnegie Mellon has formed a strong partnership with a leading game company — Electronic Arts — to enhance the game's evolution and development, Alice could serve as a model for math and science games with a more general focus.

Driving more money into the classroom

Squeezing inefficiencies out of the system

States and school districts are under increasing pressure to reduce education costs, which constitute up to half of many state budgets. Even in states without large budget deficits, money for education is always limited and rarely keeps pace with costs.

How can states and school districts respond to today's unprecedented fiscal pressures without adversely affecting educational performance?

First, they can place a greater emphasis on the correlation between education dollars and outcomes. Comparing students' scores on the National Assessment of Educational Performance with a state's education spending shows that return on investment varies greatly across states. Utah and North Carolina post a 200 percent return on their investment while other states show disappointing results. Policymakers have tended to focus too much on inputs without paying enough attention to efficiency or to ensuring that educational dollars are delivering value.

Second, states and school districts can take steps to reduce non-instructional costs. Currently, 40 cents of every dollar spent on education is utilized for non-instructional purposes. Lacking economies of scale — and often, sufficient managerial expertise — many districts find it extraordinarily expensive to provide a full array of support and administrative services in-house. Strategies to achieve economies of scale and reduce non-instructional costs include consolidation, shared services and cooperative purchasing.

In 2008, Maine consolidated 260 school districts into 80, saving $365 million.

ACTION PLAN FOR REDUCING NON-INSTRUCTIONAL COSTS

In this era of tight budgets and loud calls for results and accountability, schools need to identify every means of saving money while improving capacities. A variety of proven strategies are available to shrink non-instructional costs and drive more money into the classroom:

Provide incentives for shared services

One promising approach is to reduce non-instructional spending costs through greater sharing of services across school districts. Arrangements can be made with other school districts, among schools within large school districts or with outside entities to share services across a range of school functions: transportation, food service and nutrition, instruction, safety and security, health services, purchasing, finance and payroll, facilities and real estate, human resources, technology services and administration (see figure 3-4).

Oregon's Reset Cabinet Report estimated the state could save more than $40 million a year if school districts shared certain services.

States can help in a variety of ways to identify best practices and drive innovation in shared services at the district level. The New Jersey Regional Efficiency Aid Program, for example, provides tax credits directly to homeowners as a way to publicly reward school districts and municipalities for sharing services.

In Ohio, Governor Ted Strickland chose Greene County, Ohio in 2009 to conduct a pilot program in shared school services. The idea for the initiative came from a private citizen, a school board member who volunteered to approach local foundations for money to help fund the initiative. No tax dollars would be used. Plans called for the county's six

3-4. School functions amenable to shared services

Capability	Fit for Shared service	Savings potential (Comparative)
Direct (Services to students)		
Transportation	●	●
Food service and nutrition	◐	◐
Instructional	◐	◐
Safety and security	◐	◐
Health services	◐	○
Indirect (Services to staff or infrastructures)		
Purchasing	●	●
Finance and payroll	●	◐
Facilities and real estate	●	●
Human resources	●	◐
Technology services	◐	●
Administration	◐	◐

Source: Deloitte Research

Shifting just a quarter of tax dollars spent by school district
potentially yield savings in the range of $9 billion.

school districts to work with Wright State University's Center for Urban and Public Affairs to conduct the pilot, which would help to define models for shared services and assess the fiscal impacts in order to inform a statewide strategy. The school districts formed committees to explore the potential for sharing services in six areas: advanced placement instruction and programs, administrative and financial services, information technology, contracted services and agreements, special education instruction and programs, and transportation.

Promote cooperative purchasing

Pooling purchasing power can yield substantial savings for school districts and their partners by reducing operating expenses for such items as utilities, equipment, services and supplies. New Jersey's Shared Services Program is a cooperative effort among Middlesex County municipalities that supports the towns by providing a way to reduce daily operating expenses through cooperative purchasing. The program began in 1998 by offering towns aggregate natural gas purchasing, resulting in a 5 percent savings on electricity for public buildings during the first year of the program. The municipalities share services for water and wastewater programs and the purchasing of natural gas, electricity, equipment, services and supplies.

Tap underutilized assets

Partnering with businesses can help school districts tap into underutilized assets such as land. For example, in exchange for land, private partners have provided some school facilities with fitness centers that are used by students during the day and by private clients outside school hours.

Common public-private partnership models include the sale of development rights on unused property, and sale-leaseback or lease-leaseback arrangements. In these solutions, school districts sell or lease surplus land to a developer who builds a school and leases it back to the district. In 1996, the Houston Independent School District used a lease-leaseback arrangement with a private developer to obtain two new schools, $20 million under budget and a year earlier than originally planned.

Innovative partnerships with the private sector can be structured in a number of ways to meet school modernization objectives. Private firms typically finance, design, construct and operate a public school under a contract with the government for a given time period, usually 20–30 years. Businesses usually provide non-core services such as school transport, food services and cleaning, while the government assumes responsibility for teaching.

Reduce energy costs

The Pennsylvania Department of Education Common Cents Shared Services Initiative piloted a program to implement cost-savings strategies through several shared service opportunity areas for school districts, including energy efficiency. Common Cent's cost-saving models were derived from data and analysis provided by the school districts and then tested for efficacy. Forty-nine out of 501 districts in the Commonwealth participated in the initiative. The Pennsylvania Department of Education estimates $14.4 million in potential savings for the 49 Common Cents districts. Participating districts in Pennsylvania's Riverside Intermediate Unit 6, for example, saved 55 percent on copiers. Meanwhile, Redbank Valley School District projected annual recurring savings of $10K on fuel tank installation with bulk fuel purchasing.

What works: James Oyster School's public-private partnership

Built in the 1920s, Washington's James F. Oyster Bilingual Elementary School was on its last legs by the early 1990s — leaking roofs, building code violations and accompanying shutdowns, lack of computer hookups, and limited space. The District of Columbia simply didn't have the $11 million required to build a new school, nor did it have the borrowing power. Lacking money and borrowing power, officials got creative. What the city lacked in financial assets, it made up for in physical assets; the school sat on 1.67 acres of prime real estate within walking distance of the National Zoo. The city converted its underutilized physical assets into a financial asset by dividing the property: Half for a new school and half for a new apartment building — designed and built by the private sector. In return for the sale of the land, Washington got its first new public school in 20 years — a state-of-the-art facility with double the space — without spending a single public dollar.

1 the journey to fiscally sustainable government
2 generating jobs
3 21st century education
4 closing state infrastructure gaps
5 responding to health care reform
6 improving human services
7 technology reboot
8 innovation state
9 from big ideas to big results

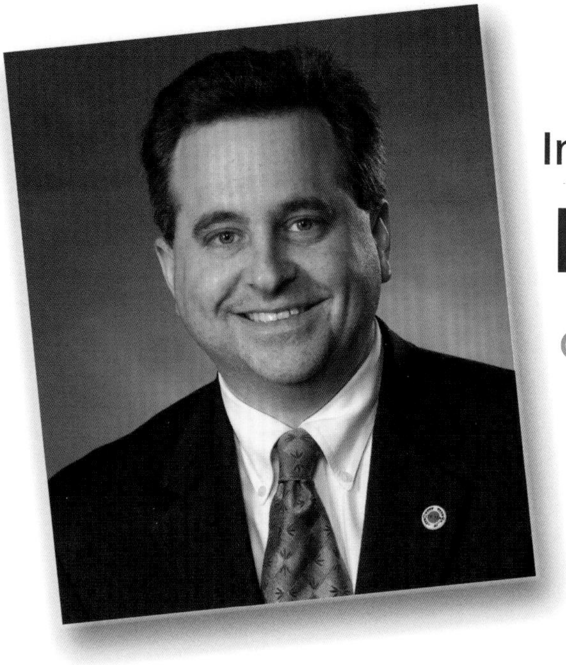

Interview with

Michael Brown

Chief Executive Officer of City Year

Q...What is City Year, and who does it serve?

City Year is a national youth service corps. We send teams of idealistic and well-trained young adults full-time into high poverty schools in urban communities across the nation to help address the nation's dropout crisis and to help turn around low performing schools. Our corps members serve as tutors, mentors and role models during the school day and then stay through the extended day to tutor students.

We work against what Johns Hopkins University has discovered are the early warning indicators that a child will eventually drop out of high school: high absences, poor behaviors and course failure in math or english. If the child has even one of those off-track indicators in the sixth grade and is in a high poverty school, they have less than a 25 percent chance of graduating with their class six years later. But if they can get to the tenth grade on time, on track with no off-track indicators, they have over a 75 percent chance of graduating from that same school system.

Q...How do you decide which schools you're going to go into?

We've analyzed the high schools in the communities where we serve that have the highest dropout rates and determined which schools, K–8, feed into them. Johns Hopkins University has published studies which show that 12 percent of the high schools produce 50 percent of the dropouts in the country. So if you can serve in the places of highest need — the worst performing schools and the schools that feed into them — you're going to have a disproportionate impact. We've found that if you can reach 25 percent of the schools in most urban centers, you can reach 50 percent of the kids who are likely to drop out.

Q...How much do schools improve when City Year corps members come in?

Last year in Philadelphia, with Talent Development Secondary and Communities in Schools, we implemented a collaborative program called Diplomas Now at the Feltonville School of Arts and Sciences, a middle school with 750 students. In one year, we were able to reduce the number of kids who were off track on attendance by 52 percent, and the number of kids that were off track on behaviors by 48 percent. The number of kids who were failing English fell by 80 percent, and the number failing math dropped by 83 percent.

Now tie that to Northeastern University studies that say that every student who drops out of high school in America costs the country about $300,000 — in lost wages, in incarceration rates, in lost taxes and in poor health. Every single grade that you keep a kid in, you're talking about huge savings in social costs.

Q...What kind of data do you have about which learning approaches work best for which individual students? And how are you able to use that data to help students?

Because City Year corps members are with students all day, every day they get a comprehensive picture of students' academic and socio-economic needs, which they can use to help improve student learning working hand in hand with teachers and other service providers. For example, every two weeks we sit at a table with a list of every single student in the sixth grade in a school, and we go through that list with the sixth grade teachers, the social workers and the City Year corps members. They talk about every single child and how they're doing against the early warning indicators of dropping out of school. And more importantly, what did we decide to do two weeks ago, and is it working? Is there something else we can learn about this child that can work?

That's where you get into best practices. You might find that this child's a kinetic learner, so we give them something to manipulate. Or this child has something going on at home that until a social worker intervenes, they are not going to be able to learn.

What this shows is that schools need data coordinators. It's one of the highest needs that I've seen in the country. If we could collect and use the data well, it would be a revolution.

Q...To what extent does the average school have data at the student level that would allow for customized learning?

Schools are at various degrees of capability with regard to data. The ones making the biggest gains are led by principals or school district leaders that get it and say, "I'm going to make sure that we have data walls and we're reviewing the data."

Governors can help by bringing in organizations at the cutting edge of building electronic data systems. They can use the bully pulpit to say to superintendents around the state, "Let's have a race to see who's going to build the best data approach to learning." And of course, they can give out innovation grants.

Q...Why is it so hard to scale these educational and social innovations? What are some of the lessons you've learned for how to do it?

One, you need to invest both in your outcomes, your product if you will, and in your systems, your capacity to deliver. Those dollars for capacity building are sometimes the hardest to get. Government, in particular, likes to fund one more unit of end product. And only very sophisticated philanthropists understand the need for dollars to train, to create human resources capacity, to build an IT infrastructure — all of these things that it takes to actually provide scale.

Another barrier is that government has a hard time picking winners and losers. There's often political pressure to give everyone a little bit of support, and create a series of small ecosystems of mom-and-pops. It's harder for government to say, "I'm actually going to pull on a big lever and scale something." Governments need to think about that and maybe even create a tiered investment system that says, "We're going to have a certain pool of funds for innovation, but we're going to have a second one for scale."

Introduction

Rebuilding America's crumbling infrastructure

Back in the 1960s, California was known for more than just Hollywood, The Beach Boys and beautiful scenery. The state was also famous for its unparalleled infrastructure. California had one of the world's most extensive transportation infrastructure programs in the late 1950s and early 1960s, which paved the way for much of the state's subsequent economic prosperity.

Those times seem like ancient history in California and throughout America. Today, crowded schools, traffic-choked roads, deteriorating bridges, and aged and overused water and sewer treatment facilities undercut the economy's efficiency and erode the quality of American life (see figure 4-1). The American Society of Civil Engineers (ASCE) estimates that the United States currently only invests about half of what is needed to bring the nation's infrastructure up to a good condition.

The consequences of neglected roads, bridges, public transit, electricity grid and other social infrastructure (such as hospitals and schools) have not gone unnoticed by the public. An overwhelming majority of Americans — 94 percent — are concerned about the condition of the nation's infrastructure. Remarkably, 81 percent say they are willing to pay 1 percent more on their federal income tax to improve America's infrastructure.[64]

Business leaders echo the public's concern about the widening gap between infrastructure needs and current spending. Among surveyed senior business executives, 77 percent believe that the current level of public infrastructure is inadequate to support their companies' long-term growth. These executives believe that over the next few years, infrastructure will become a more important factor in determining where they locate their operations.[65]

While there is widespread agreement on the need to address the growing public infrastructure deficit, both to create jobs in the short term and as a prerequisite for enhancing economic development and competitiveness in the longer term, states find themselves in a difficult and precarious position with respect to how to pay for it.

At the federal level, infrastructure is largely funded out of general revenues and diminishing highway trust funds. While the 2009 American Recovery and Reinvestment Act (ARRA) provided an infusion of federal funds for infrastructure to the tune of $113 billion, the stimulus funds fall far short of what is required to align public infrastructure with the overall demand, which the American Society of Civil Engineers pegs at $2.2 trillion over the next five years.[66] With insufficient political will to increase the gas tax and renewed pressure to reduce the federal deficit, it seems unlikely that states will see a significant near-term increase in federal funds to help close the gap.

4-1. America's infrastructure deficit by the numbers

By 2020, **every major U.S. container port is projected to be handling at least 2 times the volume it was designed to handle.**

Railroads are projected to need nearly $200 billion in investment over the next 20 years to accommodate freight increases.

Aging sewer systems spill an estimated 1.26 trillion gallons of untreated sewage every single year, resulting in an estimated **$50 billion in cleanup costs.**

Costs attributed to airline delays are expected to triple to **$30 billion from 2000 to 2015.**

Approximately **a third of America's major roadways are in substandard condition** — a significant factor in **a third of the more than 43,000 traffic fatalities** in the United States each year.

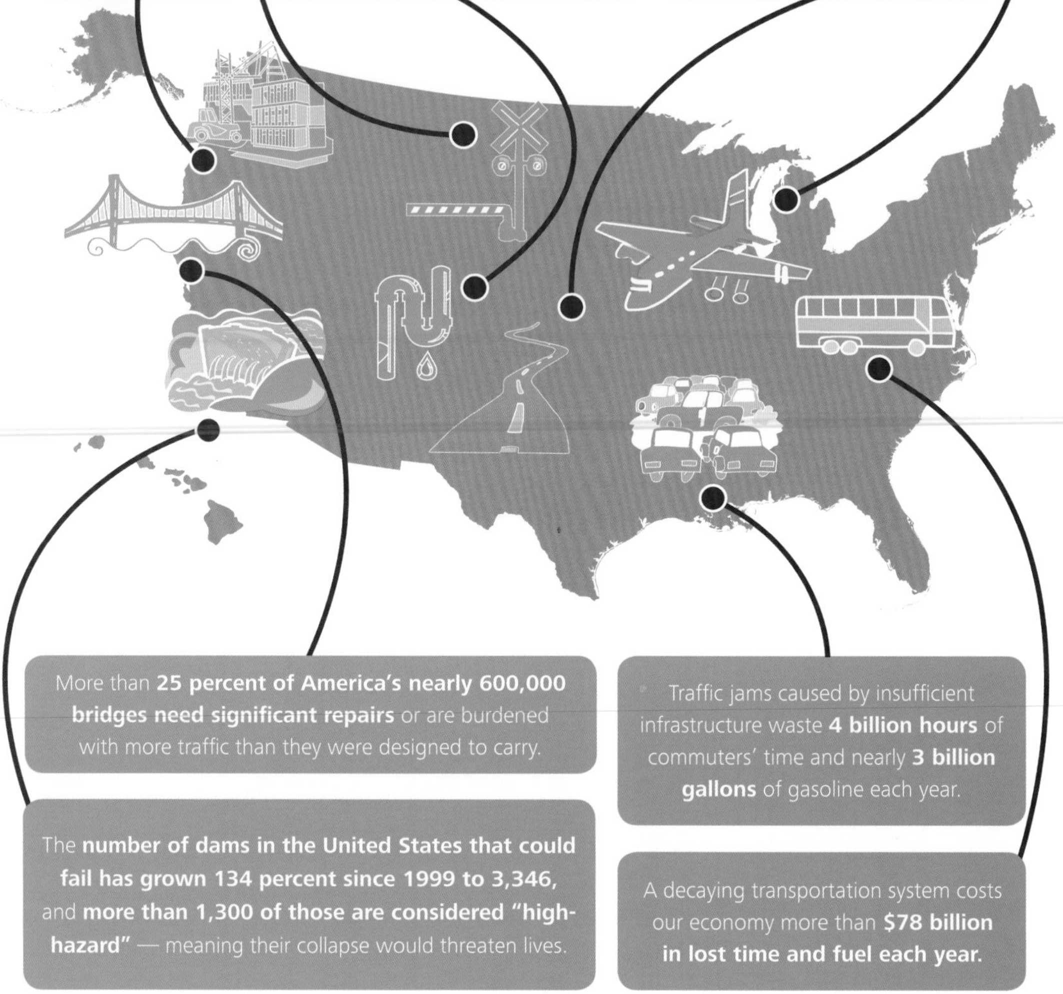

More than **25 percent of America's nearly 600,000 bridges need significant repairs** or are burdened with more traffic than they were designed to carry.

The **number of dams in the United States that could fail has grown 134 percent since 1999 to 3,346,** and **more than 1,300 of those are considered "high-hazard"** — meaning their collapse would threaten lives.

Traffic jams caused by insufficient infrastructure waste **4 billion hours** of commuters' time and nearly **3 billion gallons** of gasoline each year.

A decaying transportation system costs our economy more than **$78 billion in lost time and fuel each year.**

Sources: Eric Kelderman, "Look Out Below! America's Infrastructure Is Crumbling," Pew Center on the States, January 22, 2008, <http://pewresearch.org/pubs/699/look-out-below>; "Fixing America's Crumbling Infrastructure," U.S. Chamber of Commerce, July 2008, <http://www.uschambermagazine.com/article/fixing-americas-crumbling-infrastructure>.

"You're never going to be able to raise the gas tax high enough to provide the necessary funds. Meanwhile, there's tons of private money ready to come in and participate all over the world. The United States is a laggard in this respect, which is ironic. Here in the land of innovation, we are absolutely backwards in this respect. I still believe, however, that plain business sense, coupled with the severity of the need, will finally make private investment in public infrastructure a much more common phenomenon in our country."

~ Mitch Daniels, Governor of Indiana

At the state and local levels, the majority of infrastructure is funded through state and local budgets (taxes and user fees) and financed in the municipal bond market. Increased federal mandates for social spending, balanced budget requirements and increased competition among states to keep taxes low have put the brakes on spending at the state and local levels, while debt limitations have constrained borrowing. As a result, state leaders find themselves with insufficient resources to meet the challenges they face.

Closing the current gaps will require raising additional revenue, reducing costs and finding new sources of finance with higher risk appetite. Given government restrictions on tax-exempt bonds and the political difficulty of raising taxes to secure new revenue in the current economic climate, a viable option for states is to engage the private sector in transforming existing assets and/or service provision and developing new capacity across the infrastructure landscape.

If infrastructure gaps are to be narrowed, the public sector must respond with solutions that can evolve with the changing environment. The old delivery models must give way to new, innovative models and a portfolio of hybrid approaches — from modifications in traditional procurement through to public-private partnerships.

Leveraging public-private partnerships

Engaging the private sector to help close the infrastructure gap

Increasingly, governments around the world (including state and local governments in the United States) are turning to the private sector for some, or all of, the five basic elements of infrastructure projects: design, construction, service operation, ongoing maintenance and finance (see figure 4-2). Once rare and limited to a handful of jurisdictions and infrastructure sectors, these public-private partnerships (PPPs) have emerged as an important alternative model that governments are utilizing to improve project delivery and, in some cases, close a gap between infrastructure needs and the public sector's capacity to address them. While the United States has been slower to adopt this trend, this is rapidly changing. More than half the states now have PPP-enabling legislation on their books, with states like Virginia and Florida particularly active in using PPPs.

Public-private partnerships are unlikely to fully replace traditional financing and development of infrastructure, but, for certain projects with the right characteristics, they offer several benefits to governments trying to address infrastructure shortages or improve the efficiency of their organizations. First, because the destination, not the path, becomes the

4-2. The five components of an infrastructure project

Design. Under virtually any partnership structure, the responsibility for design will be shared. For instance, even in partnership structures with high degrees of private responsibility, the public sector's articulation of performance specifications will limit the range of design options. In many projects, the need to ensure compliance with broader planning and environmental guidelines results in a significant degree of public sector design.

Construction. This component includes the construction of the physical asset(s) over a prescribed period of time, generally at a prescribed cost. Which party assumes the impact of construction cost overruns and time delays must be considered.

Service operation. Operating the asset may include various activities from general management of service provision and revenue collection to performing soft (or non-core) services associated with an asset, such as laundry services within a hospital. Operation typically begins at the end of construction, upon agreement that the construction has been satisfactory. In PPPs, the private partner's compensation is dependent on the achievement of performance standards.

Ongoing maintenance. Generally, there are two principal types of maintenance to be considered in any infrastructure project: ongoing regular maintenance (or operation maintenance) and major refurbishment, often called life-cycle or capital maintenance.

Finance. This component generally includes financing for the capital costs of construction as well as working capital requirements.

Source: Deloitte Research

> "To provide the kind of infrastructure that Americans need and deserve, we must find innovative ways of paying for it. One tool — private investment — must play a larger role in delivering projects. We must embrace the private sector to help leverage scarce federal and state dollars."
>
> ~ Ed Rendell, Governor Of Pennsylvania

organizing theme around which a project is built, public-private partnerships enable the public sector to focus on the outcome-based public value they are trying to create. Second, PPPs transfer certain risks to the private sector and provide incentives for assets to be delivered on time and on budget, and to be properly maintained over time. Third, public-private partnerships can lower the cost of infrastructure by reducing both construction costs and overall lifecycle costs. Fourth, because the private sector is often willing to take on higher levels of debt and to provide upfront equity capital, public-private partnerships can allow infrastructure project delivery to be accelerated by years compared to traditional municipal bond financings. Finally, in addition to providing higher-quality infrastructure at lower cost, governments can use PPP transactions to unlock the value from undervalued and underutilized assets, such as land and buildings, and use those funds to help pay for new infrastructure.

Despite current challenges in the credit markets, private equity capital has continued to flow in the direction of infrastructure. Over the past several years, an estimated $190 billion has migrated to infrastructure funds globally, which could theoretically translate to more than $950 billion of leveraged purchasing power.[67] It behooves government leaders to look closely at how to make limited public dollars go further by using private resources to narrow such bedeviling infrastructure deficits.

While PPPs offer significant benefits, formidable challenges abound. Lessons learned from PPP leaders worldwide suggest several strategies that foster success. First, governments need a clear framework for partnerships that confers adequate attention on all phases of a life-cycle approach and ensures a steady stream of potential projects. This can help avoid problems of a poor PPP framework, lack of clarity about outcomes, inadequate government capacity to manage the process and an overly narrow transaction focus. Second, a strong understanding of the innovative PPP models developed to address more complex issues can help governments achieve the proper allocation of risk — even in conditions of pronounced uncertainty about future needs. This allows governments to tailor PPP approaches to particular situations and needs. Third, a clear PPP procurement process and apportionment of final decision-making authority is necessary to ensure that private sector participants feel confident that the significant investment in preparing a bid will not be wasted by a broken procurement process. Last, an open, honest, direct and timely communication program with all affected stakeholders can be of critical importance, as PPPs can be politically controversial and difficult to execute in certain circumstances.

It is important to note that PPPs, while they may incorporate many of the tools of traditional public finance and procurement, are a new way of doing business, with the public and private sectors sharing and apporting project risks over the life of the project. Without seeing these PPPs as true partnerships — not simply a different type of transaction — and adopting a tailored approach

4-3. The "availability payment" model

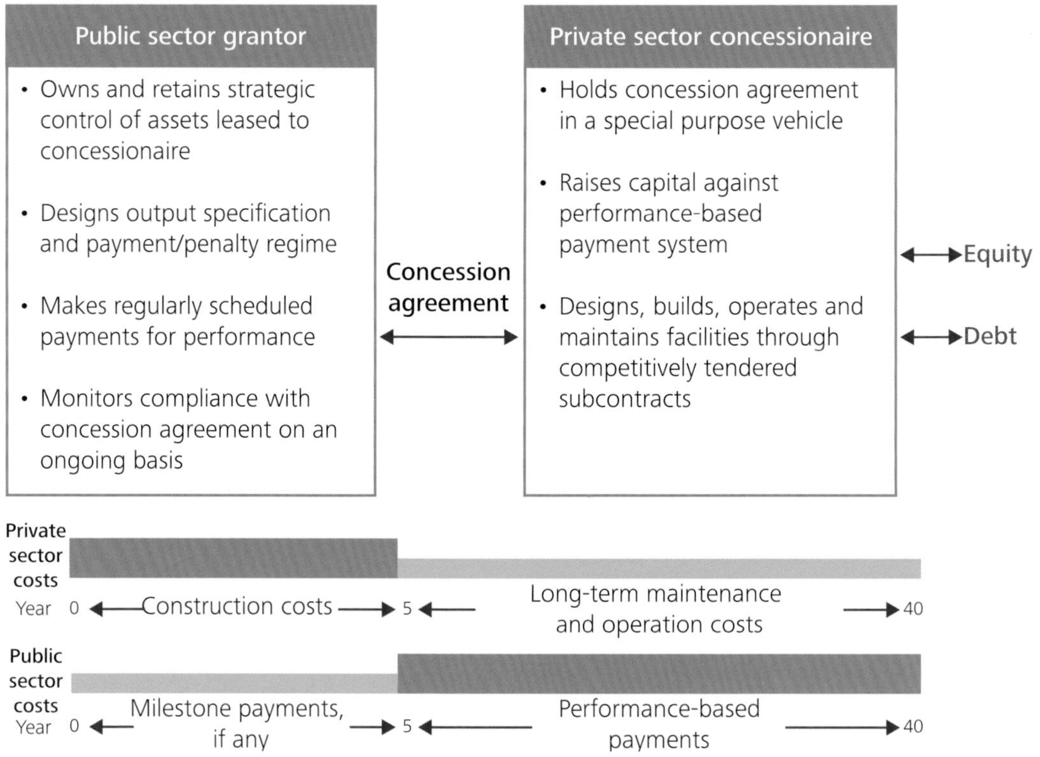

Public sector grantor
• Owns and retains strategic control of assets leased to concessionaire
• Designs output specification and payment/penalty regime
• Makes regularly scheduled payments for performance
• Monitors compliance with concession agreement on an ongoing basis
Concession agreement
Private sector concessionaire
• Holds concession agreement in a special purpose vehicle
• Raises capital against performance-based payment system
• Designs, builds, operates and maintains facilities through competitively tendered subcontracts
Equity
Debt
Private sector costs
Year 0
Construction costs
5
Long-term maintenance and operation costs
40
Public sector costs
Year 0
Milestone payments, if any
5
Performance-based payments
40

Source: Deloitte

that suits the relative uncertainty and scale of each project at hand, governments are likely to make the same old mistakes. By using the full range of delivery models that are available and continuing to innovate — learning from failure instead of retreating from it — the public sector can maximize the likelihood of meeting its infrastructure objectives.

ACTION PLAN FOR LEVERAGING PPPs

Closing state infrastructure gaps will require innovation in service delivery and funding/financing models as well as forceful leadership from governors. The following strategies form the foundation of a balanced program to incorporate PPPs:

Articulate the importance of infrastructure investment to voters

Politically, the common characteristics of infrastructure — namely, that it is expensive and time-consuming to produce — can make public investment a difficult sell, particularly at a time when budgets are being slashed and popular programs are being eliminated. Yet, there are compelling reasons to invest in infrastructure that need to be articulated to constituents because of what is at stake for the U.S. economy. In particular, a series of large-scale investments over time are needed to modernize the foundation of the U.S. economy and to help the country keep pace with foreign competitors. An ample supply of well-maintained infrastructure is table stakes for competing in an increasingly flat world.

Create a favorable legal climate for PPPs

A key requirement for attracting private capital to infrastructure projects is to establish the necessary legislative and regulatory framework to support a successful PPP program, with clear processes, decision-making criteria and authority to execute transactions. With governments worldwide competing to attract investment capital, a poor legislative and statutory environment will stymie a state's efforts to engage private firms in planned PPPs.

"We traditionally have looked at PPPs for the large projects with high price tags, where the state has a limited amount of money we're looking to leverage. But we think there are also some great opportunities for PPPs among the smaller projects. And along with road projects, we think opportunities exist in our port, aviation and rail projects."

~ Sean Connaughton, Secretary of Transportation for the Commonwealth of Virginia

The Commonwealth of Virginia has one of the country's best PPP-enabling laws. Legislation has given the Virginia Department of Transportation authority to form contractual relationships by entering into partnerships with private sector firms and units of government and removed barriers to the formation of PPPs. The program also allows for fast-track study, design, funding and construction of state highway projects that are independent of the normal state procurement process. All in all, Virginia's law creates a platform for constructing new transportation infrastructure projects that might otherwise be decades away or might not be constructed at all.

Create a strategic procurement and finance unit in each department with a significant capital program

In contrast to the development of a single cross-government unit with expertise specific to a particular procurement approach, these new department level units would be fluent in all the best approaches for procuring and financing infrastructure — from traditional procurement to public-private partnerships. Additionally, because the unit would be housed at the department level, staff would have the relevant sector expertise needed to account for the risks that are unique to each class of infrastructure (e.g. roads, prisons, wastewater facilities, schools, etc.).

Make full use of the wide range of delivery and funding/financing options available

Choosing an appropriate model requires understanding the broad range of delivery options available, including new, innovative PPP models developed to address more complex issues such as proper risk allocation. Any procurement decision should be derived from a robust appraisal of all the options, based on the specific circumstances in which a project is being developed. In addition, since the financial markets began undergoing

What works: Florida Department of Transportation's "availability payment" model

In early 2009, the Florida Department of Transportation (FDOT) entered into a $1.8 billion 35-year concession with a private consortium headed by ACS Infrastructure Development to build and operate high-occupancy toll lanes near Fort Lauderdale. In this PPP, the FDOT will set toll rates, retain all revenues and make annual "availability payments" to the private concessionaire out of all of its revenues (including state appropriations, tax revenues and tolls). This structure is designed to retain as much public sector control over rate-setting as possible while also ensuring that the private concessionaire is incentivized to operate and maintain the road efficiently at the desired standard. The project represents the first U.S. toll road PPP structured with performance-based availability payments (see figure 4-3).

The California legislature has authorized regional transportation agencies and Caltrans to enter into an unlimited number of PPPs through 2017.

radical changes in 2008, the financing market for PPPs has seen significant evolution. Moving from a market primarily characterized by scarce equity capital and financings executed in the bank loan and project finance markets, recent transactions have included funding and financing from Private Activity Bond allocations, TIFIA loans, federal and state grants, ARRA money and equity from concessionaires, infrastructure funds and direct investment by pension funds. Flexible and creative use of funding and financing tools available to state and local issuers can provide lower costs of capital to a project and create more opportunities to deliver infrastructure.

Adopt a full life-cycle perspective

Diving head-first into anything without a proper understanding of what you're getting into is usually a recipe for disaster. The same is true of entering into new partnerships. Governments need a full life-cycle approach (e.g., a clear framework) for infrastructure partnerships that confers adequate attention to all phases of the project — from policy and planning to the transaction phase, and then, to managing the concession (see figure 4-4).

Roadblocks to overcome

Politics

Political factors often determine the extent or nature of private sector involvement. For instance, the Commonwealth of Pennsylvania was unable to garner sufficient legislative support to enter into a concession agreement for the Pennsylvania Turnpike that would have raised $12.8 billion to meet other pressing transportation needs.[68]

Goldilocks syndrome

There can be a tendency in partnership structures to transfer either too much or too little risk to the private sector. For example, public sponsors often look to PPPs to save upfront or total project costs, sometimes resulting in too much risk being transferred to the private sector. Optimal risk transfer ensures that there are enough high-quality bidders to reap the benefits of robust competition and that the public sector does not "overpay" to transfer risk that it is better suited to retain (see figure 4-6).

What works: Indiana toll road lease

The Indiana Department of Transportation partnered with the Cintra-Macquarie venture to operate and maintain the Indiana Toll Road, paying the state $3.8 billion to lease the toll road over the next 35 years — a windfall of cash that's being reinvested in the state's 10-year "Major Moves" transportation plan. As a result, Indiana is one of the only states in the country with a fully funded transportation investment program.

4-4. Infrastructure project life cycle

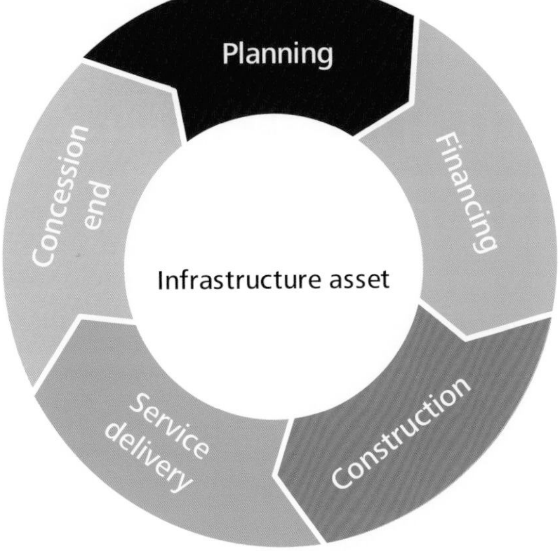

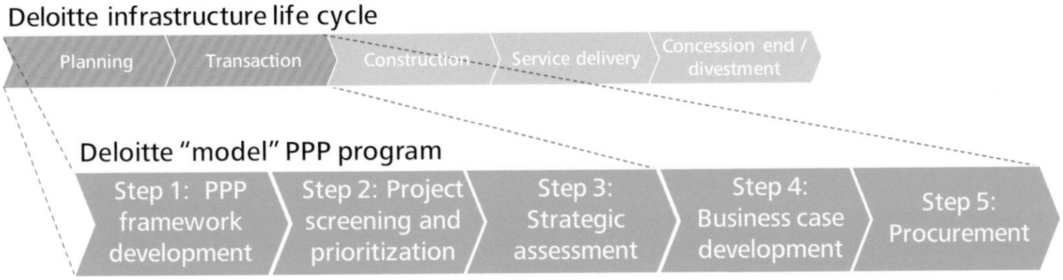

Description:

Step 1: PPP framework development

- Develop and publish a PPP framework document that:
  - Lays out organizational and project objectives for PPPs
  - Identifies key PPP constraints (legal, political, financial, practical)
  - Articulates expected PPP costs and benefits
  - Establishes a risk allocation philosophy
  - Establishes principles for a screening and prioritization methodology

Step 2: Project screening and prioritization

- Develop and implement specific screening and prioritization criteria for each type of asset
  - Should be able to be implemented with available or easily collectible high-level data

Step 3: Strategic assessment

- Develop preliminary commercial / financial structures for high priority projects
  - Costing analysis
  - Risk analysis and preliminary allocation
  - PPP partnership structure analysis
  - Market soundings
  - Financing options analysis
  - Financial modeling

Step 4: Business case development

- Develop detailed business cases for projects that present the highest risk-adjusted expected value in the Strategic Assessment
  - Full Public Sector Comparator / Value for Money analysis, including detailed risk modeling
  - Procurement strategy development

Step 5: Procurement

- Execute procurement process
  - Commercial / financial structure finalization and preparation of suite of project documents
  - Tender document preparation and process execution
  - Bid evaluation
  - Conclusion of partnership agreement

Source: Deloitte

Partnering for value:
Determining the right mix of public and private involvement in infrastructure financing and delivery

All too often, public sector entities are unaware of the myriad available alternatives or of the considerations involved in selecting the most appropriate delivery models for their capital projects. This has resulted in less-than-ideal outcomes from traditional procurements and public-private partnerships alike.

The central question government leaders have to answer in order to address the longer-term issues associated with pursuing their infrastructure objectives is not whether to involve the private sector in infrastructure projects, but rather: *What is the optimal mixture of public and private sector participation in any given project to maximize public value?* There's no one-size-fits-all answer for every situation. Most infrastructure projects are composed of five elements for which responsibility must be assigned: design, construction, operation, maintenance, and finance. Theoretically, any of these elements and their related risks can be allocated to either the public sector or the private sector. The shape of that allocation determines the structure of the partnership.

Dividing up these responsibilities in the best possible way for any given project is not easy. It requires careful qualitative and quantitative analysis. Short-cutting this process could result in suboptimal allocation and lost value. How, then, can public sector entities decide which project responsibilities they are best suited to retain, and which they are better off shifting to the private sector? Jurisdictions can determine the best mix of public and private resources for a given infrastructure project by following these three steps (see figure 4-5):

4-5. Determining the right mix of public and private involvement in infrastructure financing and delivery

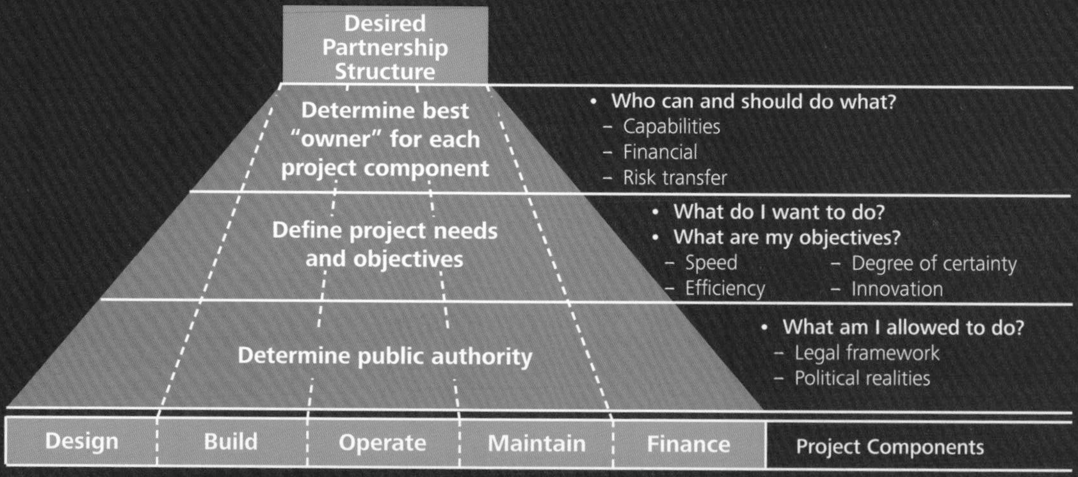

Source: Deloitte Research

4-6. Optimizing risk transfer to maximize Value for Money

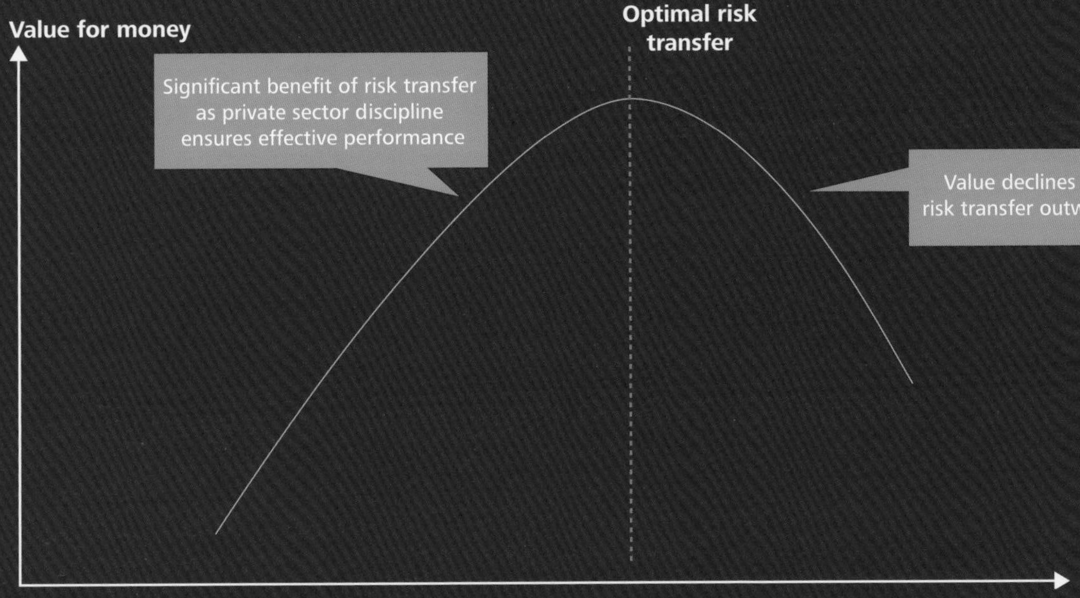

Source: Deloitte Research

Step #1: Determine public authority
Exploring the laws and policies that exist regarding the involvement of the private sector in the financing and delivery of public infrastructure allows for the narrowing of the pool of potential partners. Furthermore, it ensures that the partnership won't stumble on political constraints further down the road.

Step #2: Define project needs and objectives
Once a public sector entity has determined what it is permitted to do, the next step is to define the project goals. First, define the need. Then, define the service solution to meet that need. Lastly, policymakers must determine the asset(s) required to support the solution.

Step #3: Determine the best "owner" for each project component
Determining what you have authority to do and what you want to do will begin to narrow the options for structuring the relationship between the public and private sector. Then, sort out who can and should do what, using three basic criteria: 1) the in-house capabilities to deliver and/or manage, 2) the best financial options, and 3) how risks should be allocated between the public and private sector to maximize public value (see figure 4-6).

By applying a bottom-up approach to the development of a partnership structure, the public sector can deliver projects in a way that most closely approximates the optimal solution for any given jurisdiction. Careful, informed analysis at the outset of a project will help to ensure that limited resources are put to their best possible use, while putting government organizations in the best position to achieve their infrastructure objectives in today's challenging climate.

Interview with Sean Connaughton

Secretary of Transportation for the Commonwealth of Virginia

Q...Virginia has achieved considerable success with public-private partnerships (PPPs) over the years in administrations of both parties. What has enabled Virginia to do this?

Virginia has a constitutional mandate that it have a balanced budget every year. That requires the state to look for ways to be innovative. Second, the state limits public debt to about 5 percent of general revenues. That makes state agencies look for ways to maximize revenues and look for private partners to take on debt and do projects on their own. Virginia is a pro-business state. We welcome the chance to get the private sector involved in our projects.

Q...What are some of the key factors that have separated Virginia's successes in the PPP space from its transactions that haven't gone so well?

Over time, instead of actively and aggressively identifying PPP projects, we started relying on unsolicited PPPs. That has slowed down the process, because often, we have not done the necessary environmental and other studies, or preliminary engineering or scoping, or even thought about how to fund some of these projects. We're refocusing our whole effort to incorporate the PPPs in our planning and programming, where we identify revenue streams to fund the projects. And then, we identify where we think a PPP makes sense and then solicit private partners.

Q...Are there any specific types of assets and transactions where you see the most benefit in procuring under a PPP paradigm?

We traditionally have looked at PPPs for the large projects with high price tags, where the state has a limited amount of money we're looking to leverage. But we think there are also some great opportunities for PPPs among the smaller projects. And along with road projects, we think opportunities exist in our port, aviation and rail projects.

Q...For your HOT lanes projects in Northern Virginia, you're using private activity bonds and also had the public sector take a real equity stake by sharing the upside. What broader lessons does it provide for other states?

This will be the first HOT lanes project that attempts to manage traffic flows as well as provide free service to carpools. We think this will be a model for other urban areas that wish to bring market forces to bear on transportation assets. We also believe that there are a lot of other places where we can do this in the commonwealth. Even on the free lanes, we would like to look for ways to manage the current capacity. We believe that the new operations center that Transurban is putting in place in Northern Virginia to manage the HOT lanes will become a test bed for how to get better utilization out of our existing free lanes.

Q...Are you considering in the future moving away from the gas tax toward, say, the use of more dynamic, GPS-based, per-mile pricing?

Even though we have more cars being registered in the state, and we have more vehicle miles being traveled, our gas tax revenues are going down. We think that's due to the better fuel efficiency of newer vehicles, changes in driving habits and the impact of alternative fuels and electric and natural gas cars. These vehicles have the same impact on our transportation infrastructure as a gasoline-driven car, but they pay no taxes to support the system. We are looking at all the different options because in the long term, the gasoline tax is not a sustainable revenue source. I'm interested in how I can use technology to control traffic and get the most out of the current capacity.

Q...You have proposed a state infrastructure bank initially funded via sale of state liquor stores. Why do you believe the bank is needed?

We currently have a small, federally qualified state infrastructure bank, but we would like to establish a $1 billion infrastructure bank that does not use federal dollars and is not restricted by federal rules. It would be patterned on the TIFIA (Transportation Infrastructure Finance and Innovation Act) program at the U.S. Department of Transportation, but it also would enable us to lend money out and use the principal and interest payments to multiply into other projects. Then, we could lend out even more money and potentially provide guarantees or other techniques to leverage the first billion dollars three to five times. We think this is a great way for the government to multiply limited funds to get projects done and to provide credit during a period when it's difficult for the private sector to do so.

Q...What are the advantages of doing this without federal dollars?

It would allow us to move faster. And we could utilize it for projects that are not strictly highway projects. Also, an infrastructure bank without federal dollars would allow us to establish our own credit facilities based on what we think are the market needs. Maybe in certain instances, we're going to do direct loans; in other instances, we may be a guarantor; in other instances, we may be backing certain credit facilities.

Q...What other innovative things is Virginia doing?

We're establishing a standalone PPP office to deal with PPPs in road, rail, transit, aviation and ports. We're making it easier for our research programs to get the products of their research into our procurement system and our daily practices, setting aside $10 million to $20 million a year to provide incentives for using the results of our studies. We're also looking into how to make sure that our Metropolitan Planning Organizations, which get federal funding, and the state are spending their money cooperatively, not in isolation from each other.

Q...Have you found innovative ways to reduce costs or enhance revenues?

We did an aggressive operational and performance audit, which found more than $1.5 billion in unused federal obligation authority, federal toll credits and cash buildups in our construction programs. We will put out on the street in the next six months $614 million more than we had originally planned, thanks to the money we found in this audit. In addition, we're pursuing a transportation reform package in our general assembly that will update archaic regulations and policies. We're proposing that our general assembly clean up these things to give us more flexibility to spend the money we have.

Q...Looking at transportation issues three or four years into the future, do you see any big game-changers on the horizon?

The first big issue is where the federal program goes. The second is how the ever-increasing efficiency of vehicles and the use of alternative fuels is going to impact the basic funding mechanism for the entire U.S. transportation program.

When the economy improves and trade increases, it will have a major impact on the transportation network around large ports in Virginia and elsewhere. I think the environmental issues are going to come storming back when the economy improves, so the ability to expand transportation facilities will become a major issue. And we'll need to grow the intercity passenger rail systems that can move people into very heavily urbanized areas.

PART III: TRANSFORMING HEALTH AND HUMAN SERVICES

Introduction

A new era of State responsibility in health care

The 2009 federal health care reform law marked a new era of state responsibility in health care — the most significant since the advent of Medicaid. The state's role in health care will be larger than it has ever been before. While state governments' role as a payer is expanding, the most significant transformation is their overall role in the health care environment (see figure 5-1). Recent activity in health information technology and new responsibilities related to high-risk pools and insurance exchanges place states at the center of one of the most significant transformations of health care in more than four decades.

The full implications of legislative and regulatory initiatives affecting health care will unfold over the next decade and beyond. Certain components of the Patient Protection and Affordable Care Act of 2010 (PPACA), such as expanded access for children and disabled adults and regulatory reforms in the health insurance industry, must be developed and implemented swiftly. Delivery system reforms involving doctors, hospitals, long-term care and allied health professionals, the individual mandate, and employer penalties, to name a few, will involve a complex set of state decisions and long-term planning and implementation.

5-1. States will need to coordinate with stakeholders across the health care environment

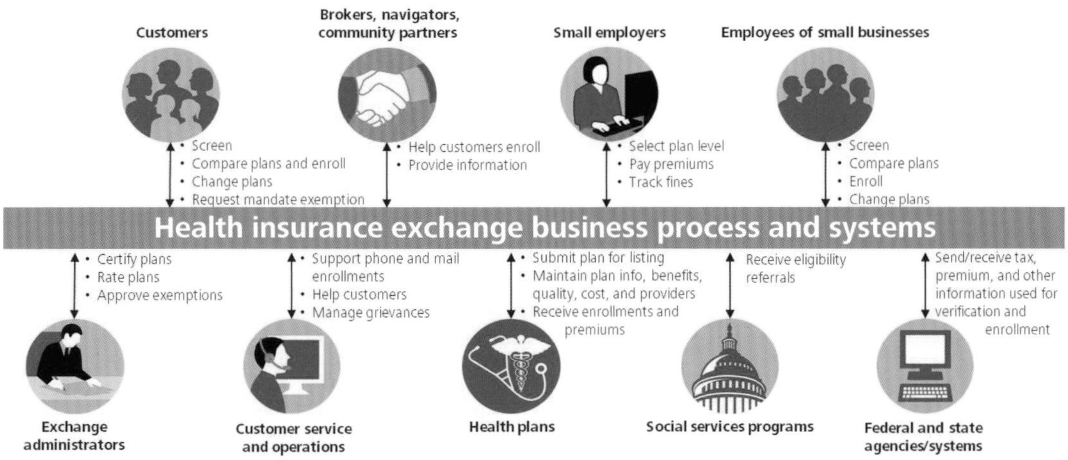

Source: Deloitte

Much of the action and implementation responsibilities of health reform will reside with the states. Just as states have previously assumed responsibility for expanded Medicaid programs and the Children's Health Insurance Program, they will now be responsible for many newly eligible citizens as well as the technology and business processes that support the reform program. Americans who previously went without health care insurance will go to their state government to enroll for coverage, have eligibility determined and seek referrals to managed care plans. The states are also where the health information exchanges will be established, as well as the technology developed to capture information on these new entrants into the health care system.

It will not be easy. Planning for this dramatic change must occur in a period of unprecedented Medicaid growth (see figure 5-2), driven by continuing economic challenges and a downward spiral of employer-sponsored health coverage. Most states are still struggling to cope with the recent surge in Medicaid caseloads as out-of-work Americans by the million look for help paying their medical bills. As a result, many states have cut back on other vital programs to try to balance their budgets. The new health care reform law will expand Medicaid enrollments in 2014, increasing states' costs, even with enhanced federal support.

Beyond the expansion of Medicaid programs, escalating expenses associated with delivering long-term care (LTC) to a growing number of enrollees add to the significant challenge of reining-in costs. State-administered Medicaid has become the nation's primary funding source for LTC. Prior to 1995, elderly residents exceeded 15 percent of the population in only five states; by 2025, the elderly will exceed 15 percent in every state except California and Alaska. Moreover, the health status of both child and adult Medicaid enrollees is lower than that of populations covered by private insurance, making medical management of Medicaid populations more problematic.

5-2. Medicaid enrollment has increased by nearly 6 million since the start of the recession

Monthly enrollment in millions

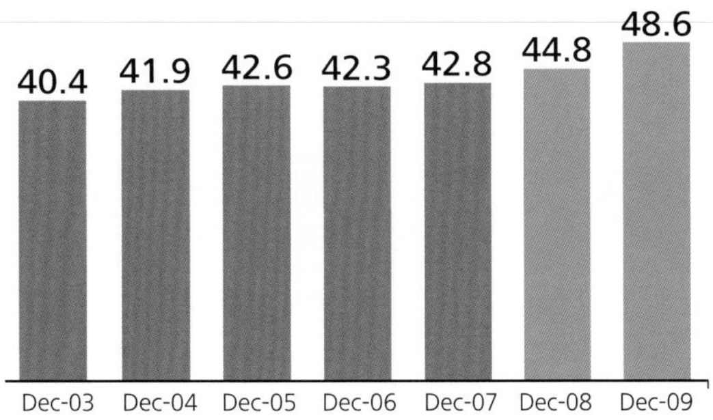

Source: Kaiser Family Foundation

5-3. Medicaid 500

MEDICAID 500

By virtue of their sheer size, more than half of state Medicaid programs have expenditures comparable to the revenues of the largest U.S. corporations and may indeed trump some of the largest corporate entities in size in 2014 when health reform legislation takes effect.

Rank	Company	$ millions
1	Wal-Mart Stores	408,214.00
2	Exxon Mobil	284,650.00
3	Chevron	163,527.00
4	General Electric	156,779.00
5	Bank of America Corp.	150,450.00
53	Kraft Foods	40,386.00
54	**California**	**39,903.00**
56	Apple	36,537.00
63	Aetna	34,764.10
65	**New York**	**32,428.00**
66	Caterpillar	32,396.00
84	Delta Air Lines	28,063.00
88	American Express	26,730.00
100	Amazon.com	24,509.00
124	Nike	19,176.10
127	**Pennsylvania**	**18,750.00**
130	AFLAC	18,254.40
143	**Florida**	**16,119.00**
144	Capital One Financial	15,980.10
162	**Illinois**	**14,488.00**
163	**Texas**	**14,471.00**
165	Loews	14,123.00
166	**Ohio**	**14,051.00**
170	Viacom	13,619.00
220	**North Carolina**	**10,721.00**
221	**Michigan**	**10,551.00**
223	Texas Instruments	10,427.00
239	Progress Energy	9,885.00
240	**New Jersey**	**9,851.00**
241	Starbucks	9,774.60

Rank	Company	$ millions
266	**Massachusetts**	**8,688.00**
269	**Missouri**	**8,619.00**
270	Nordstrom	8,627.00
284	Whole Foods Market	8,031.60
287	**Arizona**	**7,972.00**
288	Ameriprise Financial	7,946.00
297	**Georgia**	**7,615.00**
308	Estée Lauder	7,323.80
309	**Washington**	**7,223.00**
334	Goodrich	6,685.60
336	**Minnesota**	**6,658.00**
339	**Louisiana**	**6,558.00**
343	Yahoo	6,460.30
345	**Maryland**	**6,353.00**
352	**Wisconsin**	**6,198.00**
356	**Virginia**	**6,079.00**
356	KeyCorp	6,068.00
372	Barnes & Noble	5,596.30
373	**Indiana**	**5,595.00**
373	Newell Rubbermaid	5,577.60
378	**Kentucky**	**5,509.00**
428	**Alabama**	**4,871.00**
428	Foot Locker	4,854.00
443	Health Management Associates	4,687.30
446	**Connecticut**	**4,671.00**
455	Washington Post	4,569.70
480	**South Carolina**	**4,562.00**
494	Electronic Arts	4,212.00
495	**Mississippi**	**4,203.00**

Source: Deloitte Research

5-4. Health reform timeline

	2010	2011
Insurance markets	• Dependent coverage to age 26 • Prohibition of rescissions • No lifetime benefit maximums • Limits on annual benefit maximums to 2014 • No pre-existing condition exclusion for children • Temporary high-risk pools • Temporary reinsurance program for early retirees • Limitations on cost sharing for preventive services • Internal & external appeals processes required • Premium increase rate reviews • State ombudsman program	• Minimum MLRs and rebates • CLASS Act - LTC insurance
Government programs	• Medicare market basket update reductions and other payment changes • Filing period reduction for Medicare FFS claims • New office & programs created to better manage dual eligibles • Changes & increases to Medicaid drug rebate percentages • Medicaid overpayment collection extension due to fraud • CHIP expansion & eligibility maintained until 2019 • Web sites to compare plan options with standard ways of describing benefits • Prevention and public health fund for prevention & wellness, etc. established • Maternal & child health funding • Funding for community health centers • Workforce development program improvements • CMS systems modernization • State medical malpractice reform demonstrations • Wellness grants for small employers • Biosimiliar access • Biologic data exclusivity	• Medicare Advantage program payment changes • Medicare Advantage quality bonus payments • Medicare bonus payments to primary care & gen. surgeons in medically underserved areas • Coverage for health risk assessments & annual prevention plan (Medicare) • Preventive health co-pays eliminated (Medicaid) • Part D "donut hole" elimination • Medicare Innovation Center in CMS • Medicaid LTC & community-based care programs & pilots created • Medicaid mandatory use of National Correct Coding Initiative • Medicaid provider termination if terminated under Medicare or other state plan • RAC audit expansion • Integrated data repository, data sharing & reporting extension • Increased fraud and abuse detection, prevention programs • Residency positions reallocated • Nursing home "compare" Web site • Physician "compare" Web site • Restaurants & vending machines must publish nutritional information
Delivery systems & effectiveness	• EMR adoption subsidies • Patient Centered Outcomes Research Institute creation • Hospital pricing publishing requirements	• No federal match for Medicaid payments for hospital acquired infections • NFP hospitals required to conduct community needs assessment • NFP hospitals must charge low income patients the standard reimbursement amount • "Health home" pilot (Medicaid) • Physician self-referral restrictions & transparency • Nursing home & SNF monitoring & quality demonstration process
Revenue & subsidies	• $250 Medicare Part D rebate for beneficiaries reaching the "donut hole" • R&D tax credits for small biotechs • Small business tax credits (<50 employees) • Health insurance tax to fund Patient Centered Outcomes Research Institute	• Tax rules around FSAs, HRAs, etc. changed • Rx manufacturer fees

Source: Deloitte

12	2013	2014	2015+
Participation standards & reporting requirements for participating plans	• HIPAA 5010/ICD-10 • Administrative simplification of all provider/plan transactions • CO-OP development subsidies	• Individual mandate • Guaranteed issue and renewal • Rating restrictions (age, geography, family size & smoking) • Essential benefits package defined • No annual benefit maximums • No pre-existing condition exclusions for adults • American health benefit exchanges for individuals & small groups <100 employees • OPM contracts with two national plans to be offered on each exchange • Reduce cost sharing and OOP minimums for those up to 400% FPL • Automatic enrollment of employees for large employers • Standard electronic enrollment forms • Coverage for clinical trials participation • Free choice vouchers	• Groups over 100 employees can join exchanges (2017)
Employer wellness program – pilots, programs, etc.	• Medicare Disproportionate Share payment reductions • Medicaid Disproportionate Share payment reductions • Medicaid payments to primary care physicians increased • Preventive health co-pays eliminated (Medicare)	• Medicare Advantage MLR requirements • Medicaid minimum eligibility set to 133% FPL • Medicaid/CHIP enrollment simplification • Quality & patient satisfaction ratings published for plans • Medicare Independent Payment Advisory Board	
Hospital value-based purchasing program (Medicare) Medicaid episode-based payments pilot Medicare payments for preventable hospital readmissions reduced Independence at Home demonstration project (Medicare) ACOs that meet quality standards can share in savings	• ICD-10 requirements • Life sciences/pharmaceutical "sunshine" provisions • Medicare episode-based payments pilot	• Medicare payments for hospital acquired infections reduced	• Patient safety evaluation system requirement (hospitals with >50 beds) (2015)
	• Medicare payroll tax increase on high-income earners • Retiree Part D deduction for employer subsidy eliminated • Medical device sales tax	• Individual mandate penalty • Premium tax credits and subsidies to 400% FPL • Penalties for employers whose employees obtain subsidized coverage • Health insurance industry excise tax	• "Cadillac" tax on certain high cost employer-sponsored coverage (aggregate values > $10,200) (2018)

Knowledge of the health care system tends to be linked to anecdotal personal experiences with physicians, hospitals and plans, rather than hard data about prices, quality, outcomes and service.

The management challenge is further compounded by the sheer magnitude of state Medicaid programs, many of which have budgets the size of the largest U.S. corporations but lack the resources, tools and decision support systems available to their commercial counterparts (see figure 5-3).

Politically, health care — and specifically, Medicaid — is a spotlight issue for state governors and legislators. Systemic, sustainable cuts in health costs that do not compromise the quality and safety of care are, at best, challenging. Administrative simplification, leveraging information technologies to reduce paperwork and waste, aggressive efforts to reduce fraud, and liability reforms are important first steps, but long-term solutions require policies and incentives that align desired outcomes with spending by individuals and governments. In most cases, the tough, fiscally responsible choices that have to be made are unpopular.

Moreover, health care is complex. Most consumers and elected officials do not fully understand our $2.5 trillion system. Rather, knowledge of the health care system tends to be linked to anecdotal personal experiences with physicians, hospitals and plans, rather than hard data about prices, quality, outcomes and service. As a result, health reform is prone to strong opinions and misinformation from all sides, so emotions tend to run high.

While the complexity of implementing health reform can't be overstated, the new federal legislation offers states the opportunity to make meaningful reforms that they have wanted to put in place for years. States remain the laboratories of democracy — the place where the boldest policy innovations occur. They are also the place where voters often put problem solving abilities ahead of partisanship and ideology.

The long haul has begun. Remaining flexible over the course of the transformation is critical. When reforming a complex system, it is difficult to anticipate all of the new wrinkles that will undoubtedly emerge along the way.

Implementing reform

A new era of state responsibility in health care

The passage of the Patient Protection and Affordable Care Act of 2010 (PPACA) marks perhaps the most ambitious transformation effort undertaken by government in recent times (see figure 5-6). While controversial, the motivation was to create an inclusive health care system that ensures access to affordable, quality care. The change was fueled by the economics of the existing health care system and antiquated incentive structure that produced endless cost escalation without actually improving outcomes.

Nonetheless, new federal legislation is creating as many questions as answers. Perhaps foremost on the minds of Medicaid administrators is how states will cope with the expanded role for Medicaid included in the recently enacted federal health care reform. Expanding Medicaid to cover all Americans up to 133 percent of the federal poverty level is one of the two major reform approaches to solving the problem of high uninsurance rates (see figure 5-5). While Medicaid expansion under the PPACA does not take effect until 2014, states will need the intervening time to prepare adequately for the transformation of Medicaid programs.

Beyond the significant expansion of Medicaid, the health care reform law puts enormous responsibility on states to create health exchanges, oversee new insurance industry regulations, upgrade health care workforce training programs through licensing and medical education, and oversee the integration of public health programs with local delivery systems. Furthermore, states are major employers, so every element of coverage for employees, dependents and retirees must be revisited to align with PPACA requirements (see figure 5-7 for an illustrative roadmap of the states' role in implementing health reform).

PPACA raises four big questions: Will individuals buy insurance according to the mandate? Will employers maintain coverage or pay the penalty and walk away? Will delivery system reforms result in lower costs? Will states be able to deliver on their obligations?

Every stakeholder — providers, payers, regulators, consumers, states — has to reduce health costs, but cost reduction is little more than table stakes. It does not guarantee success or even survival. States will be successful to the extent status quo approaches and barriers to change are set aside for fresh ideas and bold leadership. For states, innovation in medical management, public-private collaboration, leveraging technology and engaging legislators in a nonpartisan process of health system redesign are imperatives. Health is too important for states to let it be a partisan sideshow.

The 2010 federal health care law raises four big questions: Will individuals buy insurance according to the mandate? Will employers maintain coverage or pay the penalty and walk away? Will delivery system reforms result in lower costs? Will states be able to deliver on their obligations?

ACTION PLAN FOR IMPLEMENTING HEALTH CARE REFORM

The federal health care reform legislation will be enormously complex for states to implement. Driving much of the decision making is a calendar requiring certain features be up and running at certain times, whether it's the health insurance exchanges or the eligibility protocols.

Beyond merely complying with federal health reform mandates, states must build a solid foundation for systemic reform if they are to control costs and improve health outcomes. The health care reform pyramid reflects the essential, interdependent relationships among four key focus areas: health care information technology, comparative effectiveness, coordination of care and consumerism (see figure 5-9). The strategies outlined below can help states get a handle on the complexity of health reform.

Develop an implementation roadmap

The first step for governors and their health and Medicaid directors is to develop an enterprisewide implementation roadmap laying out a holistic view of the plethora of requirements from the legislation and how they're going to approach them. Soon after PPACA passed, the State of Maine developed an encompassing roadmap across the full spectrum of health care reform, from health benefits exchanges to the American Recovery and Reinvestment Act (ARRA), from health information exchanges to Medicaid expansion. Maine's roadmap looked at current operations and then laid out an imple-

5-5. Changes to program structure under PPACA

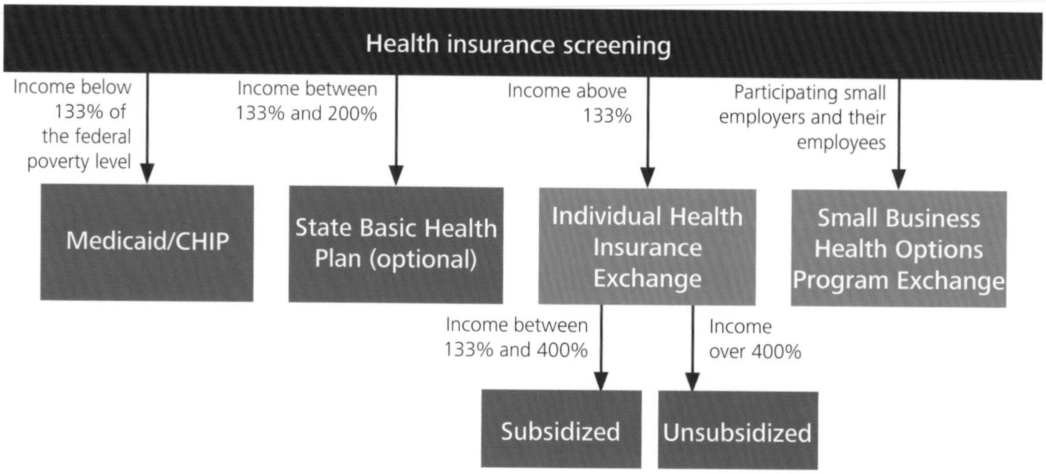

Source: Deloitte

responding to health care reform

5-6. State government at the center of health reform

States are at the center of a dramatic transformation of the U.S. health care system that's driven by federal legislation, budget pressures and consumer demand for quality, cost and access.

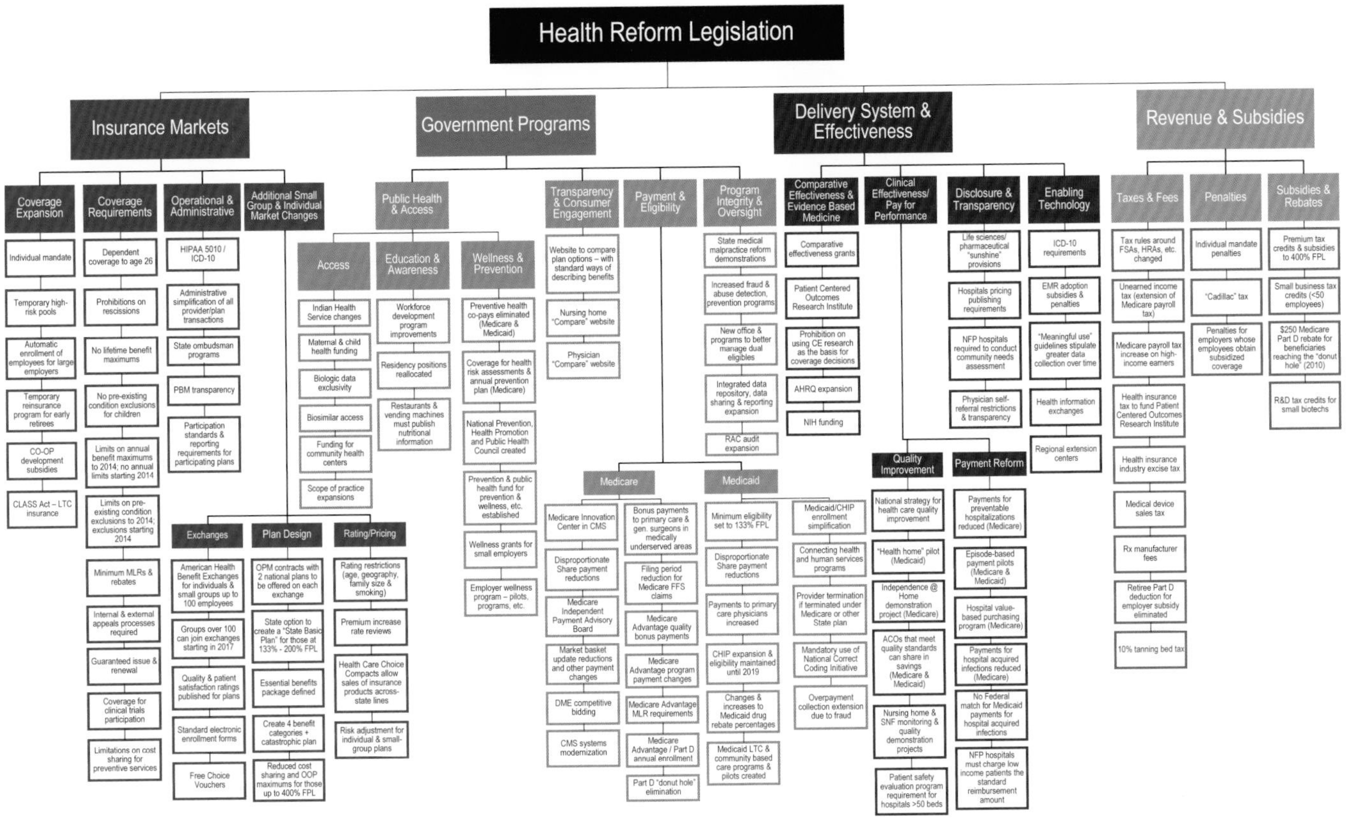

Note: The Health Reform Legislation map contains certain key provisions from the Patient Protection and Affordable Care Act (PPACA) passed on March 23, 2010 (Pub. Law No 111-148), the corresponding Health Care and Education. Reconciliation Act (HCERA) passed on March 30, 2010 (Pub. Law No 111-152), and other reforms from the American Recovery & Reinvestment Act (ARRA) passed on February 17, 2009 (Pub. Law No 111-5).

Source: Deloitte

Roadblocks to overcome

How to expand Medicaid

Determining how to absorb the influx of new enrollees will be one of the greatest challenges states face across the next few years, particularly given the strain Medicaid budgets already experience and the impact the recent economic crisis had on both tax revenue and eligibility.

Oversee a surge of new market entrants

As was the case with previous health reform efforts, a large number of new commercial entities will likely enter the market with varying levels of experience and capabilities. To avoid the performance shortcomings of the past, states will need to carefully evaluate the experience level, management capacity, and financial wherewithal of new entrants into the market.

5-7. Illustrative state roadmap for health reform

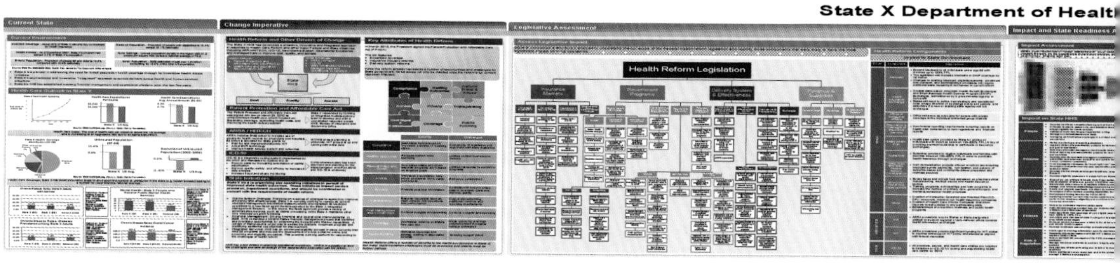

Source: Deloitte

mentation strategy for how all the reforms can be accomplished in an integrated, coordinated fashion.

Design your health benefit exchange to meet the unique needs of your state

The PPACA mandate to establish insurance exchanges in each state by January 1, 2014 is one of the cornerstones of reform. It is also among the most challenging and uncertain implementation priorities. The exchanges must publish information that enables consumers to compare plans, establish call centers to answer consumers' questions, and determine eligibility for subsidies and exemptions from the penalties imposed on people who opt to forgo insurance. Moreover, the exchanges will need to develop new IT systems that enable the exchange of data between state Medicaid agencies, insurance companies, employers and federal agencies.

While the Massachusetts Connector and the Utah Health Exchange provide two real-world examples, the individual health benefit exchanges are likely to look and operate quite differently from state to state. It is common to hear exchange proponents express their hope that exchanges will resemble Orbitz or Expedia for health insurance. While that vision is technically possible, the investment and change required to achieve that vision should not be underestimated.

Once the U.S. Department of Health and Human Services finalizes requirements and associated funding, states must evaluate how to develop their exchange(s) to meet their unique needs. Should they combine the individual and small group product lines and operations within the exchange? Should they join with other states in a regional approach? Should they maintain direct operational control of the exchange or form a nonprofit entity to carry out the requirements? Or, most dramatically, should a state stay out of the exchange business altogether, simply allowing HHS to run the exchange?

Invest in IT infrastructure to support reform

Given the considerable technology challenges of health information exchanges and providing important information on health conditions and outcomes across providers, a significant level of capital investment in health information technology will be required to meet the objectives of the federal health care legislation.

California Insurance Exchange Legislation

On September 30, Gov. Schwarzenegger (R) signed legislation establishing a health insurance exchange in California. The exchange will create a Web-based insurance plan marketplace for residents, offering standardized and detailed information about available plans, as well as a toll-free hotline to help consumers understand their options. Approximately 8.3 million residents are expected to be eligible for coverage through the exchange. The program is expected to bring as much as $10 billion in subsidies for the state over 10 years.

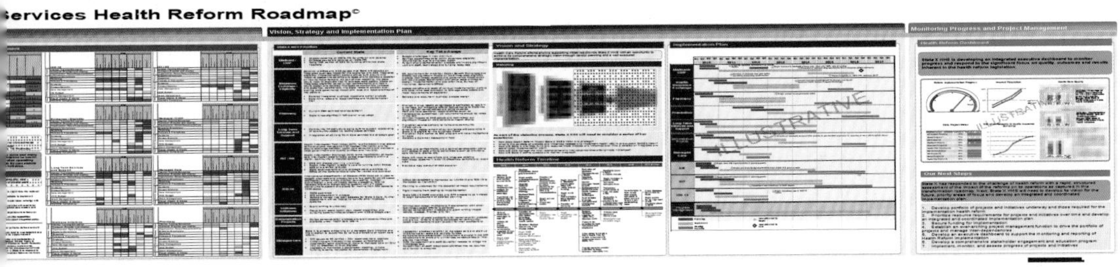

Enhance health care information technology (HCIT)

Thanks to HCIT, tecnology-enabled care coordination such as e-prescribing, which saves money and improves safety by limiting adverse drug events, is possible. Furthermore, adopting HCIT can reduce administrative costs. Other forms of electronic health records make it possible to share patient information between sites, reducing redundant paperwork and unnecessary tests.

In 2009, 18 percent of all prescriptions were electronic, up from 6.6 percent in 2008.[69] Across the U.S. there are a number of state initiatives underway aimed at increasing the percentage of electronic prescriptions. Delaware's Medicaid program, for example, funded startup costs for e-prescribing software and training for the state's top Medicaid providers. So far, a fifth of Medicaid providers have adopted the technology.[70] On the other side of the country, the California Public Employees' Retirement System (CalPERS), Anthem Blue Cross, Medco Health Solutions and Blue Shield of California have joined forces to form California's largest e-prescribing initiative, which will monitor and report on participating physicians' use of e-prescribing.[71] States should properly fund investments in HCIT as a necessary foundation for reform.

Improve the link between health expenditures and outcomes

States need to adopt new incentive structures rather than maintain a system that rewards a higher volume of tests and procedures at the expense of evidence-based and cost-effective treatment. Too many procedures are conducted without a compelling clinical basis. Drawing upon research to tease out which costly treatments have proven unnecessary could make a huge dent in the spiraling costs that plague health care. The health care reform bill allocates more than a billion dollars to sponsor research into how to improve the link between health care expenditures and outcomes.

What works: Patient-centered medical homes (PCMH)

A 2010 study led by researchers at Harvard Medical School analyzed seven PCMH programs to assess features of those deemed successful (see figure 5-8). Sponsors of these programs included prominent commercial health plans, integrated health systems and government-sponsored programs.[72] The selected programs were measured based on improvements in the number of hospitalizations and savings per patient. Despite the sample's heterogeneity, the research team concluded that four common features were salient to the seven programs' success:

- Dedicated care managers
- Expanded access to health practitioners
- Data-driven analytic tools
- New incentives[73]

In the current economic climate, more states are cutting in-home community services. These cuts will further aggravate state Medicaid performance since community programs are less expensive to provide and, in some cases, reduce the need for institutional care.

Promote new ways of coordinating care

Health care delivery in the United States tends to be fragmented and inefficient. Patients are handed from doctor to doctor with little regard for the broader care plan. This system not only leads to imperfect health outcomes, but also results in higher expenditures through duplication or mere negligence. By delivering more coordinated care, states can improve population-based health outcomes and reduce demand for more expensive acute services. Moreover, electronic health records can facilitate the delivery of more thoughtful, coherent care plans.

The patient-centered medical home (PCMH) is a new way of organizing primary care. Patients receive care coordinated by a primary care physician who is supported by information technologies. The care is then actually delivered by a multidisciplinary team of allied health professionals who adhere to evidence-based practice guidelines. The goal is to deliver continuous, accessible, high-quality, patient-oriented primary care that replaces the current high-volume approach many primary care physicians are forced to practice.

Encourage greater consumer engagement

Health care consumers can be enlightened consumers through the use of personal health records (PHRs), heightened transparency and incentives for primary care. Nine of the 15 reasons for hospital admission involve the progression of chronic conditions that are not treated. By combining primary care with incentives and technologies that support consumer engagement, states could dramatically reduce costs while improving health outcomes.

5-8. Analysis of seven PCMH pilot programs

Pilot	Results		
	Hospitalization Reduction (%)	ER visit reduction (%)	Total savings per patient
Colorado Medical Homes for Children	18%	NA	$169–530
Community Care of North Carolina	40%	16%	$516
Geisinger (ProvenHealthNavigator)	15%	NA	NA
Group Health Cooperative	11%	29%	$71
Intermountain Health Care (Care Management Plus)	4.8–19.2%	0–7.3%	$640
MeritCare Health System and Blue Cross Blue Shield of North Dakota	6%	24%	$530
Vermont BluePrint for Health	11%	12%	$215

Source: Adapted from Fields D, Leshen E, and Patel K. "Driving Quality Gains and Cost Savings through Adoption of Medical Homes," *Health Affairs*, May 2010; 29(5): 819-826. Appendix Exhibit 1.

When designed and implemented correctly, consumerism has been shown to reduce both health care utilization and costs. For example, when consumer-driven health care (CDH) is offered on a full-replacement basis, actuarial studies have shown that CDH plans lower discretionary and potentially unnecessary utilization and reduce employer health care expenses by as much as 10–15 percent in the first year of implementation. After the first year, the cost trend is generally 3–5 percent lower than the marketplace, but greater reductions are sometimes achieved.[74]

5-9. The health care reform pyramid

By focusing on four areas, government leaders can build a solid foundation for systemic reform. The essential, interdependent relationships among these focus areas is reflected in this diagram.

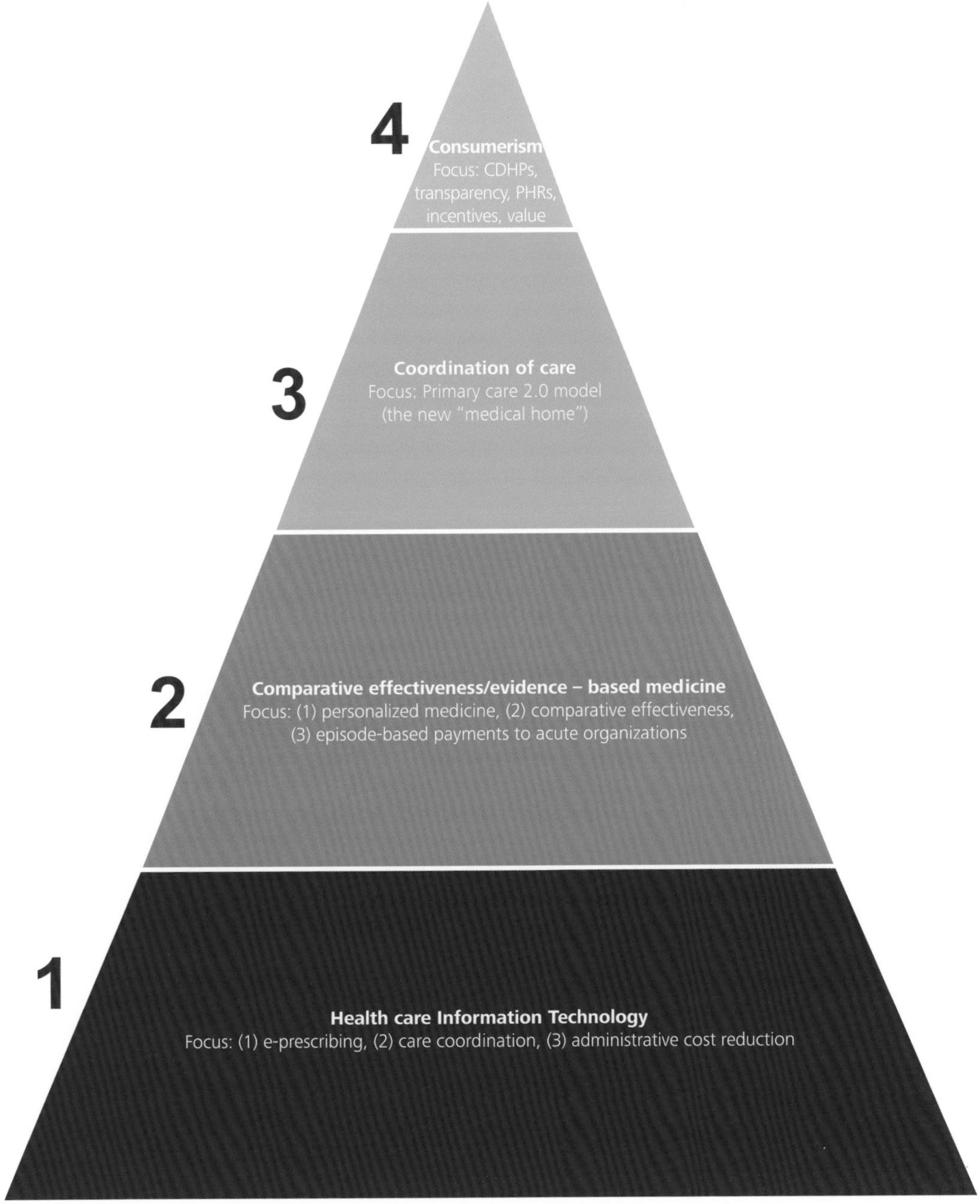

Source: Deloitte Center for Health Solutions

Controlling long-term care costs in Medicaid

The ticking time bomb

There is currently no coordinated, comprehensive system for the provision and financing of long-term care (LTC) services in the United States. For the disabled and elderly who lack personal financial resources, navigating the complexities and regulations associated with LTC decisions can be extremely challenging. No less daunting is the task facing state policymakers, whose decisions on behalf of these vulnerable populations directly and dramatically affect state budgets.

Medicaid has become the nation's primary funding source for LTC. Over a third of all Medicaid expenditures are for consumers who need long-term care services. Because Medicare does not provide long-term nursing home benefits or home and community-based services, Medicaid is in essence the long-term care provider for an increasingly large percentage of the elderly population. As a result, the pressure on states to control costs while making effective decisions regarding the provision of community versus institutional LTC services presents an opportunity to transform LTC as a whole. This transformation assumes a sense of urgency as state governments face new and growing fiscal challenges generated, in part, by the needs of the aging Baby Boomers.

Indeed, time is of the essence. The expected increase in Medicaid enrollments resulting from aging populations and increased eligibility from health care reform add to the urgency with which this escalating problem must be addressed. Left unattended, states' obligations to their LTC Medicaid enrollees resemble a ticking time bomb, one that will wreak havoc on already-strained budgets.

Ensuring a more favorable balance between institutional and community-based LTC services is an important place for reformers to begin. Recent research shows that individuals may be cared for in community settings without sacrificing quality and with increases in beneficiary satisfaction. However, in the current economic climate, more states are cutting in-home community services. These cuts will further aggravate state Medicaid performance since community programs are less expensive to provide and, in some cases, reduce the need for institutional care.

ACTION PLAN FOR MANAGING THE COSTS OF DELIVERING LONG-TERM CARE

The long-term care system in the United States is fragmented, complex and historically focused on the provision of institutional care. If private or family-supplied funding is not available to the elderly or disabled who require LTC, state Medicaid funds are required to support those needs. Every state has its own specific eligibility criteria for Medicaid and a complex set of other agency programs. States need to be actively engaged in initiatives to control LTC expenditures while maintaining or increasing quality. These strategies can form the foundation of a plan to better control their LTC costs:

Increase community-based care options

Research shows that individuals may be cared for in community settings without sacrificing quality and, in fact, with an increase in beneficiary satisfaction. Despite the evidence, states seeking to make cuts are reducing budgetary allocations to these cost-effective, in-house measures. States should examine all of the available options for keeping long-term care patients away from institutional settings and, where appropriate, encourage wider adoption of community-based care.

The State of Washington uses a single, comprehensive, automated assessment tool called CARE to assess the most appropriate care setting for LTC recipients. The results are used to jumpstart discussions regarding delivery options, helping to collaboratively develop the most appropriate, patient-specific care plan. The tool also monitors the receipt of services and flags individuals whose needs are expected to change. This ensures that they receive appropriate support to make the transition to institutional settings at the appropriate time.

Develop citizen-centric approaches

States and local agencies that provide assistance for individuals who require LTC services have historically not been visible to those who need help. Both funding and fragmentation issues have plagued the relationship between resource groups and potential recipients of these services. States need to develop a delivery model that addresses the unique needs of each citizen. A more personalized model would result in more satisfied consumers and may reduce the need for expensive institutional care.

Expand chronic disease management

Approximately 39 million Americans with chronic care conditions require LTC services, which includes support for activities of daily living. Yet, despite the great expense attached to these sorts of patients, these individuals often have multiple care providers and multiple treatment and medication plans. This lack of coordination often leads to otherwise preventable emergency department visits, hospitalizations and nursing home admissions. States should develop chronic disease management programs that better coordinate care, which can help to bend the cost curve.

Strengthen the long-term care workforce

To absorb the impending demographic bulge created by the Baby Boomers, states will need to take steps to avoid caregiver shortages. To lessen the demands states should encourage informal care networks, providing financial resources that allow for more flexible arrangements in the community. Modest resources reallocated to a community setting that permit informal caregivers (e.g., family members or others) to better provide for their loved ones can significantly reduce costs associated with institutional care.

Many public and private partnerships are developing to improve the quality of long-term care, control spending and allow for more community-focused, personalized, long-term care systems.

Roadblocks to overcome

Controlling rising LTC expenditures

The Centers for Medicare and Medicaid Services (CMS) project that future LTC spending will increase at an average rate of 8.6 percent per year.[75] This projection is based on expected continuing increases in the use and cost of LTC as well as projected increases in enrollment — especially for aged and disabled beneficiaries.

Absorbing aging Baby Boomers

The convergence of an aging population and health care reform's mandate for increased access to care will have especially far-reaching consequences for Medicaid and long-term care. Census data indicate that the number of Americans aged 65 and older will more than double in at least 20 states by 2025. This demographic bulge will force budget-conscious state administrators to examine how to address the full range of elderly needs with limited resources.

What works: Expanding community-based care in Vermont

The State of Vermont adapted its Medicaid program to let consumers hire independent providers — either family members or others — to assist in delivering community-based care. Allowing seniors to self-direct funds has proven to be more effective than more traditional arrangements in meeting individual needs and reducing the emotional, physical and financial stress experienced by informal caregivers. More than 60 percent of personal care hours are now self-directed.

Increasing the focus on Medicaid medical management

Softening Medicaid's impact on state budgets

In many states, Medicaid is the single largest expense category in state budgets. Governors and legislators face tremendous challenges in managing their Medicaid programs. Each year seems to bring climbing enrollments, soaring costs, more complexity in enrollee health problems and a shrinking pool of providers who agree to treat enrollees.

Medicaid spending jeopardizes myriad important budgets items — increased pay for teachers, improvements in general services, required compliance with federal mandates and infrastructure investments to streamline government.

The effective management of Medicaid programs across the country is also a politically charged issue. Policymakers understand their obligations to the program and its recipients, but identifying solutions that balance reduced cost and appropriate care is difficult.

With the recent enactment of the PPACA, the number of Medicaid beneficiaries is likely to grow considerably. As it stands, the elderly and disabled populations currently contribute 76 percent of the growth in Medicaid spending, and their numbers will increase substantially with the aging of the country's Baby Boomers.

Medical management of the Medicaid population is a tough business. The design and delivery of health services to Medicaid enrollees presents particular challenges — enrollees don't regularly use the system; risk factors and social issues render treatment plans ineffective and complicate diagnoses; and, in many states, doctors and hospitals will simply not treat enrollees because of liability concerns. A new approach is needed.

Successful Medicaid medical management programs use information systems to segment patients into groups according to their health risks, enroll patients and providers in appropriate care programs, promote accountability and reward it with incentives and measure results. These programs maintain a clinical focus while investing in the administrative structures necessary to optimize cost-effectiveness and quality.

ACTION PLAN FOR MEDICAID MEDICAL MANAGEMENT

State policymakers can better manage Medicaid's costs by focusing on two areas: clinical population care management and administrative considerations (see figure 5-10).

Develop clinical population care management plan

This refers to how health problems in the Medicaid population are diagnosed, interventions are planned and care is coordinated. States should develop a comprehensive program targeting preventive health care and healthy living as a necessary foundation for Medicaid medical management.

The provision of care drives Medicaid costs. A medical management program can favorably impact these costs.

On top of that, states should focus their efforts on disease management to reduce medical costs for chronically ill patients with the goal of slowing disease progression and avoiding costly hospitalizations and complications.

For the sickest 1 to 5 percent of Medicaid enrollees who drive a large portion of controllable costs, states must focus on case management. A key program element is a one-on-one, nurse-to-enrollee care management model that follows an individualized care plan.

Roadblocks to overcome

Unsustainable spending patterns

Accounting for around 22 percent of the "average" state budget, Medicaid is the fastest growing line item. By 2015, total Medicaid spending is projected to double from its 2007 levels and reach $670 billion. On average, states pay 37 percent of the costs of Medicaid; the federal government pays the balance, though the formula varies by state.

Growing enrollment

With the enactment of federal health reform, the number of Medicaid beneficiaries is projected to increase from 58.8 million today to 76 million as the PPACA provisions kick in.

5-10. Key impact areas: Medicaid medical management

Clinical considerations	Administrative considerations
• Risk stratification and predictive modeling • Preventive health, screenings and education • Chronic care management for type II diabetes, heart disease, depression, COPD, asthma and other conditions • Case management for the frail elderly, recently discharged and severely disabled	• Integrated care team design and oversight • Medication management and formulary design • Single point of entry systems • Medical management information system for program management and quality control • Nurse-staffed call center to support medical management • Integrated care program for dual eligibles • Evidence-based guidelines and process for coverage and denial management • Provide: credentialing, payment and performance reporting services

Source: Deloitte Center for Health Solutions

Develop single point of entry systems for Medicaid

Administrative medical management refers to how states and health plans operate the program to optimize enrollee patient care and satisfaction while reducing costs (such as policies, procedures, infrastructure and management). Medicaid enrollees' complex medical and psychosocial issues require care teams that include physicians, behavioral health professionals, pharmacists, family and other patient caregivers. These teams can motivate and coach participants, collaborate to share ideas and advocate for participants to identify additional resources to help address their myriad needs.

To help coordinate health care, Medicaid administrators and plans should focus on developing single point of entry systems (SPOEs) to provide a centralized, trusted, one-stop portal to access all administrative program functions. Combined with the Internet, these systems could enhance enrollee engagement and self-care. Several states and the District of Columbia offer SPOE systems for Medicaid enrollees (see figure 5-11).

5-11. Examples of Medicaid single point of entry systems

Single Point of Entry System	Description
Wisconsin www.dhfs.state.wi.us/ltcare/Generalinfo/rcs.htm	Provides information and assistance regarding public benefits that may be available as well as area programs and services.
Oregon www.oregon.gov/DHS/index.shtml	Provides centralized information source for needs assessment and eligibility, pre-admission, screening, case management and service plan authorization, counseling, adult protective services, and after-hours, on-call support.
Massachusetts www.mass.gov/?pageID=eohhs2homepage&L=1&LO=Home&sid=Eeohhs2	Provides centralized access, medical eligibility determination, service authorization and case management.
Michigan www.michigan.gov/mdch/0,1607,7-132-2943_4860---,00.html	Provides centralized access to eligibility determination, information and assistance programs.
Maine www.maine.gov/dhhs/index.shtml	Provides centralized access for medical assessments of enrollees and unique issues for each patient enrollee.
Washington, D.C. www.adrc-tae.org	Based on the Wisconsin model. Site streamlines eligibility determination, acts as a central point of data collection and analysis, and provides centralized information and assistance services to long-term-care enrollees.

Source: Web sites indicated in table

What works: Predictive modeling at Blue Cross and Blue Shield of Tennessee (BCBS TN)

BCBS TN uses predictive modeling to help stratify the Medicaid population by looking at an "impactability index" to identify which members have gaps in care, then prioritizes outreach. Member adherence to care plans and provider adherence to clinical guidelines is a new contractual requirement for BCBS TN. The predictive modeling process gives BCBS TN the ability to identify gaps in care to share with physicians in the plan.

The predictive modeling works by looking at five key indicators to total a score:

1. Estimated cost for next year
2. Preventive gaps in care (such as pap smears and mammograms for women)
3. Chronic gaps in care (the model can pick up one or more conditions)
4. Is a client "impactable?" (Can something be done to help prevent rapid deterioration?)
5. Is a client "movable?" (Will risk increase if nothing is done now?)

BCBS TN can use these scores for more than live referrals. They also ensure results that both disease management and case management programs can use to intervene in health care.

Interview with

Alice M. Rivlin

Senior Fellow at The Brookings Institution

Q...Although the health reform law is a federal statute, it grants states considerable leeway in its most important provisions. Can you describe the discretion states are granted within the new law?

One of the most important ones is to set up the exchanges on which individuals who are eligible for federal subsidies will purchase health insurance. That was left to the states but with a proviso that states could opt out of it, in which case the federal government would come in.

States are also allowed to join together to set up exchanges where there isn't a critical mass of population as in some sections of the country. They may want to do that.

I think the exchanges are an extremely important part of health reform. It's basically a free market approach to health coverage, which allows individuals with federal subsidies to choose among health plans on an exchange and health plans to compete for business on the exchange.

The reform won't work well unless the states set up very robust exchanges where there is plenty of information about the plans, their costs and their outcomes. That's not going to be an easy task. The governors are going to have to turn to and start working on the exchanges fairly soon.

Q...What steps can states take to avoid some of the problems associated with choice overload that we saw with the rollout of Medicare's prescription drug benefit? How do states ensure that new entrants into the health care system have access to comprehensible choices when they go to buy health insurance?

Well that's one of the big challenges. And states have to make sure that there are rules that make it easier for individuals who are choosing to see what they're buying. Past experience shows that it is hard to set up new marketplaces like this.

The governors can learn from some of the states that have already done it, especially Massachusetts. They can see what Massachusetts did well and what they did badly and try to set up exchanges that improve on the Massachusetts experience. There are other states that have tried it, but Massachusetts has been a lead.

Q...How do state leaders balance their new responsibilities associated with health care reform and their ongoing budgetary and programmatic responsibilities with respect to managing health care costs?

Some states are deep in the question of managing health care costs already and are using innovative ways to reduce the cost of serving Medicaid beneficiaries effectively. I think they have to learn from each other and pick out the things that have worked well. For example, what kind of managed care works well in Medicaid and what have the states that have been most successful in holding down the costs while increasing service actually done?

Q... You recently served on the Robert Wood Johnson Foundation's Commission to Build a Healthier America. One of the Commission's chief findings was that while preventive and primary health care are important that "most prevention activities occur outside the traditional medical care setting, in the places where we live, learn, work and play." What does that conclusion imply for states?

The Commission emphasized that we could be a much healthier America not just by providing better health care but more importantly by changing lifestyles, diet, exercise, early childhood development and the kind of neighborhoods that people live in. Some neighborhoods are a lot healthier than others.

If you are going to have a healthy diet, you have to have access to fresh fruits and vegetables. And there are parts of major cities that are food deserts. They don't actually have places where people can buy fresh fruits and vegetables.

Some states are working hard on this and some cities, Philadelphia in particular. Another major example is exercise. Much of the problem is with young people who aren't exercising as much as they used to and are increasingly obese. The schools have to put into their school day regular exercise for young people. Exercise doesn't have to be expensive or involve a lot of equipment. It just requires taking time out of the school day to make sure that younger kids are running around and older kids are actually doing physical activity.

Q...One of the fastest growing sources of health care expense is the provision of long-term care. Medicaid is in essence the long-term care provider for an increasingly large percentage of the elderly population. What advice would you offer state leaders with respect to the very difficult issue of containing costs in this area?

This is a very difficult national problem. And it's going to get worse. The need for long-term care will escalate over the next decade or two or three as the Baby Boom generation moves into the high care age group. That hasn't actually happened yet. The leading edge of the Baby Boom is still in their 60s. And need for long-term care increases as people age and it's particularly high among people in their late 70s, 80s and up.

So this is a wave of need that's going to come. Health reform has not satisfactorily dealt with how we are going to pay for long-term care. Medicaid is carrying the bulk of the public cost at the moment, but it's going to get larger if we don't do something different and it's not clear what that can be. Efforts to sell private insurance have had limited success and the new part of health reform called the CLASS Act doesn't come into effect for a while and may not be the long-term answer to this problem.

Q...What opportunities does the new health care legislation offer states to start making reforms or put pilots in place in this area?

It's full of pilot programs for experimenting with new delivery systems and new ways of paying for health care. And the states should look very carefully at what kinds of pilot programs they're eligible for under the act and try to do a good job running them.

Introduction

Federal legislation is shifting responsibility for navigating stand-alone benefit programs and services from individuals to the state

With the economy still underwater, anti-poverty programs have never been more popular. The Great Recession left unprecedented levels of genuine need in its wake. Unemployment continues to hover around the 10 percent mark, and one in seven U.S. residents can't cover the basics.[76] As a result, human services programs — which now serve a record one in six Americans[77] — are becoming profoundly expensive (see figure 6-1). These programs are a critical safety net for individuals and families that need help. Increased access to government aid when citizens need it most is a noble undertaking from a public service perspective, but these commendable initiatives are placing additional strain on already-bleak budgets.

Federal assistance under the American Recovery and Reinvestment Act (ARRA) helped states accommodate increased demand during the recent recession, creating temporary breathing room that allowed states to avoid more significant cuts to programs that serve vulnerable individuals and families. Unfortunately, it also helped many states defer tough restructuring decisions. With much of this aid set to expire in 2010, the onus will be on cash-strapped states to find creative ways to reduce the costs associated with delivering human services programs while accommodating increased demand.

Federal health reform is shifting responsibility for navigating benefit programs and services from individuals to the state, thus prompting states to make their health and human services system more accessible to citizens. Previously, disparate benefits and highly idiosyncratic processes to determine eligibility kept penetration rates artificially low in many state programs. With the "no wrong door" vision of the legislation, participation rates in health and human services programs are likely to increase as those who are eligible for multiple programs are automatically enrolled, regardless of which door they come through.[78]

Thanks to the emergence of Web 2.0 technologies, delivering suites of interrelated health and human services programs to support the unique needs of each citizen and family has become more feasible. Service integration is complicated and will require HHS agencies to reexamine delivery strategies, business processes and personnel policies, but providers can now use Web 2.0 tools to work much more collaboratively with the network of government agencies, third-party providers and community partners responsible for delivering services. Moreover, collaborative technologies enable citizens themselves to play a more direct role in shaping the services they receive.

6-1. Federal costs (in billions) for anti-poverty programs have soared since fiscal 2008 began in October 2007

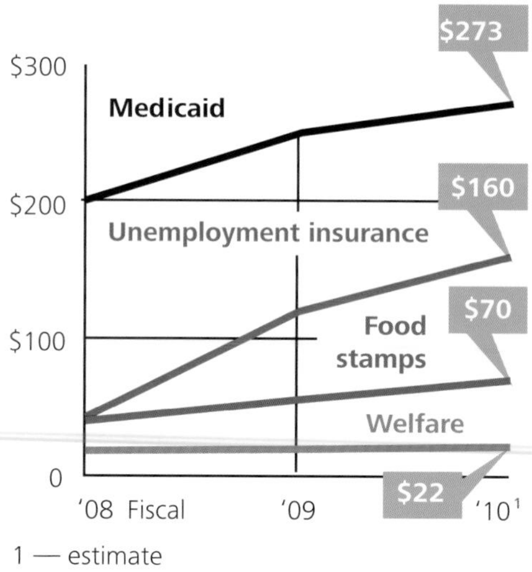

Sources: Congressional Budget Office and Heritage Foundation
By Julie Snider, *USA Today*

Human services programs have been overshadowed in recent years by more cumbersome, unfunded obligations such as Medicaid and public pensions. While human services may not garner the same level of attention as these mandates, the effectiveness of these programs remains a highly visible way to measure the success of a governor's administration. Reducing the cost to deliver these critical services and improving outcomes will be an important priority for states struggling to balance their budgets while meeting the needs of recession victims.

Almost ironically, human services providers find themselves struggling with the same situations as many of their clients: reduced cash flow, decreased credit availability and difficulty creating long-term financial stability. Because of changes in the way states finance human services, providers are being stretched to the breaking point. Innovation is more likely to wither on the vine than to spread from state to state as programs are created and dismantled based on funding streams rather than need. The time is ripe for states to explore how best to financially empower human services providers to increase capitalization and scale and foster program innovation.

Likewise, flexibility and local innovation — with a focus on outcomes — produced incredible results when welfare reform was enacted in the mid-1990s. But in the last decade, as the pressure to work subsided and the economy worsened, some of the initial gains made by the state-administered Temporary Assistance for Needy Families (TANF) program were lost. By renewing the work focus of the TANF program, states can rekindle the momentum behind welfare reform. At the same time, advocating for more flexibility in programs like child welfare could serve to jumpstart the post-welfare-reform level of innovation in programs that could benefit greatly from modernization.

The next sections address reform strategies that could be pursued by new governors and their teams to drive state human services reform and integrate health and human services.

Driving state human services reform

Refocusing programs on delivering their intended outcomes

State human services departments are confronted with the same mandate most state government agencies face today: the need to do more with less. While federal stimulus aid has temporarily reduced budgetary pressure in a number of human services programs, states will find themselves hardpressed to meet the increased demand for services as this aid dries up (see figure 6-2). As such, states have a short window of opportunity to start preparing to accomplish more with fewer resources down the road. Governors and legislative leaders should seize this opportunity to modernize human services, reduce the costs associated with delivering them, improve the use of technology and refocus programs on delivering their intended outcomes.

Finding ways to work smarter by using technology to automate business processes so that critical human resources can be redirected to the front lines is central to bringing the delivery of human services programs into the 21st century. Business process reengineering can help to identify more efficient ways of delivering human services by streamlining processes and eliminating duplication. Both Michigan and Texas, for example, have made noteworthy progress in driving integrated human services enrollment and delivery.

To ensure greatest impact, steps should be taken to adopt new workflows that account for changes associated with the technology solutions that are introduced. Additionally, by simplifying rules and procedures, human services offices can reduce the volume of office calls or visits.

The success of human services programs in an era of austerity doesn't simply rely on figuring out how to respond to increased demand with fewer resources. Success also hinges on refocusing programs on their intended outcomes: reducing dependence and promoting self-sufficiency. Providing flexibility with respect to how those outcomes are achieved and holding programs accountable for results can help to realize these outcomes.

Looking beyond the expiration of American Reinvestment and Recovery Act funds, states have a more significant opportunity to reform the way health and human services programs are delivered. Health care reform has provided a platform for state administrators to finally integrate health and human services. While states have made progress in better integrating stand-alone benefit programs and services in recent years, historically, there has been a very loose link between the two. Given their common underlying mission — ensuring the basic well-being of society's neediest citizens — strengthening the linkage between the two would catalyze a more fundamental shift in focus from delivering stand-alone programs to helping people on their path to self-sufficiency.

6-2. "Low-Gap" scenario: State general revenue minus expenditures with and without federal stimulus

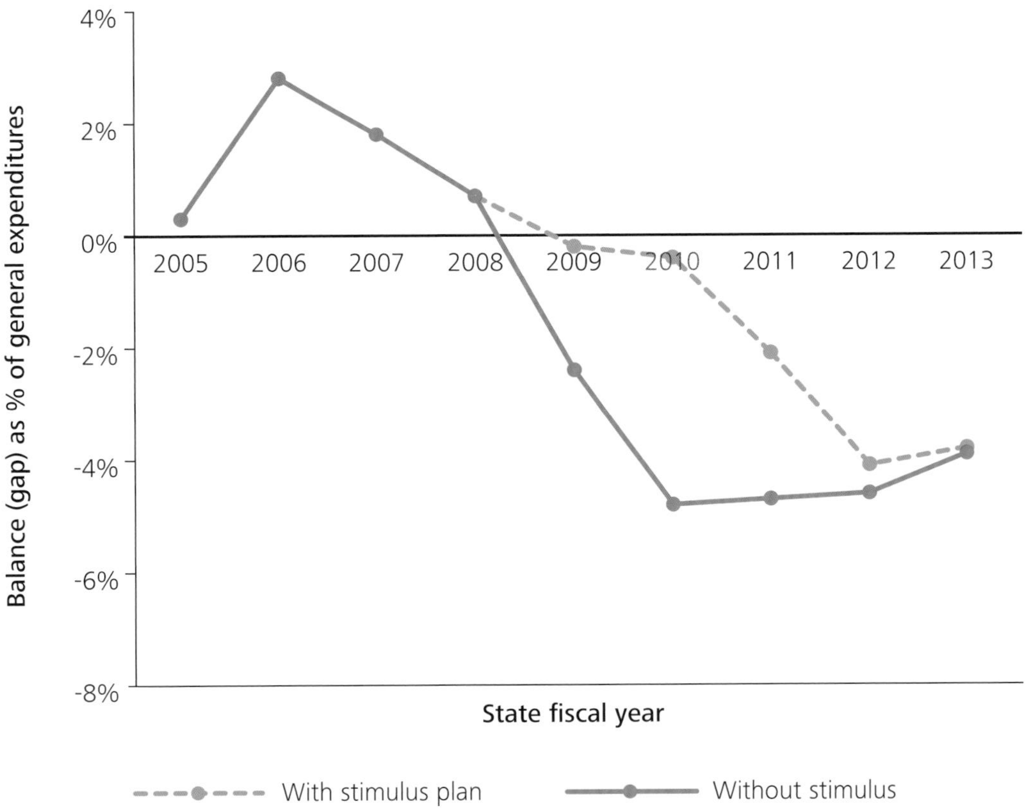

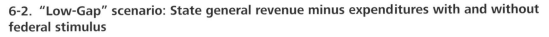

Source: Donald J. Boyd, *Coping with Effects of Recession in the States*, presented at the Governmental Research Association Annual Conference, The Brookings Institution, Washington, DC, July 27, 2009.

ACTION PLAN FOR REFORMING HUMAN SERVICES

Transforming human services against the backdrop of today's bleak fiscal outlook will be challenging. Recognizing that enabling legislation, existing eligibility and scope of service policy vary by state, here are a set of strategies that can help drive change. These reforms can all be accomplished without large funding increases, adopted within the first year or two of the administration, and in most cases should, in time, result in significant cost savings and service improvements.

Increase focus on client outcomes

Today, not enough focus is placed on outcomes. Human services agencies must determine how to reframe their attention on achieving the stated aims of their programs — helping clients achieve greater self-sufficiency. The first step is to develop the right outcome metrics.

The second step is to engage citizens in shaping the services they receive, making them more active stewards of their own journey. HHS clients want to play a bigger role in determining what services they need from government. They want to compare experiences with their peers and obtain advice on similar cases. Wikis, blogs and other HHS-focused social networking activities won't just boost citizen satisfaction; they'll improve outcomes by making clients smarter consumers of services.

Equip frontline workers with modern tools

Frontline human services workers have historically been constrained by the information they can carry with them at any one time. Mobile technology has the potential to give frontline human services workers real-time access to information that enables better decisions, which may, in turn, produce better outcomes. More so, mobile devices permit frontline workers to tap into the expertise of peers, drawing upon the collective experience of a community of workers rather than the judgment of an individual.

The State of Florida has streamlined foster care caseworkers' workloads by equipping them with mobile computing devices that permit information sharing and the upload of crucial data in real time. Smart phones and laptops with built in cameras have been distributed to more than 2,300 caseworkers. Using remote data capture, caseworkers take digital images that immediately upload to the state's child welfare online system, cataloging the date, time and location. The objective is to enable caseworkers to spend more time with children and less time consumed by paperwork.

Increase flexibility to innovate in child welfare

Child welfare is one policy area that has seen minimal advances in recent years. Innovation has been constrained by federal funding streams that support the cost of providing foster care and associated administrative costs but not the delivery of these services. As a result, child welfare departments are challenged to find money to improve service delivery. Allocating modest funds for this purpose, or encouraging more federal flexibility on how to spend federal funds, could help spur innovation in this area.

Several years ago, the State of Florida negotiated a temporary statewide waiver on the use of federal IV-E money, giving it added flexibility to direct federal funds to the delivery of child welfare

Preparing now to accomplish more with less later

Working smarter:

- Conduct business process reengineering (BPR) analyses to create more efficient ways of delivering human services by streamlining processes and eliminating duplication and stovepipes
- Create more understandable client notices that reduce calls to workers

Using technology:

- Invest in automation technologies for things workers do manually
- Reduce customer-worker interactions through creative use of self-service mechanisms and the leveraging of community partners
- Reduce overhead costs by implementing document imaging, scanning, indexing and content-management solutions
- Streamline client information access by implementing enterprise information sharing across different systems, divisions, agencies and, potentially, partner agencies

6-3. TANF work participation rates, FY 1997 – FY 2008

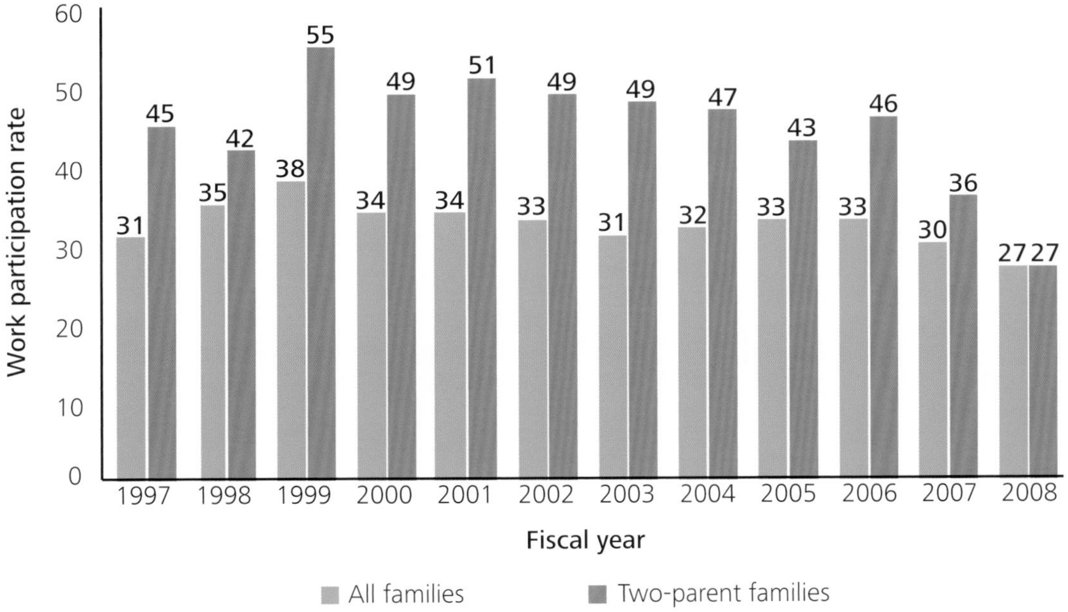

Source: Office of Family Assistance, Administration for Children and Families, U.S. Department of Health and Human Services, <http://www.acf.hhs.gov/programs/ofa/particip/indexparticip.htm>

services. The added flexibility allowed the state to move to a community-based care system with some privatization and more local authority. As a result, the state witnessed a dramatic 30 percent decrease in kids participating in their foster care program. Petitioning for the removal of federal funding constraints would give states more flexibility to allocate money to local innovation.

Innovation in child welfare can also be spurred by evaluating funding streams from the state to local governments. Faced with seemingly endless increases in spending on children and family services (one of the state's largest line items) through the 2000s, the Commonwealth of Virginia did something quite clever. Instead of simply indiscriminately cutting money for children and families and letting the pain fall where it may, the state did a careful analysis of the entire structure of children and family services spending, including where and why money was being spent. What officials discovered was a perverse set of funding incentives that actually drove local governments (which administer children and family services programs in Virginia) to channel kids into more expensive and clinically less effective congregate care (group homes and other institutional settings). The problem: Under the state's reimbursement formula, local governments were actually getting more money for institutional placements than for lower-cost placements in foster homes.

Realizing that the state was, in essence, incentivizing local governments to make bad clinical decisions about foster care placements, the legislature in 2007 voted to reverse the formula. The effect on the budget and on children was immediate: For the first time in decades, the costs of children and family services actually went down, while outcomes for kids improved. "We saved $100 million in the first two years alone — nobody expected that," says Republican Senator Emmet Hanger, who was instrumental in pushing the new funding formula through the Virginia Assembly. And while some of those savings were being banked by the state in tough fiscal times, some of the savings were also reinvested in more clinically proven and cost-effective community-based care.

Revive work focus of TANF programs

Recent data suggest a growing disconnect between citizens receiving TANF benefits and their active search for employment, which has been the overriding objective for welfare reform (see figure 6-3). Devising incentives that place greater emphasis on securing a new job would draw a more direct link between benefits received and enrollees' demonstrated commitment to finding employment. By renewing the work focus of the TANF program, states can start to reverse this trend and continue the momentum behind welfare reform.

Reinvent human services financing models

States must determine how best to empower nonprofit and public sector providers to scale and sustain program innovation. Right now, financial models for human services embrace cost reimbursement contracting that favors short-term efficiency over long-term effectiveness. The inflexibility has reduced focus on service quality and outcomes, promoting the status quo over innovation. Program sustainability is threatened as providers move from one grant cycle to the next, creating and dismantling programs based on funding rather than need. The challenge is to figure out what financing mechanisms can be created to increase capital flow to underfunded nonprofit human services providers. One state to watch is the Commonwealth of Massachusetts, which has slowly been moving health and human services providers off cost reimbursement to performance-based contracting.

Roadblocks to overcome

Reducing administrative costs
A disproportionate amount of human services time is devoted to administrative tasks that do not contribute directly to positive client outcomes. Protocols are often confusing, resulting in as many as twenty correspondences every month between a typical household and office. The volume of traffic and additional time spent processing paper prevents human services staff from spending their limited time on service delivery.

Managing an increasing number of beneficiaries
State budgets are further strained by a growing number of citizens becoming eligible for human services benefits. Increased unemployment resulting from the recent recession has put a tremendous burden on already scarce resources available for unemployed citizens, a problem whose time horizon remains uncertain given the slow pace of economic recovery.

What works: Alliance for Children & Families' "Ways to Work"

The Alliance's "Ways to Work" program is a character-based lending initiative that is a classic "hand up, not hand out." Ways to Work lends money to those with bad credit or no credit history so that they can purchase a used car to get to work. The program charges a maximum interest rate of 8 percent, which covers administrative costs, as opposed to the payday loans that typically charge an exorbitant 25–30 percent interest rate. Ways to Work loan recipients realized a 41 percent increase in earnings, and the program enjoys an 88 percent repayment rate, which remained unchanged during the recent recession.

Integrating health and human services delivery

Making services citizen-friendly

Health and human services agencies face tremendous pressure from elected leaders to deliver more effective services to clients who need them. Over the past few years, this has triggered a drive toward service integration — the idea that formerly stand-alone benefit programs and services should be linked together in ways that magnify their impact and improve their usability. Now, the emergence of Web 2.0 technologies presents an opportunity for HHS agencies to work much more collaboratively with the citizens they serve.

To do it right, three critical elements must be addressed: service offerings, technology and workforce management (see figure 6-4). Virtual organizations will gradually replace physical locations for service delivery within the network. Effective agencies will evolve toward a "civic switchboard" concept — where HHS clients are connected to resources both within and beyond traditional government entities — to define and deliver the appropriate set of services for a household and its members.

Under this new paradigm, technology takes the next step after moving to the Web by linking HHS providers within and beyond government. Service delivery encompasses a growing network of public and private organizations to create a service delivery network. Furthermore, as HHS agencies start to feel the effects of a massive wave of retiring Baby Boomers, they will need to revamp hiring and growth plans, provide tools to encourage collaboration across organizational silos and capture institutional knowledge.

ACTION PLAN FOR INTEGRATING HEALTH AND HUMAN SERVICES

The following four strategies can help state leaders make the vision of integrated health and human services delivery a reality:

Create client-centric access to HHS programs and information

HHS agencies, while remaining responsible for delivering services, need to make information and services available through a variety of different channels — even if public agencies don't own or directly control some of those channels. These new channels will complement existing HHS portals and other e-government initiatives, and over time, they may begin to replace government-only efforts.

ACCESS Florida, a Web-based application designed to meet the increased demand for public benefits following the 2004 and 2005 hurricane seasons, simultaneously cut the state's HHS workforce in half. Call centers were established, and community partnerships across the state helped citizens with the new online process for applying for benefits.

Empower citizens with self-service options

Human services employees devote considerable time to helping citizens with tasks that don't require their assistance. Expanding automated self-service options for human services clients would reduce administrative work for staff, freeing them to allocate time to more meaningful work. Even more importantly, involving citizens directly in the process turns otherwise passive recipients of aid into engaged individuals who are actively trying to become self-

6-4. Service integration 2.0

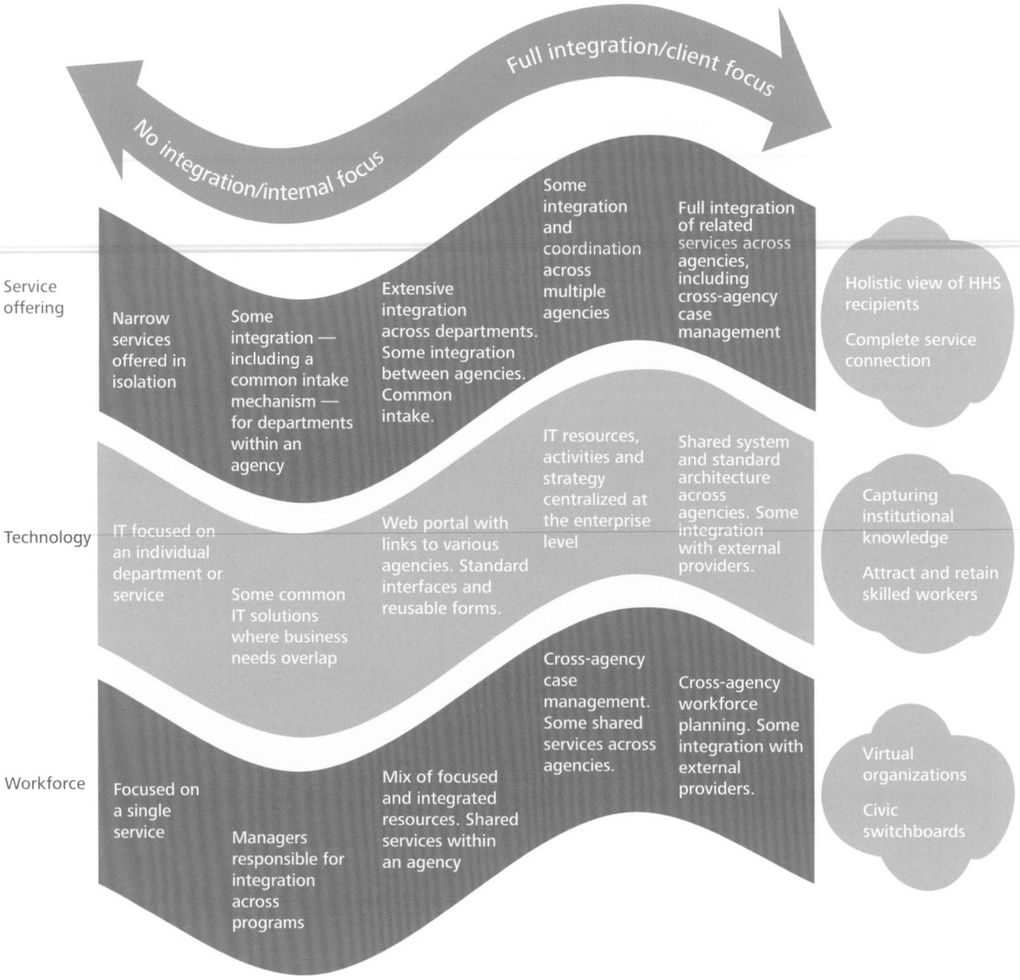

Source: Deloitte Research

sufficient. Massachusetts' Virtual Gateway is an online portal that serves as a single front door for health and human services programs. The Gateway streamlines the application procedure and reduces the time and effort required to access services.

Promote cross-agency collaboration

A lone human services organization can't address all the needs of clients and their families, so single-agency portals don't adequately support service integration. HHS agencies should explore the development of mashups — compilations of Web services that are managed by different agencies or organizations and delivered through a single online location.

Develop financing models that encourage service integration

Disadvantaged individuals and families often have multiple needs, while government funding is allocated in discreet streams that discourage holistic service delivery. Fragmentation of funding sources places an unnecessary administrative burden on human services providers and consumes resources that would be better spent on the provision of actual client service. A statewide human services strategy — a common approach to human services planning across government departments and agencies premised on serving the individual or whole family — would go a long way in addressing service integration issues.

Roadblocks to overcome

Simplifying the bureaucratic maze

Citizens often face a bureaucratic maze that can make it hard to access the services they need. This fragmentation of human services agencies hinders impactful service delivery and frustrates everyone involved: caseworkers, clients, politicians, care providers and taxpayers. Organizational silos stifle employee opportunities to take a more holistic approach to their cases. Shortcomings in organization undermine the very mission of health and human services: making life better for people. States must therefore overcome the disparate nature of these agencies.

Defining what service integration means for your state

HHS agencies struggle with the exact meaning of service integration. Some define it in terms of combining related services — for example, combining all state health care programs like Medicaid, the Children's Health Insurance Program (CHIP) and disability services — into a single offering. Others see it as grouping different departments and agencies under a single umbrella organization. And to many, service integration is simply a common Web portal with links to various agency Web sites. States must determine what service integration will look like for them.

Interview with

B.J. Walker

Commissioner, Georgia Department of Human Services

Q...What are the biggest challenges you see facing human service departments over the next few years?

One big challenge is how to serve more people with fewer resources. And how do you bring in state-of-the-art technologies to support that need when there are no resources to pay for technology? A second challenge is how to make changes in the way state government agencies are organized, and what they provide to the public. Who is willing to have the difficult conversation about which services government is not going to perform anymore?

Q...In Georgia, have you found radically different ways to provide human services that allow you to accomplish more with fewer resources?

The biggest thing we're doing in Georgia involves restructuring the back office support required to deliver services. For example, we are restructuring food stamps administration, with different specialists responsible for different aspects of approval and delivery. We're also having customers input their own initial data, either by scanning their documents at kiosks or entering their information when they apply online.

For every service that's delivered according to the "one customer, one caseworker" model — such as Medicaid or TANF — there might be ways to create a new back office model that focuses on efficiency rather than on personal contact. Rather than assuming a face-to-face transaction all the time, we should save face-to-face — which is the most expensive transaction — for when we actually need it.

Q...In child welfare and family services, some governments are starting to make wider use of mobile technology, with data analytics and collaboration tools to transform the way caseworkers do their jobs. What is Georgia doing in that respect?

We are using tablets so that caseworkers can plug back into our Statewide Automated Child Welfare Information System while they're engaged with families. There are probably a thousand other ways to use technology to enhance those transactions. The challenge is how to keep the practice current with the available technology. In government, we have to go through a thousand hoops to get a new system, and then we wind up with systems that are already obsolete, or certainly not on the cutting edge. Every day, we're doing critical transactions with people's lives, and we're operating with systems that are almost always way behind the times.

Q...Have you thought about other models for technology, other than today's model?

If the Feds are setting the standard, and if the Feds are approving all these customized models, why not simply say, "Here's the frame of what we would want you to use"? Or, why don't they pick three, or four, or five frames? From the standpoint of those of us who have to jump through the hoops and have old systems that we cannot afford to replace, it would make more sense.

Q...What are some of Georgia's bigger human services successes over the last few years?

When we need to drive our performance it's usually framed through values. In each of the programs where we've seen significant enhancement of our performance, I attribute it to the value that we explicitly drove into how we ask the workforce to approach the work. For example, when I came here, there were about 29,000 work-eligible adult households on TANF. There are now fewer than 3,000. We recognized that our work participation rate at that time was only 19 or 20 percent, and we had not spelled out for the caseworker or the customer why it was important to work. So we started to articulate that welfare is not good enough to raise children with. The caseworker now had a reason to drive the customer base into work participation, and we had a value to articulate to the customer about why we were doing that. It was very hard for anybody to argue with the values, and that forced a level of performance.

Q...Your work participation rates are among the highest in the country. What are some lessons from Georgia for other states?

We really pay attention to people when they walk in the front door. We engage them from day one in work participation, identifying potential jobs in the community and taking them right to a job that day if we have to. If a caseworker knows there's a job at Waffle House down the street, we'll drive them down there on day one. Some may say Waffle House is not a good enough job. I say — if it's good enough for me to eat there — it's good enough for someone to work there.

Q...Getting back to values, did you use that lens to drive changes in child welfare?

The value was that any move of a child out of the home of their parents is a move to do active harm to the child. That's not typically a child welfare value. We always thought we were rescuing children from bad adults — sometimes, we do need to do that. But we never thought about the consequences of our actions on the actual child.

Once you start to frame that value with the caseworker, now every time I make a decision to move a child is a decision to do harm — whether you move the child within the foster care system or whether you move the child from home into the system. That value asks the caseworker to step back and examine their decisions.

Q...How do you drive innovation in today's economic climate, and what are some of the big challenges of doing so?

We try to give people a wide berth to design locally what works for them, with some guidance about what we want. That's why we go so much from a value base. A lot of public sector workers are operating outside their real, concrete value system because they think policy, regulation and bosses are supposed to tell you what to do. But if you say, "We've got to collectively decide what values we are operating from," then you start to engage people at a depth of themselves that was never called on before. And as long as you're not standing there with a policy book to smack them back down, they pretty much will design for you.

Mid-level managers often don't see the work on a day-to-day basis, and they haven't done day-to-day work in a long time. Their eyes are so focused on what they are trying to tell me or their staff, that they miss stuff under their feet. So we're very particular about them taking a look at a certain number of files a week, and trying to understand what kind of practice is going on in their house. We try to stay as close to the front line practice as we can and give front line workers a reason to come to work every day that isn't just tied to somebody else's vision of what they ought to do.

PART VII: OVERHAULING STATE OPERATIONS

Introduction

Emerging technologies will fuel a fundamental transformation of government. They will also introduce new risks.

Consultants, technology firms and analysts love to produce annual laundry lists of technology trends that will change the world, usually with "flying car" glimpses of a magical new future. This chapter takes a different tack by offering an agenda that's designed to help state governments solve their most pressing policy and operational challenges.

The technology trends we examine are clustered in two categories: emerging enablers and disruptive technologies.

Emerging enablers are core disciplines that have evolved within organizations — capabilities, skills and philosophies that are critical for partnering, innovating and creating more value. These include enterprisewide IT consolidation, server virtualization and cybersecurity. Though some have already been addressed at length by state governments, they deserve a reevaluation by governors and CIOs based on evolving technologies and work environments. This chapter examines two of these in more detail: IT consolidation and cybersecurity.

Disruptive technologies are trends that present significant new opportunities for improving how government operates and delivers services. Disruptive technologies include cloud computing, mobile computing, machine learning, deep data analytics and social media, which will be covered in chapter 8. Individually, these technologies may not be disruptive; but deployed together they may positively disrupt the cost, capabilities or even the core operating model of IT and the deployment of services. In this chapter, we examine two of these disruptive technologies in more depth: cloud computing and data analytics.

"CIOs should be thinking in terms of how to transform the operations of government and how to extract redundancies from today's broken, out-of-date, 1950s-era model."

~ Gopal Khanna, CIO, State of Minnesota

For state governments, when deployed effectively, these emerging enablers and disruptive technologies can simplify non-essential critical tasks through automation and transform the very business of government. Technology solutions are often expensive, however, and the laundry list of failed state IT projects would deter executives in any industry from allocating scarce dollars. However, state agencies that successfully harness information technology's potential to reduce cost and improve service delivery have demonstrated the value of thoughtful, purposeful adoption of new technology.

Two-thirds of CIOs expect lower IT budgets through 2013.[79]

There is no shortage of challenges ahead for governors and their state CIOs. Technology introductions invariably disrupt the status quo and therefore must be managed with great care. Not only will they change the way state governments operate, but they also present new dangers, particularly in terms of how we safeguard data and handle the constant threat of cyberattacks. Though there are many hurdles ahead, sitting on the sidelines is not an option. State governments must carefully navigate this changing terrain, making smart investments in technology solutions.

7-1. Emerging enablers and disruptive technologies

Emerging enablers	Disruptive technologies
IT consolidation	Cloud computing
Virtualization	Machine learning
Cybersecurity	Mobile computing
Enterprise information management	Deep data analytics
IT governance	Social media

Source: Deloitte Research

Cutting fat through IT consolidation

Taking the costs out of information technology

IT consolidation has risen to the top of most state CIOs' agendas.[80] The impetus behind consolidation is clear: the piecemeal development of many states' IT infrastructures has inadvertently created an inefficient and duplicative web of systems that don't communicate with one another. This evolution has been aggravated by a historically fragmented priority- and budget-setting process at state and federal levels around IT and has further divided siloed state IT shops. As more and more citizen data are kept in digital form, the need for IT transformation and consolidation is even more compelling.

In 2009, state CIOs listed consolidation as their #2 priority, after budget control.[81]

Without consistent IT standards, protocols, systems and coordinated approaches to investments in IT, states will be stuck devoting scarce time and resources to fixing legacy systems and searching for data, rather than administering programs or introducing innovation into their services. Even more discouraging, two-thirds of public sector CIOs expect further budget reductions for IT due to the recent economic downturn, only enhancing the case for timely IT consolidation.[82]

ACTION PLAN FOR CONSOLIDATING IT

With nearly all states having taken on some form of consolidation activity, clear lessons have emerged in how to successfully execute this transformation:

Customize your approach

Successful state consolidations vary greatly. Approaches include total centralization, federation, hybrid models and outsourcing. Some states have conducted their consolidations piecemeal over time; others took more of a "big bang" approach to implementation.

Georgia opted for a big bang approach. The state determined that it could most effectively provide consolidated IT services by outsourcing them. Georgia selected one organization to manage infrastructure and associated services, and a second for network and telecom services. The state technology authority, which focuses on service delivery and quality, maintains governance and oversight of IT services. Thirteen departments were consolidated, and staff was reduced by more than 70 percent. The $203 million in savings from consolidation (over eight years) also enabled the state to modernize its IT assets.

Massachusetts took a very different approach. The state's federated consolidation model balances gains from economies of scale with the business needs of individual state departments. This model designated a CIO for each of the executive departments and developed coordinated cycles for strategic planning and sharing of common needs and best practices. Massachusetts implemented consolidation without making significant layoffs or reducing current levels of service.

Address where you are *and* where you'd like to go

Take time for both high-level and detailed consolidation planning, focused on both immediate and future needs. A forward-thinking consolidation roadmap can enable advanced planning for technology changes, growing populations, emerging citizen needs and service-improvement opportunities. It can also make the plan "administration proof" and keep it from being merely the policy program du jour.

Examine the opportunities to consolidate systems

Illinois, too, has gone the infrastructure route, consolidating servers into two primary data centers, with an ROI since 2006 of some $11 million. But the state has also focused on revamping its application development and management. A study by the University of Chicago found that 25 percent of the families served by the state's various health and human services agencies represented about 85 percent of program usage. "What that told us was that on the IT side, we needed to focus on commonalities across programs," says Greg Wass, the state's CIO. "They all have an application intake process; they all have an eligibility layer; they all have some kind of casework or case management layer."[83] So over the past two years, the state has launched an effort to turn its program silos into what Wass calls "service horizontals." The idea is to build IT services — beginning with a single client ID service, an eligibility rules engine, and a provider management system — to be used by all subscribing state agencies.

What works: Michigan's IT consolidation

Michigan was one of the first states to go down the consolidation path. With the strong support of then-governor Jennifer Granholm, the state consolidated 19 agencies, reduced 40 data centers to 3, and reduced staff by nearly 15 percent when nearly all state IT functions were reassigned from various departments to the state's central IT organization. This model created a single source of authority and integrated strategic planning. Consolidated operations have resulted in an estimated $100 million in savings for the state. "We had a clear vision that a consolidated computing environment was the right choice," says Granholm.

Illinois is working with four other states and the federal government to take the connected services technology concept to the next level — across states. Minnesota, Oregon, Utah and West Virginia are collaborating with Illinois to obtain a federal innovation grant to develop a service that can be shared among multiple states. The START project (Strategy to Apply Reusable Technology) could dramatically change the way some large state technology programs, particularly health and human services, are planned, developed, funded and managed in the future. Current federal spending on 50 state health and human services systems exceeds $11 billion annually. While technology to support these programs has improved greatly in recent years — from paper to mainframe to client-server to Web-based platforms — the underlying architecture of "one program, one system" has remained frozen in time. The potential for service improvements to clients and cost savings for state governments from a service-oriented approach is tremendous.

Gather wide participation

An effective consolidation will consider how to actively engage a wide range of stakeholders, as well as how to consolidate infrastructure and assets. In Massachusetts, for example, many agencies balked at a plan to move all state government data to secure managed storage, since their current, informal

management processes cost them nothing from an ongoing budget perspective. To persuade those agencies to participate in this seemingly cost-prohibitive change, the state's Information Technology Division devised a medium-term chargeback structure, bringing infrastructure into a secure state while also meeting participants' cost constraints.

Don't underestimate the human resources factor

IT consolidation is as much about the movement of human resources and financial assets as it is about the convergence of desktops, servers and systems. Thus, even if the consolidation plan involves no outsourcing or layoffs, human resource issues will be critical. Understanding the capacity, roles and responsibilities of IT staff, and building that into the consolidation plan, will help ease the challenges of organizational design and change later on. Communicating transparently and regularly with staff can limit confusion and rumors and increase support for a new program.

Roadblocks to overcome

People transition issues
Consolidation will likely change the number of jobs and types of activities conducted by IT staff, potentially creating resistance and confusion. Additionally, states possess many legacy systems and programs that require special skills held by specific employees. Maintaining the right institutional knowledge over assets can prove challenging in a consolidation.

Inventorying IT assets
Inventorying IT assets is a complex, time-consuming project, especially if states do not have strong asset management practices in place. States often lack enterprisewide insights into what IT assets they have, where they reside and how they are maintained, providing another challenge to successful consolidation. Tools exist however to automatically scan and maintain IT asset inventories.

Transition and replacement costs
Many crucial state technology assets reside in poorly managed server closets or under desks, with few information security protocols. Replacing, re-engineering or virtualizing these resources may require costly investments in technology, resources, facilities and time.

What works: Minnesota's e-licensing consolidation

Minnesota's e-licensing portal allows citizens and businesses to apply for, renew and manage licenses with 22 state agencies and boards. Previously, agencies and boards used more than 60 separate licensing systems. These increased the complexity of the licensing process and were costly to maintain. Also, aging systems posed a risk of system failure.

Implemented in phases, the Minnesota Electronic Licensing System (MNELS) includes a single customer-facing e-licensing solution that allows citizens and businesses to log into one online system to manage all professional and business licenses. Standardizing licensing transactions makes it easier for customers to do business in and with the state, along with improving regulatory and enforcement capability for state agencies and boards.

Cybersecurity

Making cybersecurity a priority before your state becomes a target

People put a lot of trust in state governments to collect, maintain and protect the appropriate information necessary to execute their programs, protect individual rights and ensure public safety. The volume of that information expands at an ever-increasing pace, and maintenance and protection of that information, particularly where it involves personally identifiable information (PII) and personal health information (PHI), becomes more and more challenging. It is especially challenging when privacy needs to be balanced with freedom-of-information mandates and online government access.

> Security researchers now uncover nearly 100,000 new malware samples each day.[84]

State agencies possess treasure troves of medical, financial and other personally identifiable information, not to mention sensitive business data and information relevant to national security. In fact, states likely have more citizen data than any other level of government. This information is under direct and focused attack. A scan of public data-loss notification Web sites indicates that more than one-fifth of reported data breaches in 2009 occurred in the state and local government sectors.

Cyberthreats are increasing in sophistication and force. The threat of participation of some foreign governments and organized crime has added another element to the array of cyber risks; potential traps for sensitive consumer information are multiplying.

While states have established chief information security officer (CISO) positions over the last decade and worked hard to secure state-maintained networks and systems, the ever-increasing number and nature of threats have created an evolving landscape in which vulnerabilities continue to threaten the security of state government. State and local governments, federal agencies and the private sector must work together to implement tougher security safeguards, thwart these threats and be ready to respond when an attack occurs.

7-2. What major barriers does your state (or agency) face in addressing information security

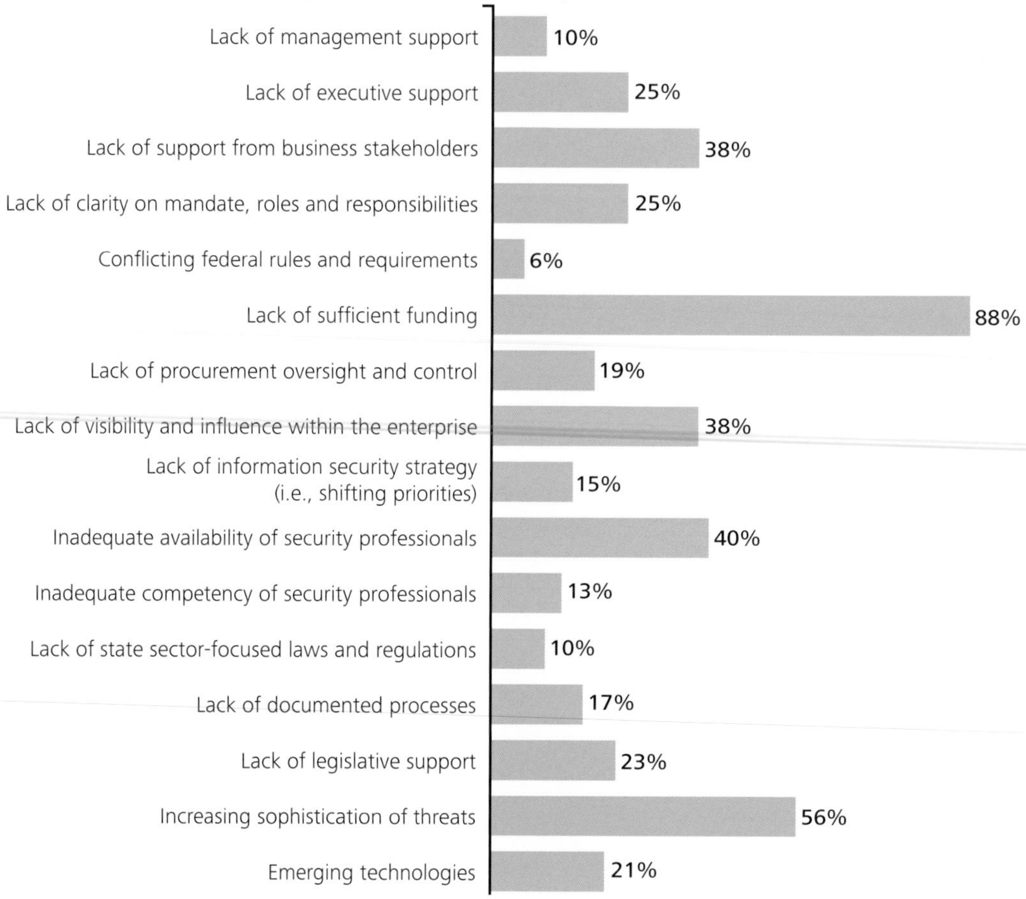

Source : NASCIO-Deloitte report, *State Governments at Risk*

Approach cybersecurity as the ongoing management of a continuous risk, not as a safeguard against specific future attacks.

ACTION PLAN FOR ENHANCING STATE CYBERSECURITY

To keep up with today's ever-increasing cyberthreats, states must step up their actions. These strategies should form the foundation of a cybersecurity gameplan:

Establish standards

Although there is no mandated state compliance platform to drive consistent security programs, adopting an understood, comprehensive and repeatable framework statewide will enable improved alignment between state agencies and business, technology and security leaders.

Make security a priority for everyone

Governors should follow the lead of the federal government and private industry when it comes to making information security a priority. First, the role of CISO should be elevated to have enterprise-level authority. Second, the CISOs should seek out the support of leadership across all branches of government, as well as influencers and other private-public stakeholders, to advance the discussions. Lastly, joining forces with attorneys general, homeland security and federal and local agencies may help raise the bar for information protection in state government.

In 2009, Michigan became the first state to announce that it would deploy the network monitoring system EINSTEIN 1, which is operated by the U.S. Department of Homeland Security. As part of the collaboration, DHS's U.S. Computer Emergency Readiness Team (US-CERT) will provide services to Michigan, identifying suspicious activity on state networks and addressing threats.[85]

Catalog all potential sources of threat

Identify key assets and likely threats; then, focus security resources accordingly. Unintentional or malicious acts from inside an organization are just as potentially dangerous as external breaches. Biometrics and smart cards can help improve internal security through stronger authentication measures and preauthorization of critical transactions.

States also need to monitor and assess security capabilities of third-party providers. State agencies rely heavily on the services and data-sharing capabilities of third-party service providers, contractors,

7-3. Level of confidence in protecting information assets from threats

Using a scale from 0-5 indicate your level of confidence that your organization's information assets are protected from threats	Not confident at all	Not very confident	Somewhat confident	Very confident	Extremely confident	Not applicable/ Do not know
Attacks originating internally	6%	19%	57%	11%	2%	4%
Attacks originating externally	4%	13%	45%	26%	9%	4%

Source: NASCIO-Deloitte report, *State Governments at Risk*

business partners and community organizations. Many of these third parties manage their own networks, receive delegated user management capabilities for state-run systems, and have access to sensitive information and equipment of state agencies. Solutions must involve not just technical tools, but also process improvement, fail-safe protection and training and awareness programs.

Coordinate across the state enterprise

Business and security must be better aligned from strategy through to execution. This makes it critical for the CISOs to fulfill their enterprisewide risk management role. Regular reporting and metrics are key parts of achieving this alignment.

Arkansas is one of several states that have created offices to coordinate cybersecurity activities across the entire state enterprise. The Arkansas Cyber Security Office establishes standards and policies for securing the state government's information technology resources. It also coordinates resources used to protect multiple state government organizations, including the Arkansas Continuity of Operations Program.

Roadblocks to overcome

Governance and funding

State CISOs lack the funding, programs, resources and tools available to CISOs of comparable federal agencies and private sector enterprises. More significant, most state CISOs lack the enterprise authority to manage the risks that threaten critical information assets spread across multiple agencies, departments, boards and other organizations that make up state government.

Internal threats

States traditionally have focused on strengthening the perimeters of their networks to keep cybercriminals out. State CIOs generally express less confidence in their ability to prevent internal threats when compared to external threats (see figure 7-3). Many internal breaches are the result of accidental breach of information, such as the accidental loss of an unencrypted laptop or hard drive. Others can be traced to the malicious behavior of employees.

Cloud computing

Making the transition to on-demand computing

Today, anyone with an Amazon.com account can rent nearly unlimited computing capacity and storage on Amazon's Web Services platform. No contracts are needed, and procurement is as simple as buying a book. Popular services such as Gmail and Flickr operate in much the same manner. Information is stored centrally on the Web, where it is accessible from any machine. This computing model is called cloud computing.

It's hard to recall a recent technological development that has generated more hype and expectations than cloud computing. Why all the excitement? It's an idea with a clear value proposition to drive customer demand. The convergence of standardized Internet technologies, virtualization and automation of large-scale data centers has created a set of software services that were unthinkable even a few years ago. The qualities that define cloud computing — on-demand service, elastic capacity and variable consumption — represent a powerful new way to deliver IT services.

Cloud computing represents a fundamentally different way for government to architect and remotely manage computing resources. It allows CIOs to leverage powerful IT infrastructures in a fraction of the time it takes to provision, develop and deploy similar assets in-house. The cloud eliminates barriers, opening up nearly unlimited computing resources at superior economies of scale. It can also create strategic, transformational and even revolutionary benefits beyond the immediate and pragmatic opportunities to improve efficiency.

These benefits led cost-conscious policymakers to recognize cloud computing as an attractive new form of low-cost IT outsourcing. If executed thoughtfully, the budget savings are considerable. Adopting cloud technologies eliminates capital and operational expenses associated with servers, software licenses, maintenance fees, data center space and the employment of IT labor. Furthermore, cloud computing permits greater flexibility and speed and the capacity to add and subtract computer power as needed. Cost pressures have led cloud computing to gain greater traction.

Cloud computing is evolving at a brisk pace. Looking ahead, a series of significant disruptions will likely emerge. These disruptions will be progressively more widespread and profound, creating opportunities to reshape not only the technology industry, but all institutional architectures and management practices in an expanding array of industries, including state government.

7-4. Types of cloud models

Vendor cloud (External)	Cloud computing services from vendors that can be accessed across the Internet or a private network, using one or more data centers, shared among multiple customers, with varying degrees of data privacy control. Sometimes called "public" cloud computing.
Private cloud (Internal)	Computing architectures modeled after vendor clouds, yet built, managed, and used internally by an enterprise; uses a shared services model with variable usage of a common pool of virtualized computing resources. Data is controlled within the enterprise.
Hybrid cloud	A mix of vendor cloud services, internal cloud computing architectures and classic IT infrastructure, forming a hybrid model that uses the best-of-breed technologies to meet specific needs.
Community cloud	Used across organizations that have similar objectives and concerns, allowing for shared infrastructure and services. Can be deployed using any of the three methods outlined above, simplifying cross-functional IT governance.

Source: Deloitte

ACTION PLAN FOR TRANSITIONING TO CLOUD COMPUTING

The transition to cloud computing represents a fundamental shift in how states provide IT. It will not happen overnight. A thoughtful, staged approach would consist of the following four steps:

Develop a cloud strategy tailored to your state

Cloud computing is not a one-size-fits-all solution. You need to tailor it to your specific environment in order to garner the greatest benefit to your government organization. Through a hybrid approach, the State of Utah is saving $4 million a year in hosting services by consolidating data centers, virtualizing servers and moving to a private cloud platform. Eventually, Utah's hybrid private cloud will deliver hosted email and Web applications to cities and counties within the state.

To ensure that cloud computing adds genuine value requires thoughtfulness about selecting the right opportunities and seeking a clear return on investment based on actual usage, not simply anticipated savings.

Start small with non-mission-critical applications

Develop a business case for a simple pilot project — preferably supporting a new, non-esential application — and follow it closely. Plan, measure and evaluate costs and benefits before, during and after implementation. Ensure that the state information technology shop understands and becomes comfortable with cloud computing before proceeding to more central, operational applications.

Gradually expand utilization of cloud computing

Once a state successfully deploys cloud computing technologies, it is time to expand to more strategic government services. This entails being more conscious of the implications of cloud computing on employee workflow and business processes. Cloud computing is an enabling technology — deploying it to central services of the government requires being conscious from the start about how that will change the way your state does things.

What works: Oregon's partnership with Google

Oregon will save an estimated $1.5 million annually by partnering with Google to offer the state's schools cloud-based computing. The initiative provides Oregon's public schools the ability to transition email, calendars, online documents, video conferencing and Web site creation to Google's Apps for Education services.[86]

Bring other government entities into the cloud

The big benefits from cloud computing will come from numerous state, higher education and local entities all sharing a common computing platform. "Eventually, there is no reason to believe we shouldn't have a common cloud platform for unemployment insurance, Medicaid and other large systems that serve multiple jurisdictions," says Gopal Khanna, the CIO of Minnesota.

The Ohio Academic Resource Network (OARnet), the technology arm of the University System of Ohio, is developing a common technology platform for itself and four other organizations involved with higher education in the state. The facility will include networked storage, virtualized servers, clustered applications and a consolidated storage area network. OARNet also will provide a common infrastructure for delivering cloud computing services to research institutions and institutions of higher education in Ohio.[87] Eventually this platform could be shared across states with other universities.

Next door, the State of Michigan plans to build a data center that will provide cloud computing services to state agencies as well as cities, counties and schools. The state will also use the new center to spur economic development by offering application hosting and data storage to private sector businesses.[88]

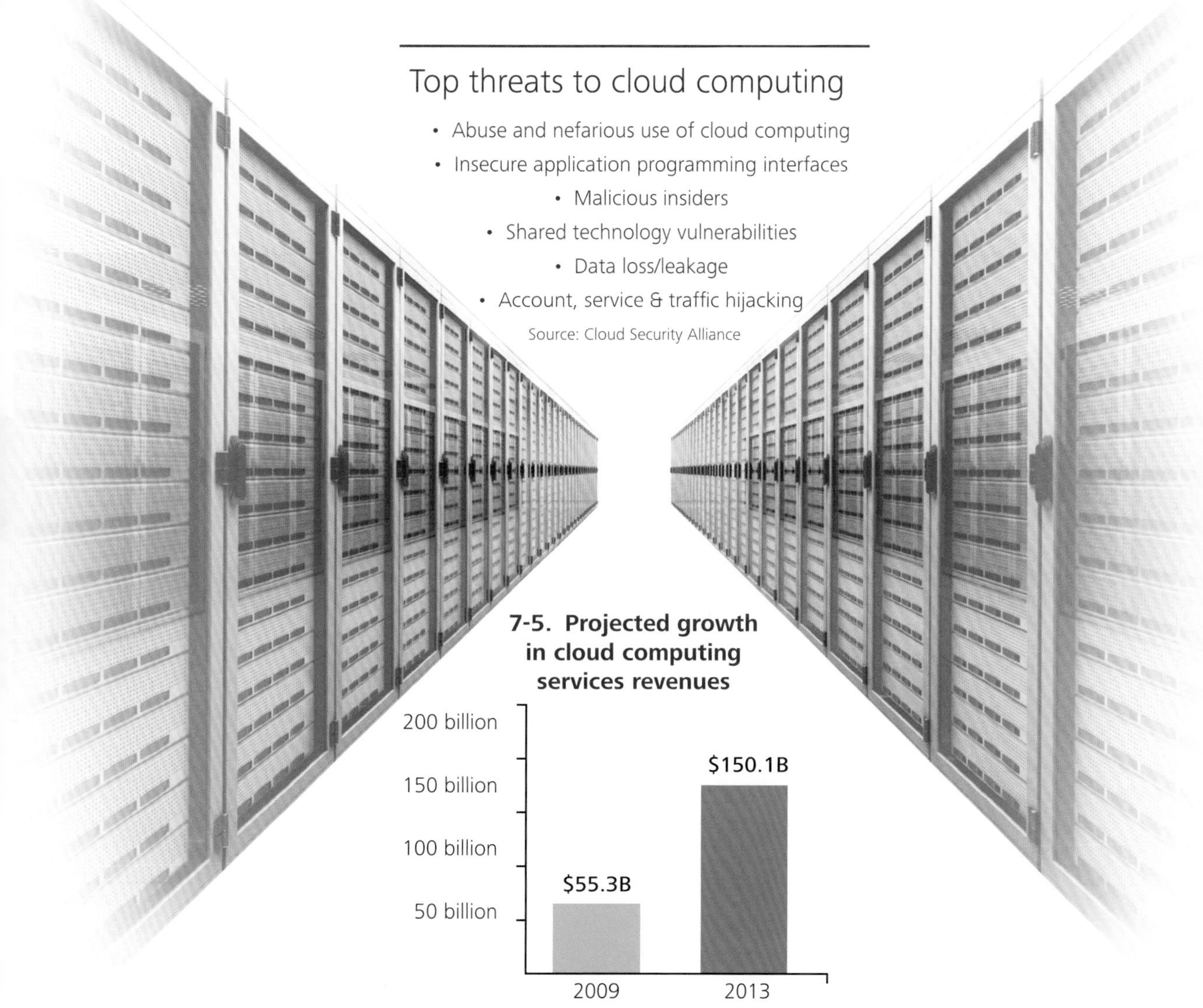

Top threats to cloud computing

- Abuse and nefarious use of cloud computing
- Insecure application programming interfaces
- Malicious insiders
- Shared technology vulnerabilities
- Data loss/leakage
- Account, service & traffic hijacking

Source: Cloud Security Alliance

7-5. Projected growth in cloud computing services revenues

Source: Gartner <http://www.processor.com/editorial/article.asp?article=articles/P3201/23p01/23p01.asp&guid=>

1 the journey to fiscally sustainable government
2 generating jobs
3 21st century education
4 closing state infrastructure gaps
5 responding to health care reform
6 improving human services
7 technology reboot
8 innovation state
9 from big ideas to big results

The promise of data analytics

Building the intelligent state enterprise

Data analytics has the potential to transform how government operates. Governments, companies and individuals, with nearly unlimited storage space, are capturing unprecedented amounts of data, which can hold immense value. Today, leading public and private organizations have overcome the tendency to make critical decisions with incomplete information. Instead, they are using analytics tools that go way beyond spreadsheets and basic reporting to mine the terabytes of data they collect to predict customer behavior, forecast events, make better public policy, predict where crime may occur and create new sources of value.

At the same time, the relationship between state governments and citizens is undergoing fundamental change. State leaders recognize that unlocking public data can fuel new levels of performance. In many jurisdictions, data is now viewed as a public asset to be leveraged by citizens, business and communities to inform decisions that can greatly enhance the operational effectiveness of government. Indeed, there is a growing consensus that data, and the evidence-based decision making it enables, leads to more consistently effective practice than reliance on conventional wisdom or "gut" instinct.

Yet, it is not enough to simply open up state government data vaults for mass consumption; state leaders must position their organizations for success in an increasingly data-driven world. To increase the utility of public and online data, state governments must develop the analytic capabilities to share and manipulate the data they collect, along with the increasing volume of unstructured data available online.

We are only starting to understand the ways in which state agencies can leverage data to improve performance and minimize risks. But we know that the potential for using mashups, crowdsourcing, analytics and other techniques to transform data into meaningful knowledge is tremendous.

> "The ability to take data — to be able to understand it, to process it, to extract value from it, to visualize it, to communicate it — that's going to be a hugely important skill in the next decades."
>
> ~ Hal Varian, Chief Economist at Google

ACTION PLAN FOR BUILDING THE INTELLIGENT STATE ENTERPRISE

State leaders have an opportunity to combine the resourcefulness of online citizens and entrepreneurs with the power of factual data to more effectively achieve their mission. These actions can help states to realize the tremendous promise of data analytics:

Educate staff and managers on what real analytics can do

Many state managers and workers don't have strong, up-to-date knowledge of the value analytics can have in transforming government. The education campaign should focus not only on training state workers in the "what" and the "how" of analytics but also more generally in how to evolve to a more evidence-based culture.

Focus analytics on your core mission

The vastness of the public data that exist can lead state agencies to lose focus on the purpose of data analytics. Efforts to develop analytical capabilities need to be driven by an agency's core mission and its most important issues and priorities. When data provide insights that challenge accepted norms, it is important to be ready to adjust strategies and tactics.

The Illinois Department of Transportation (IDOT) has built a business intelligence platform that gives employees direct access to important data that had previously been trapped in many separate information silos. Dashboards allow employees to draw data from multiple IT systems in order to perform analyses and monitor performance. For example, a fatalities dashboard allows IDOT to analyze causes connected to fatal accidents, such as speed, alcohol, weather and improper use of lanes.

> Data analytics is only as valuable as its influence on actual decision-making. Analytics capabilities and outputs need to be deeply embedded in the processes of everyday work.

Approach data analytics as a new core competency, not a new tool set

All too often, state agencies believe that the powerful tools that exist to analyze vast data stores are the sole answer. This is far from the case. Organizational competencies, data ownership policies, cultural norms and management processes all need to be rethought if analytical power is to be exploited. The Commonweath of Kentucky, for example, is not only building new analytics capabilities for the child support enforcement program, but also identifying changes to existing business processes required by implementing the new tools.

What works: Oregon Progress Board

The Web site of the Oregon Progress Board (http://benchmarks.oregon.gov/) allows users to generate reports that measure the state's progress toward three strategic goals: quality jobs for all state residents; safe, caring and engaged communities; and healthy, sustainable surroundings. The reports are based on state data on the economy, education, civic engagement, social support, public safety and the environment, along with data from the state's counties.

In 2008 and 2009, the Colorado legislature lowered the barriers to collaboration and information sharing among state agencies and then set up a structure to develop protocols for more robust sharing and use of data at all levels of government. A new chief data officer and her staff have since set out to capture all state data and work processes, with an eye toward eliminating redundancies and finding data-sharing opportunities that can boost efficiency and the quality of decision making. As an example, they developed a system to share juvenile justice information among state and local agencies and the courts — the idea being to create a comprehensive look at each youngster in the penal system and guide decisions about their education and social service needs.

Weave analytics into the fiber of state government

Data analytics is only as valuable as its influence on actual decision-making. To make a real difference, analytics capabilities and outputs need to be embedded deep in the processes of everyday work, from agency heads to the front lines.

Develop data visualization capabilities

One way to make sure the output of data analytics delivers insights state employees and executives can use is by not burying them in a blizzard of incomprehensible data. Well designed interfaces and data visualizations let users easily understand and act on the results or drill down for more

7-6. Major cloud computing categories

	Service type category	Description of the different service categories
Major cloud computing categories	Software-as-a-Service (SaaS)	A model of software deployment whereby a provider licenses an application to customers for use as a service on demand. SaaS software vendors may host the application on their own Web servers or download the application to the consumer device.
	Platform-as-a-Service (PaaS)	The delivery of a computing platform and solution stack as a service. It facilitates the deployment of applications without the cost and complexity of buying and managing the underlying hardware and software layers. It provides all of the facilities required to build and deliver Web applications and services entirely from the Internet.
	Infrastructure-as-a-Service (IaaS)	The delivery of computer infrastructure as a service. Rather than purchase servers, software, data center space ,or network equipment directly, clients instead buy those resources as a fully outsourced service. The service is typically billed on a utility computing basis.

Source: Deloitte

information. Involve the users of the data in the design. They will tell you when the amount of data they're getting is too much or too little.

Enlist key partners inside and outside your agency

The pioneers in data analytics quickly learned that the interrelationships they needed to understand required data outside their own domain. Even within state agencies, the culture of localized data ownership needs to be overcome to extract maximum data value.

In addition, the utility of previously untouched data for both citizens and government employees will depend on how easy it is for stakeholders to manipulate the data to their benefit. Finding the right format will require a more collaborative relationship among users across state, federal and local government and in the community.

Leverage the online community

The online community can be encouraged to mashup state data in innovative ways. Citizen-led data analytics should be brought into policy analysis, where feasible, given the imagination and resources that exist outside government.

Through its Data.ca.gov Web site, California makes raw state data available to citizens and organizations that want to incorporate it in their own applications. The site also provides a link to a variety of tools that allow users to query state agency databases and download raw data. The state's Apps for California competition resulted in numerous innovative approaches for making it easier to analyze state and local government data.

Roadblocks to overcome

Making data usable

State governments are drowning in data. Determining how best to harness this flood of information, much of which currently resides in disparate systems, and transferring it into an accessible, usable format will be extraordinarily difficult.

Mitigating privacy concerns

Privacy issues pose a serious challenge. Much of the data that state governments collect draw upon very personal interactions with citizens. In no area is this sensitivity greater than the health arena, where improved decision making often requires drawing upon the personal experiences of patients.

Interview with

Dave Fletcher

Chief Technology Officer, State of Utah

Q...Utah has been a pioneer among states in everything from cloud computing and IT consolidation to mobile apps and social media. Why Utah?

Back in 1993, Governor Mike Leavitt encouraged our state agencies to do innovative things like opening government data to the public — things that have only recently come into vogue. Although the public was only just discovering the Web, leaders from the governor on down started putting a lot of emphasis on how to make things happen online. On top of that, our population is pretty tech savvy. Our residents have been connected to the Internet for some time.

Q...A lot of states have found IT consolidation to be more difficult to implement than they anticipated. How did you do it?

Obviously, agencies want to be able to control their own destiny, and IT is an important part of that. It's important for IT to work closely with agencies and provide assurances that their needs will continue to be met after an IT consolidation. Our legislature passed legislation back in 2005 saying that we would consolidate IT. It was very helpful to have that encoded in law. Particularly with budget constraints, it makes a great deal of sense to consolidate. It eliminates wasteful duplication and creates opportunities to do things more cost effectively. We've reduced full-time equivalent count by about 20 percent — that's $10 million to $20 million a year.

Q...Utah is a leader in cloud computing. What are you trying to achieve, and why?

We're taking a hybrid, private-public approach to leveraging the significant benefits of doing business in the cloud. Through data consolidation and virtualization of our server farm, we've dramatically reduced our number of physical servers. And we're now able to provision virtual servers to our users in our private cloud. In the past, when an agency wanted a server, buying and installing it was a lengthy process. Now, we can do that instantaneously. We can take advantage of public cloud services in the same way.

Q...Some people believe that states could see massive savings if they developed shared, regional IT services for applications such as unemployment and child welfare. What is Utah doing in that regard?

We're working with other states on a variety of initiatives. For example, our Department of Corrections management system was developed in conjunction with about 14 other states. Right now, we've got an effort with four other states to look at a pilot MMIS system for Medicaid. Those systems generally cost upwards of $100 million. We've been working with Vivek Kundra, the federal CIO, as well as with Minnesota and other states on this project to see if we can develop a shared approach to a Medicaid information system. I think that holds tremendous potential.

Q...What about mobile? What do you see as the future of mobile government?

We were the first state to put out an iPhone app. But our goal is to facilitate services on whatever platform our users choose. Ultimately, we'd like to provide more platform-independent applications and services. We've been using HTML 5 to develop some of our apps, so eventually they will be cross-platformed to any browser that supports that standard.

Q...What do you think will be some of the big game changers in mobile government — the ones that will dramatically change the way public workers do their jobs?

We've already done some things that I think are leading in this area. For example, we've given our public safety public information officer (PIO) tools that use Twitter, Google Maps and other Web 2.0 services to provide information from the field to the media. Using an iPhone, the PIO can upload video that is then shared with TV stations and other media, as well as with the public.

Q...How would you capitalize on the vast amount of data states collect to make better decisions through data analytics?

First, we provided a front end to all of our accessible data through our Data.Utah.gov service. Internally, we take a centralized approach. We have an enterprise contract that is used extensively by both our executive branch and by public and higher education to improve their capabilities to understand the data that they control. We have a statewide financial system that's used by all of our agencies with associated analytic services that agencies use to understand the data. We have similar systems for managing our state facilities and our fleet of 7,500 state vehicles. We save millions of dollars through doing that kind of analysis at a state level.

Q...What are some of the big technology trends that you're seeing on the horizon that states need to be aware of or at the forefront of?

We need to shorten project development cycles and make development more agile and responsive to new technologies, leveraging new services as they become available and staying aware of what's happening globally. I learn a lot from innovation in Barcelona, Singapore and other areas that are doing some very creative things that make government more effective. I think we need to look seriously at the way we're doing budgeting and sometimes locking ourselves into obsolescence by conducting inflexible, multi-year projects.

9 from big ideas to big results
8 innovation state
7 technology reboot
6 improving human services
5 responding to health care reform
4 closing state infrastructure gaps
3 21st century education
2 generating jobs
1 the journey to fiscally sustainable government

Introduction

How to make state government a serial innovator

The recent economic meltdown has made an already challenging set of circumstances exponentially worse for governments, particularly state and local governments. A growing range of issues — from reforming public pensions to upgrading crumbling infrastructure — demand innovative approaches from government leaders. Existing practices will not suffice under current conditions.

While innovation is becoming increasingly critical, the public sector has yet to embrace the idea that it is a necessary discipline of government, similar to strategic planning or budgeting. Innovation in government tends to be piecemeal, short-term and narrow — focused almost exclusively on trying to figure out a way to generate more good ideas, address a crisis or leave a legacy around a specific policy position.

What's needed is a more systematic approach to innovation in government. The innovation process cannot remain an ad hoc, bureaucratic process that's disconnected from the concerns of citizens. Instead, states need to draw upon all sources of innovation — employees, citizens, private organizations and other governments — to produce regular and successful innovations. In other words, government needs to embrace and foster a culture of innovation.

To make their government a serial innovator, governors and state leaders will need to address three fundamental issues:

- How can they create a culture of innovation?
- How can they turn government data into a platform for innovation?
- How can they use Web 2.0/Government 2.0 technologies to drive innovation and help solve tough policy problems?

Building a culture of innovation

Embedding innovation into state government

The public sector tends to approach innovation as a "one-off" change, using the "big bang" approach instead of a series of new approaches that make up a broader process.

Typically, innovation in government happens in one of two ways. Either innovation intrudes itself on a public sector organization in response to a crisis, or some individual (or small group of individuals) champions a specific innovation. In either instance, the benefits are limited. Once the crisis passes or the innovation champion moves on, the organization is left with no lasting capacity for sustained innovation.

Just like strategy, planning or budgeting, innovation is a discipline. And as with these disciplines, in order for innovation to take root there needs to be an integrated approach to the innovation process — from idea generation to diffusion (see figure 8-1). Sustained innovation also requires a methodical view of the innovation process, a view that links the mission to organizational structure, processes and reward systems. Finally, the guiding principle for any initiative to generate innovation is to understand that idea generation isn't the goal, rather it is only part of the process. The real goal is to successfully implement these good ideas. State leaders need to demonstrate their support for employee initiatives and create a positive environment for innovative ideas to not only be heard, but to actually be executed and generate results.

It is only when states address these steps that they will move from a culture of "innovation by accident" to one in which a sustained organizational commitment to innovation is baked into their DNA.

8-1. The innovation process

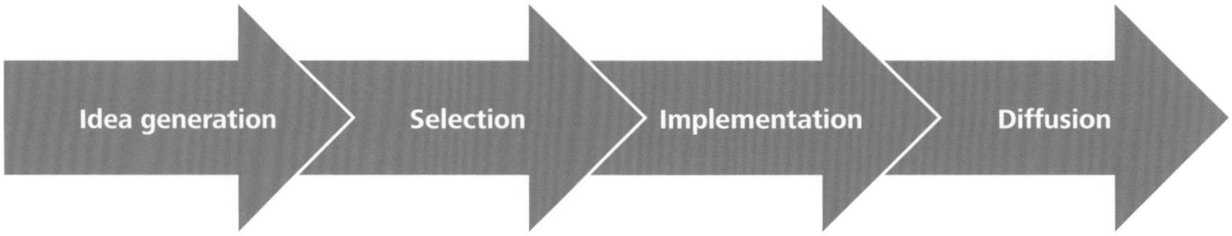

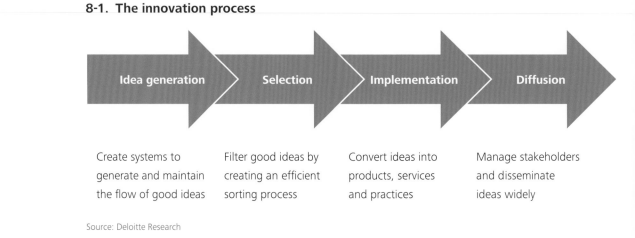

Idea generation	Selection	Implementation	Diffusion
Create systems to generate and maintain the flow of good ideas	Filter good ideas by creating an efficient sorting process	Convert ideas into products, services and practices	Manage stakeholders and disseminate ideas widely

Source: Deloitte Research

ACTION PLAN FOR EMBEDDING INNOVATION

"Innovative" is an adjective that seems more at home describing private companies, scientists and jazz musicians than it does describing government organizations. Innovative government organizations tend to pursue three fundamental strategies: 1) approach innovation as a process; 2) draw on a variety of innovation strategies; and 3) instill a culture of innovation.

Approach innovation as a process, not a one-time event

There are four phases to the innovation cycle:

1) Idea generation;
2) Idea selection;
3) Implementation (and assessment of actual results);
4) Diffusion of successful innovations.

It is in the last three phases that innovation often gets derailed in the public sector. Until a new idea delivers desirable results, it cannot be considered a successful innovation. To do that, policymakers need a clear roadmap for converting ideas into effective solutions that earn the support of stakeholders.

The U.S. Transportation Security Administration (TSA) is no stranger to such roadmaps. In April 2007, it launched Idea Factory, a secure intranet site that allows employees to submit ideas for improving agency operations and processes. By the end of January 2009, employees had submitted thousands of ideas. These led to dozens of major policy changes. Good ideas kept being submitted because these ideas were frequently implemented (and at the very least acknowledged), creating a positive environment for encouraging the submission of more ideas.

> "Creativity is thinking up new things. Innovation is doing new things."
>
> ~ Theodore Levitt

8-2. The five innovation strategies

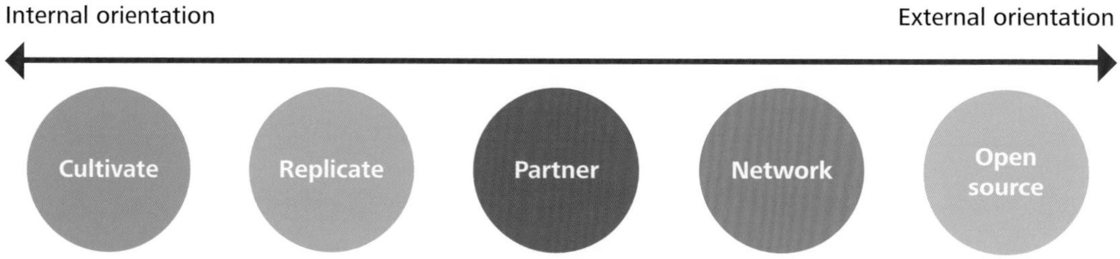

Cultivate	Replicate	Partner	Network	Open source
Q: How can the public sector alter the internal environment to overcome the hurdles of innovation?	Q: Why are some innovations replicated with speed and ease while others flounder?	Q: Can you extend partnership to "buy" innovations from best-in-class providers?	Q: How can you connect with the best ideas, engage citizens and establish new delivery mechanisms?	Q: How can you energize large groups of people from diverse disciplines to enable flexible, customized solutions?

Source: Deloitte Research

Leverage the five innovation strategies

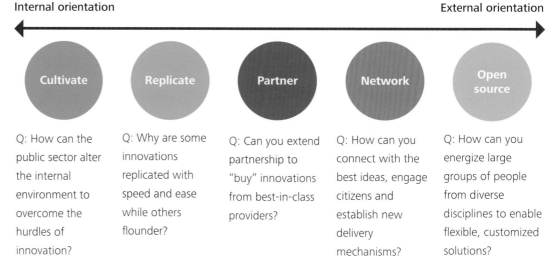

When it comes to idea generation, selection and implementation, public agencies can make use of the five innovation strategies — cultivate, replicate, partner, network and open source. An organization can and should pursue any and all of these innovation strategies. The more traditional innovation strategies (such as cultivation) and newer models (such as open source and networking) can coexist in organizations, especially those willing to break through traditional organizational boundaries (see figure 8-2).

As part of an initiative to meet tough new education attainment targets, the government of Ontario employed an open source strategy with its E-Learning Ontario initiative. It built an online repository of resources developed by teachers that can be customized to local needs to make this cache of information available to teachers and students at no cost.

Make innovation a top priority

Public organizations that have made innovation a top priority include the Canadian province of British Columbia and the state of Victoria in Australia. These public agencies make a concerted effort to instill a culture of innovation throughout the organization.

British Columbia's brand statement "Where Ideas Work" signaled the aspiration to encourage

What works: Victoria, Australia's Innovation Hub

Eschewing a top down approach, the Victoria government practices "guerilla innovation:" creating the tools, collaboration spaces and incentives to foster a culture of innovation across the Victoria public service. Victoria's Innovation Hub, a sophisticated intranet, together with the innovation festivals, contests, and more than 100 communities of practice the government sponsors, are all designed to make innovation an integral part of how state employees and managers approach their day-to-day work.

Innovation is a process, one that reflects an organization's orientation. An organization focused internally will be mired in the past. Creating a sustained capacity to innovate requires an external orientation, a willingness to draw on all sources of innovative ideas.

new ideas and to act upon them. Furthermore, senior executives were subject to bonuses and salary holdbacks of a minimum of 10 percent based on their demonstrated support for innovation and employee engagement.

Four changes can help to create an organization conducive to innovation: redefine organizational boundaries to let ideas flow in and out of the organization; build capabilities to adopt a particular strategy for innovation; transform the organizational culture; and create a flat organizational structure that offers meaning, flexibility and novelty to young workers entering the labor force.

Roadblocks to overcome

Innovation is someone else's job

The United Kingdom's National Audit Office (NAO) conducted one of the most comprehensive studies on government's approach to innovation.[89] It found that innovation is generally viewed as the responsibility of special innovation units, rather than being a core value of the organization.

Incentive structure that discourages risk taking

In most workplaces, risky suggestions reap rewards only when they lead to success. Bet and win, you're a hero. Bet and lose, you're in trouble. Governments need to provide incentives for risk taking and create mechanisms for calculating risk so that the fear of failure does not trump the desire to create new initiatives. In general, the bigger the change, the higher the risk.

Fear of failure

Innovation is about experimentation. Experiments often fail. A can't-afford-to-fail environment is not very conducive to making ambitious decisions or investments. It also seldom results in a high-performance organization. Successful innovations tend to be unpredictable. Innovative organizations often build failure into their systems of innovation. The idea is to fail quickly if you have to, learn from the experience and move on to the next big idea.

Unlocking state government

Turning government data into a platform for innovation

Since the census takers of early civilization, governments have been collecting data. Over much of that time, the primary users of publicly collected data have been limited to governmental entities and elite cadres of academics and researchers interested in government policymaking. In more modern times, governments produced statistical reports in prepackaged formats and charged users fees for standard reports and special data extracts. By the late 20th century, governments began to use the Internet as a "single window" for public information and services. Information was prepackaged and tightly controlled, without much thought given to the best format for broad public consumption or to the ways data might be repurposed by its consumers.

Today, government leaders are embracing the principles of openness and collaboration that characterize the open source movement and underlie the concept of Web 2.0.

An increasing number of public officials are signing onto the idea that public data should be broadly available in a usable format. Public leaders increasingly see data transparency as an opportunity to engage citizens, nongovernmental organizations, businesses and other governmental entities in the design of new services and the resolution of old problems. Rather than view the changing relationship between government and its stakeholders as a threat or an inconvenience, they see transparency as crucial to making governing a more collaborative enterprise between government and its citizens.

Leading governments are pursuing a range of initiatives aimed at making government more open than ever before. These "Open Gov" initiatives are largely focused on four areas: 1) cataloging sources of data; 2) aggregating raw data into a single platform; 3) encouraging users to develop nontraditional applications with government data; and 4) mashing it up in ways that make it more meaningful to its consumers. From Massachusetts to California, literally hundreds of applications have been built off government data in recent years, enhancing services and transparency for everything from public transit to where to recycle household goods. Going forward, the key will be to use the lessons learned from these early initiatives to inform the next wave of the transformation taking place – the ways in which greater openness drives disruptive innovation and enhances mission performance.

Leading organizations often build failure into their systems of innovation. The idea is to fail quickly if you have to, learn from the experience and move on to the next big idea.

ACTION PLAN FOR UNLOCKING GOVERNMENT

State leaders have before them an opportunity to combine the resourcefulness of online citizens and entrepreneurs with the power of factual data to more effectively achieve their mission. These steps can help states achieve the promise of open government while operating in difficult financial times:

View data as a public asset

Rethinking data ownership extends well beyond even the bigger boundaries of the "whole of government" enterprise. Increasingly, governments and citizens are starting to view public data as a public asset, to be shared broadly rather than limited to a select few.

8-3. State, local and tribal government open data sites

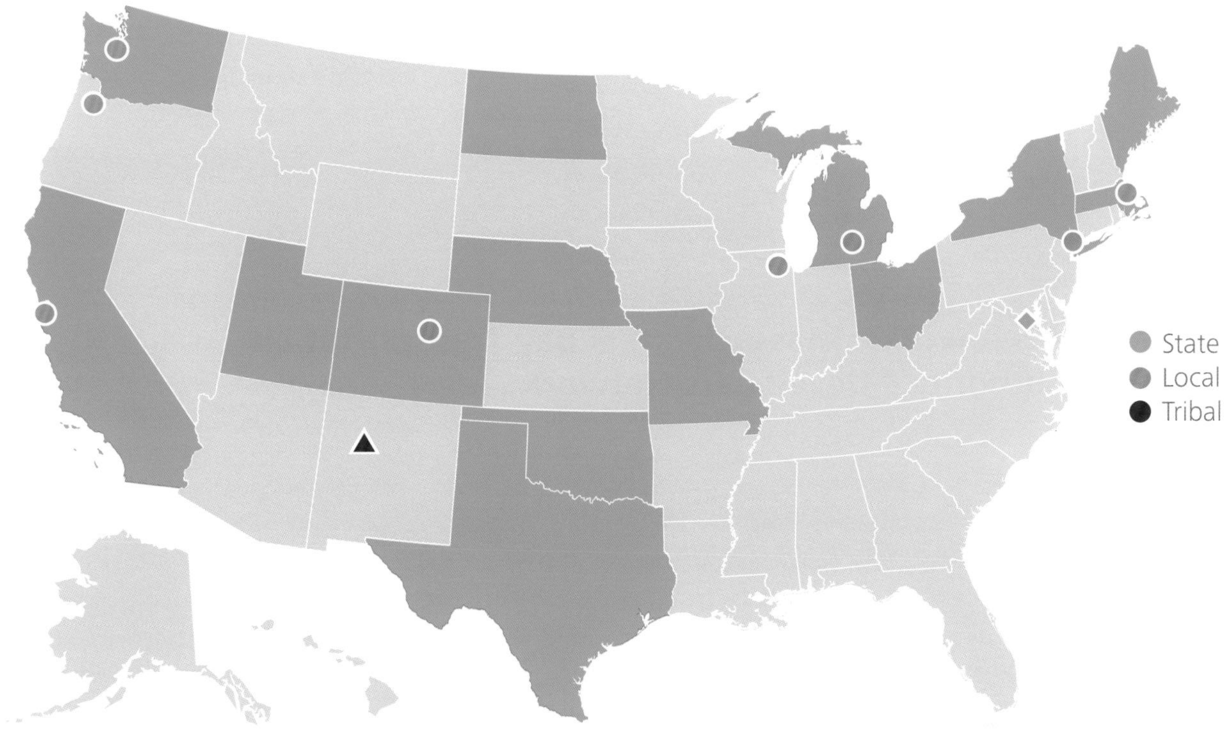

Source: Data.gov

Rethink data ownership across the enterprise

Traditionally, data have been owned by program managers within units or subunits of state government who have been tasked with controlling and limiting access. This narrow definition of data ownership is now outdated. In fact, data should be viewed as state enterprise assets, to be leveraged by the state as a whole and by its stakeholders. This means that state governments may need to rewrite current practices, policies and even legislation to enable the power of data sharing and analytics.

Make raw public data easy to access and manipulate

In their pursuit of increased transparency and accountability, governments previously have focused mainly on improved public reporting of financial information and, where feasible, program outcomes. The unlocking of government through the release of raw transaction data represents a fundamentally new form of openness. It will place state governments under an unprecedented level of scrutiny and accountability, while offering the potential to improve public services.

The District of Columbia was the first government to systematically open large amounts of data to the public, starting in 2007. Its Data Catalog provides more than 200 data sets that can be mashed up to provide insights on crime, properties, construction projects, businesses and much more. The data are

What works: Massachusetts Bay Transportation Authority's Developers Network

After a successful experiment opening basic mass transit trip planning information to applications developers, the Massachusetts Bay Transportation Authority (MBTA) decided to see what it could do with real-time bus and train information. So in November 2009, it held a developers' conference to announce a real-time status feed for five of its most-used routes. An hour later, a developer had the buses up on Google Earth. ''It's a little quicker than standard procurement,'' Joshua Robin of the state DOT told the Gov2.0 conference in May 2010. Within a week, there was a desktop widget to let riders know where buses were; in four weeks, a countdown sign built for thousands of dollars less than the agency had thought possible; a week after that, an iPhone application was up and running; and two weeks later, a text message alert service. Not surprisingly, the MBTA has decided to open real-time information about all its bus routes to developers.

8-4. Open government: From legacy to leading

	Legacy	Learning	Leading
Strategy	• Compliance with legal obligations (such as freedom of information laws, other government reporting requirements) • Standard structured performance reporting (such as annual reports that outline expenses and results)	• Pockets of organizations sharing select data • Fragmented approach without a systemwide or centralized strategy • Primarily concerned with providing more data through internally designed applications intended to improve service	• Agencywide strategy and policy of providing open access to data • Actively promoting (in media and online) government openness • Encouraging citizen participation and engagement
Culture	• Data is made accessible as required or in response to unavoidable public pressure (for example, from political scandals over travel expenses) • Default positioning on data is that they are not shared unless they need to be	• Cautious approach to data sharing — still concerned with avoiding full accountability and potential embarrassment • Officials keep coming up with reasons NOT to share data, rather than reasons to share them	• Belief that unless there is a specific reason for not doing so, data should be made available to the public • Culture of improved transparency and accountability driving more effective policies
Access	• Data are owned by government • Data provided on static Web sites • Updated infrequently (for example, annually) • Read-only formats from which data cannot be parsed	• Data are owned by government • Structured data provided selectively through interactive online applications (such as maps combining geographic data with land zoning information) • Data sets updated more frequently (monthly, weekly or sometimes in real time) • Absence of raw machine-readable data	• Data are viewed as a public good • Centralized, organized access to government data • Data updated very frequently, often in real time • Some applications are designed, but the primary focus is on providing access to raw, useful data that citizens can use to design applications

Source: Deloitte Research

available as a live feed or for download. By providing data in raw form, this Web site has helped to set the standard by which open government initiatives are judged. The next stage for the DC government is to see how they can work with developers and entrepreneurs to solve some of the core challenges of government efficiency and effectiveness.

Let the users design

Tapping the creativity of citizens allows governments to offer services that citizens want without further straining public resources. Governments can make vast stores of data available, at relatively low cost, and let users design innovative applications using public data. One benefit to letting users design is that businesses and citizen groups do not feel the constraints that traditionally have made it hard for different agencies or jurisdictions to collaborate.

Officials with the City and County of San Francisco concluded that it is not enough to make raw government data available to the public; it also is important to provide tools that encourage application development. In developing DataSF, a central repository for machine-readable city data, city officials decided to provide an open source, easily replicated standard API and platform for data distribution. By making it easy for developers to work with data, DataSF helps lay the groundwork for others to develop innovative applications that increase the utility of public data.

Tune into social networks

Data generated through social media interactions provide a previously untapped source of user feedback for state agencies on everything from service quality to programmatic changes, often in real time. For government organizations to leverage the rich data that reside online, they need to mimic the social marketers that have come before them, proactively searching for structured and unstructured data on how citizens are interacting with state public services.

Roadblocks to overcome

Making data personal

A common argument against sharing of public data is a concern about disclosure of personal information. Clearly, privacy issues pose significant challenges. But the impetus to shift control of data from service provider to citizen is strongest in the area that citizens consider very private indeed – their personal health. Here, citizens are demanding access to personalized health information and, in many jurisdictions, they are receiving it. Citizens soon will start to expect similar access to personal information in other areas, such as support services for children with special needs.

Keeping pace with changes in technology

For the most part, governments' approaches to transparency have not kept pace with advances in technology and social media norms. Requirements that data and information be made public have typically meant only that they be accessible somewhere in hardcopy. In other cases, governments have put data online but dispersed the information across numerous agency Web sites. Moreover, the data are often in formats that are not directly compatible with each other or that make the data difficult to analyze and manipulate. All of this makes it difficult for interested citizens or agencies to extract useful knowledge from the raw data.

Realizing Government 2.0

Using crowdsourcing and collaboration to drive innovation and engage citizens to help solve the state's toughest problems

Gone are the days when state Web sites were mere repositories of pages and information. The advent of Web 2.0 technologies introduced interactive, collaborative spaces that allow users to participate more actively in the process of creating and sharing content. Public organizations trying to become more innovative would be hard-pressed to find more fertile ground for generating ideas, designing policy and deploying services. Governments are using a wide range of Web 2.0 technologies that bring citizens, government employees and external partners together to improve government functions throughout the policy life-cycle, from idea generation and problem identification to evaluation and refinement (see figure 8-5).

With the adoption of Web 2.0 technologies, the public sector is on the verge of a fundamental shift in the way government agencies conduct their business. In a summer 2010 survey of 43 states and territories, the National Association of State CIOs found that nearly all were using social media to boost citizen engagement, and most were using it to advance the cause of open government.[90]

Moreover, public pressure to explore Web 2.0 use will surely grow. "While states or individual programs may have gotten into social media simply in an effort to stay current with leading-edge technologies," NASCIO's report argued, "in point of fact, the technologies have proven enormously popular across multiple levels of age and income."

But this shift won't happen with the introduction of Web 2.0 technologies alone. Underpinning the successful development of a collaborative government capability are the difficult, albeit necessary, governance and organizational changes that Web 2.0 technologies merely enable.

Before state leaders rush to install the latest collaborative technologies in their own organizations, they must first step back and understand both the business case and the requisite organizational and governance changes that a shift to mass collaboration entails.

Instead of a threat, public leaders increasingly se nongovernmental organizations, businesses and othe the resolution of old problems.

ACTION PLAN FOR REALIZING GOVERNMENT 2.0

Government 2.0 has acheived substantial momentum in the U.S. and overseas in recent years. More than most government reforms, much of this momentum has been driven from the bottom up, by public servants, entrepreneurs and activists with a passion for making government more open and collaborative. Those on the forefront of Government 2.0 have been successful by deploying these strategies:

Enhance idea generation and problem identification through bottom-up innovation

The more input you receive — the more data points, opinions, complaints, suggestions — the more likely you are to get at the truth of a situation. By soliciting input from a broader group, government officials gain a richer understanding of the world in which they operate. Such insights foster better decision making. Blogs, wikis and other forums for the exchange of ideas can help government develop this kind of awareness. The Substance Abuse and Mental Health Services Administration garnered more than 700 ideas and 26,000 votes from citizens and stakeholders by opening up their strategic planning process.

Collaborate on policy development

Big challenges demand far bigger responses than any one agency or body of experts can provide. Web 2.0 technologies provide ways for a broad array of experts and stakeholders to pool knowledge and resources. In the U.S. Environmental Protection Agency's (EPA) Puget Sound Information Challenge, participants in the 2007 National Environmental Information Symposium shared their best information resources, tools, ideas and contacts to help protect the Puget Sound environment in the northwestern United States. Participants were urged to invite other people in their own networks to join the collaboration. The EPA received 175 contributions in the 48-hour time frame allotted for making contributions.

The New York State Senate's "Open Senate" initiative, launched in January 2009, allows users to quickly search legislative particulars, Senate documents and administrative information, and public events. In 2010, the Senate created a set of mobile apps for Android, the iPhone and the iPad, allowing users to find and comment on bills, get votes and transcripts, read senators' blogs, and watch session and committee videos. The apps were built using open source code, and the Senate's CIO is making them available free in the hope that other states will adopt them.

overnment 2.0 as an opportunity to engage citizens, overnmental entities in the design of new services and

Engage the crowd to help solve long-standing challenges

State leaders could take the idea of the open data apps contests a step further and solicit a list of problems that would potentially benefit from being put out to the crowd to solve. NASA recently began looking outside the organization's boundaries for answers to perplexing problems like how to keep food fresh in space. Through InnoCentive, an organization whose mission is to connect solution "seekers" to problem "solvers," the space agency is posting its challenges online for a network of more than 180,000 self-enlisted solvers to tackle. If NASA selects one of the proposed solutions, the solver will receive a cash prize in exchange for the intellectual property.

8-5. How Web 2.0 can transform state government

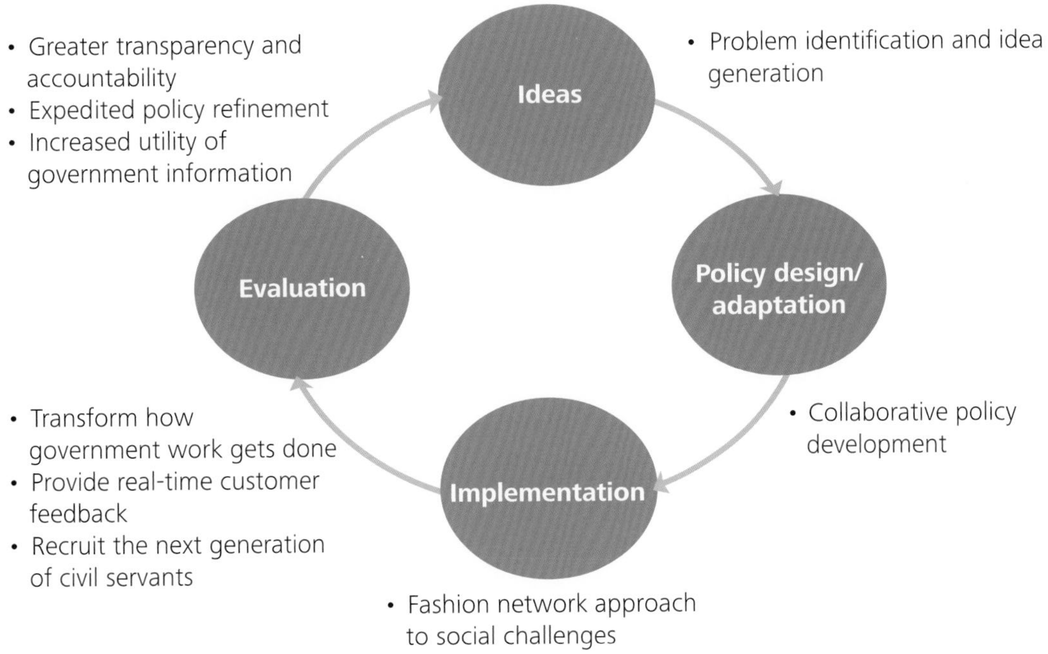

Source: Deloitte Research

Transform how government work gets done

Stovepiped organizations and rigid hierarchies keep individuals from putting their heads together to share information and solve common problems. Web 2.0 can foster collaboration across the entire state organizational chart and beyond. The U.S. General Services Administration's (GSA) OpenGSA initiative uses collaboration tools to solicit ideas and input across more than 22 federal agencies on everything from ways to improve U.S. industrial capability to how to make GSA a more sustainable workplace.

Collaborative technologies also allow employees to reorganize around specific projects and problems.

Develop public servants into social media knowledge workers

As the social media craze has spread, many governments have struggled to define the role of public servants in this environment. To achieve the promise of Government 2.0, state leaders must view public servants as social media knowledge workers. This means not only allowing managers and staff to use social networks for sharing public data and harvesting insights into how programs are performing — but requiring it. At the same time, managers must deal with legitimate concerns about what kind of communication is appropriate on a public network.

What works: Alabama Department of Homeland Security's use of Google Earth to improve disaster response

The Alabama Department of Homeland Security developed Virtual Alabama, an online platform that uses Google Earth to merge government-owned data from across the state. When disaster strikes, first responders are able to quickly access information on everything from flood zones to the location of water, power and gas lines. This collaboration has yielded dramatic results. For instance, it now takes five hours, rather than two weeks, to assess the damage after a tornado.[91] More than 1,450 agencies across the state now make use of the platform.

Recruit the next generation of civil servants

State government employers must figure out how to attract the next generation of government workers. Members of the Millennial Generation see Web 2.0 technologies as indispensable, and they assume their workplace will make these tools available. For governments trying to engage young people as employees and constituents, Web 2.0 may help lure the next generation of civil servants into government organizations and heighten retention for those who have already come through the doors.

Missouri, for example, established its own island, Eduisland 3, in Second Life, a popular 3-D virtual community with nearly 10 million residents — including the tech-savvy twenty and thirty somethings that governments are eager to attract — to host a 21st century job fair.

Roadblocks to overcome

Security concerns

As long as governments keep Web 2.0 applications confined behind firewalls, they can control the flow of data and information just as well as on any other internal system. But when they start opening communications with other organizations and the general public, security risks increase.

A culture that discourages collaboration

A culture of hierarchy doesn't fit well with the organizational flattening and individual empowerment that are hallmarks of Web. 2.0.

Fear of stepping out of legal bounds

The idea of allowing employees throughout an organization, or in many organizations, to share whatever is on their minds, with no filtering by intermediaries, scares many managers. What if someone passes along information that violates someone's privacy? What if someone spreads false rumors? Government seems better organized to tell people what they cannot do than what they can, and agency officials contemplating Web 2.0 worry about getting entangled with agency lawyers.

Interview with

Jennifer M. Granholm

Governor of Michigan

Q...You have had to address more dire fiscal challenges for a longer period of time than perhaps any other recent governor. What role should innovation play in helping to address budget gaps?

Innovation is at the heart of the answer. My cabinet will tell you that I continually challenged them to find innovative ways to do business. If you look at the way we did business eight years ago compared to today, you'll find big differences. More and more services online, the lowest number of state employees in more than 40 years, improved energy efficiency, innovations in technology ... the list goes on. But I can also tell you that innovation is not the only answer. Innovation can only go so far.

Q...One of the biggest obstacles to innovation in government is the lack of risk-taking caused in part by a fear of failure. What can governors do to change this risk-averse culture?

It's all about what you value. Governors can set the expectation for innovation, and they can encourage creativity and risk-taking, empowering employees to make decisions. That doesn't mean there's not a role for establishing operational procedures to minimize risk, but it does mean that governors should encourage innovation, being careful not to punish or discourage when we fail to meet a risky goal.

Q...What role should self-service and Government 2.0 play in empowering the constituents of government?

More and more citizens are finding face-to-face intake to be an antiquated model — they want to save time and eliminate travel, and they want around-the-clock availability. Government access and services need to be easy for families working multiple jobs, juggling day care needs and trying to find transportation. The Michigan Business One Stop is a great example of the power of self-service, making it easier for businesses to interact with Michigan government — eliminating their concerns about information being in too many places, having too many places to call and government processes being too slow.

Our research also shows a steady migration to mobile devices. Government must continue to expand self-service channels to allow citizens to use mobile devices to apply for licenses or seek information. All of our online lookups and applications should be able to run on any mobile device.

Q...You've said that state government was designed for a different age and that it needs to be redesigned to be more in tune with the 21st century. What are some of the changes needed?

Citizens need better forums for exchanging ideas with the executive branch and the legislature as well as with their local government. That information can then be used to help redefine government, and a more transparent government can then be held accountable for its performance.

A citizen simply doesn't care which level of government provides a service or where the service comes from — they just want the service. This means all levels of government must come together in a collaborative way to provide the services that the citizens have helped define. It's a lofty goal, but it's achievable, especially in times when budgets are short and all levels of government are looking for better and more efficient ways to provide their services.

Q...Michigan is one of the first states that put in an executive order to consolidate agencies. What were the benefits of doing this?

When I stepped into the job, state government had 20 departments, the constitutional maximum. We now have 15 departments — a 25 percent reduction. While combining "two buckets into one" doesn't create automatic savings and benefits, it does get people working differently, creating a more matrixed environment where new ideas and innovations are born.

Look no further than our formation of the Department of Technology, Management and Budget (DTMB). We not only had immediate efficiencies from the elimination of high-level positions, but we also had efficiencies from combining areas like human resources, budget and finance, legislative affairs and public information. DTMB eliminated 560 forms across state government, and the addition of a new, automated purchasing form resulted in greater ease and faster service for all government agencies. We've had process innovation where we leverage technology to deliver even better services.

Q...What can government learn from the private sector about innovation?

We could learn from the private sector when it comes to funding strategies. Many private sector companies have large investments in research and development — investing billions into future product development, sometimes for products that never see the light of day. With one huge, successful product (or innovation if you will), five years of lost investment is quickly forgotten. Contrast that with state government where we have a one-year funding cycle with revenues that can't support all of our current programs. The idea of setting aside significant funding for future development (innovation) is a difficult proposition. We need mechanisms and a budget cycle that allow us to make investments that will pay off in the future, rather than a tunneled focus on the short term.

Q...What about vice versa? Are there some areas the public sector is very innovative in that the private sector could learn from?

Because of the competitive nature of business in the private sector, they tend to function in an isolated and proprietary fashion. Take sharing of services. At this year's digital government summit in Lansing, we saw clear examples of how state, county, city and township governments are coming together to share services and resources. Be it video arraignment of prisoners, sharing of data centers between levels of government, sharing of networks and fiber between levels of government — all are examples of how governments have come together to innovate, share services, significantly reduce costs and develop new ways of doing business and providing services. We are breaking down silos and partnering, a huge step for government and one that the private sector could learn from.

Q...Any other advice you would give to incoming governors?

Roll up your sleeves and get to work. You've been called to serve at an extraordinary time, so don't let the crisis go to waste. Know that there are no quick fixes and no magic wands when it comes to creating jobs in a global marketplace. One thing is certain, however – education is key. The competition is no longer just with Indiana and Kansas, it's with India and Korea. So don't waste your time on the millions of nonessential tasks that come to your desk. Take the long view, focus on the essential and continue working on economic diversification, education and leveraging technology to streamline government to better serve our citizens.

PART V: GETTING IT DONE

Introduction

Turning big ideas into big results

This chapter is about accomplishing what you set your mind to do. It concerns how to translate your big policy ideas and campaign promises into successful results because, at the end of the day, results are all that really matters.

Tolstoy once observed that every happy family is happy in the same way, while each unhappy family is unhappy in its own particular way. So it is with public undertakings. We studied more than 75 major initiatives since World War II, including more than two-dozen large state initiatives. While these undertakings vary in specifics, nearly all of them follow a predictable path from idea to results. There are lots of ways a given state initiative can end in disaster, but to have a happy ending, several things *must* occur:

- The undertaking must start with a good **idea**.
- The idea must be given specifics, often in the form of legislation, that become an implementable **design**.
- The design must win approval, as when a bill becomes a law, signaling a moment of democratic commitment, or what we call "**Stargate**" because it instantly takes the process from the political universe to the bureaucratic universe.
- There must be competent **implementation**.
- The initiative must generate the desired **results**.

In addition, to be successful in the long run, a major state initiative large public undertaking requires one more step:

- Over time, the results and the methods of the initiative must be **re-evaluated**.

Nearly all public undertakings follow this predictable path. The State Journey to Success map helps to visualize the journey from idea to results as a continuous process.

9 from big ideas to big results

Source: Deloitte Research

MANAGE
RISK
TAKE FAILURE SERIOUSLY
WHY WAIT? Get Yours
HERE
SS OVER CONFIDENCE
BEWARE THE SILO TRAP
SISYPHUS TRAP
RESULT
ALM of BUREAUCRACY
COMPLACENCY TRAP
THIS WAY TO REEVALUATION

from big ideas to big results

Having a map of a public undertaking won't ensure success any more than having a map of Mount Everest will ensure you'll make it to the top. A map can help, but every step along the way requires skill. What the map does is provide a framing tool for visualizing the journey from idea to results, enabling those engaged in state initiatives to prepare for the rigors of the journey.

The potential for failure lurks at every phase along the journey to success. Any one of several recurring pitfalls can bedevil significant change efforts in state government. Time and time again, state policymakers fall into the same traps, a set of snares that doom their well-meaning initiatives to failure. Unfortunately, these traps do not announce themselves with trumpets blaring. The most dangerous aspects of the journey come from the hidden snares embedded in the public sector's taxing terrain.

Creating meaningful results will happen when initiatives stop falling prey to the same old traps.

The sections that follow are intended to augment your understanding of how to translate big policy ideas into results and bring these hidden traps to the forefront. Don't expect miracles. There are no guarantees, no magic formulas and no sure-fire recipes for success. Major state government initiatives are hard, and a healthy respect for the challenges along the road is essential.

Opening up the ideation process

Breaking free of bias and inviting in new voices

Ideas are the first phase in the public policy process. You can't have a successful result if you begin with a flawed idea. In many state capitals, when people think about ideas, they generally focus on ideology and fight over whose world view is right or whose ideas manifest the purest intentions.

Bad ideas generally become reality when they aren't exposed to external criticism. This phenomenon is called the Tolstoy Syndrome, and it's the biggest trap in the idea phase. It occurs when people or groups shut off the voices of critics. We ignore evidence that doesn't fit our preconceived notions about the world and cast aside inconvenient facts that challenge existing beliefs.

Overcoming the Tolstoy Syndrome is all about listening and confronting information that makes you uncomfortable. If we think we know the answer, we close off avenues of exploration, and fail to invite people with different skill sets to apply their unique combination of knowledge, wisdom and experience to work with us. Beating the Tolstoy Syndrome means breaking across all kinds of professional, psychological and organizational boundaries. It means letting your customers design your products, letting frontline workers set your policies and letting the private sector help solve public problems.

GUIDING PRINCIPLES FOR STATE LEADERS

Fight confirmation bias

Embrace the ethos of the scientific method. Don't ignore data that contradict your preconceived notions. Actively test your idea with skeptics. Be data-driven, and eschew policymaking by ideology.

Find the right, diverse people

Look to other fields and disciplines. Subject matter experts should be joined up with systems thinkers and other smart people with diverse interests. If your problem is in transportation, ask: how can I involve non-transportation people in my problem? An interdisciplinary team might include management consultants, investment bankers and anthropologists.

> "The simplest thing cannot be made clear to the most intelligent man if he is firmly persuaded that he knows already, without a shadow of a doubt, what is laid before him."
>
> ~ Leo Tolstoy

Deepen the idea pool

The technologies of Web 2.0 make it easier than ever to tap into the potential of large numbers of "experts" — the customers and workers closest to the problem.

Reach across boundaries

There are no such things as Republican ideas or Democratic ideas. An idea doesn't care if it came from an economist, a public manager or a politician.

Find areas of agreement

Can't agree on a solution? Bring opponents together to agree on data. Make sure you understand the concerns of others. Listen. Role-play and articulate the opponents views until they know you understand their position. Shift from position bargaining to interest bargaining. Have stakeholders illustrate their view of what stands in the way of the solution. This will help to surface some of the assumptions and preconceptions people bring with them.

the trap

Tolstoy Syndrome (also known as confirmation bias)

It was Leo Tolstoy who popularized the notion that we see only what we are looking for, often while staying blind to what is really in front of us. Our preexisting mental maps prompt us all — liberals and conservatives, businessmen and bureaucrats — to discover in the world exactly what we expect to find. The Tolstoy syndrome causes enormous problems in execution.

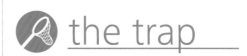

TOOLS AND TECHNIQUES

Turn data into information

Find skilled professionals who know how to move up the cognitive food chain — from data to information, from information to knowledge, from knowledge to wisdom.

Construct an idea-generating environment

Create opportunities to encourage wild ideas, sketches and wild scenarios. An approach such as Deloitte's "Deep Dive," for example, combines brainstorming, prototyping and role playing to help teams generate solutions for specific challenges.

Translate the problem into a design challenge

Doing so helps articulate the problem you are trying to solve and the constraints that must be taken into consideration in the ideation process.

Look for the opposite of an idea

Find someone getting the results you want, and then work backwards. Prototype and let "end users" surprise you.

Web 2.0

Seek ideas from customers, staff and citizens using Web 2.0 technologies. Let the best ideas rise to the top through organization-wide voting, and then have leadership select the best of the lot. Use the wisdom of the crowds as a way of testing your predispositions.

Get ideas from partners

Give the problem to someone else to solve. Let your network of partners, both governmental and non-governmental, help to develop new solutions to old problems. NASA posts some of its biggest challenges online for a network of more than 180,000 self-enlisted solvers to tackle.

Get out of your office

Change the physical space. Talk to users. If you're working on recycling policy, go visit a smelter. Talk to the truck driver who delivers scrap metal.

Use mashups

Combine ideas from unrelated fields to create new solutions — free market environmentalism, for example, to promote acid rain reduction. Another mashup is Virtual Alabama, which merged Google Earth 3-D visualization tools with emergency response data to create a state-of-the-art disaster response system (www.virtual.alabama.gov).[92]

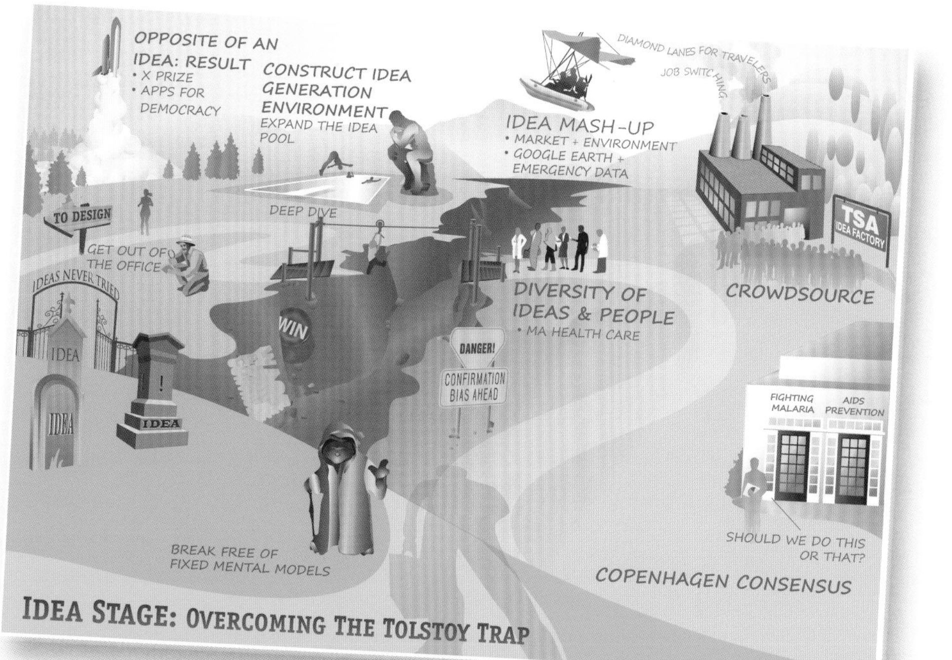

Source: Deloitte Research

Developing state policy that works in the real world

Treat policy design as a process that brings lawmakers together with implementers

Many large public failures are rooted in a failure of policy design. The Design-Free Design Trap occurs because the work of drafting a bill that launches a major initiative isn't generally treated like the design process it truly is. Instead of a sound, executable design, the goal of the legislative process is often to produce a passable bill that can be sold to constituents back home. Laws often aren't subject to the sort of exacting scrutiny they deserve.

Too frequently, the result is legislation that shows fundamental flaws in the real world. The bill gets passed, but the design is unworkable. A bad design will always undermine a good idea. The design flaws may not make themselves known until the policy is implemented; nonetheless, the failure is rooted in the design.

In the private sector, the design process is an area of expertise in and of itself. Rather than relying on the aesthetic sensibilities and whims of a designer, designs are tested and retested to see how real people react to them. The political process generally lacks this sort of scrutiny. Just as a building department reviews the design of a house before deciding whether to issue a permit, state lawmakers might uncover at least some of the design flaws if they had to submit large and complex initiatives to the scrutiny of a feasibility analysis conducted by implementation-savvy experts.

the trap

The Design-Free Design Trap

Many legislators and other public officials don't see the legislative process as a design process. Most policy ideas go straight from the idea stage to legislation drafting without ever going through the exacting design process that occurs for nearly every good or service launched in the private sector. Overcoming this trap requires a fundamentally different mindset, one based on designing policy for implementation first and foremost and passage through the legislature second.

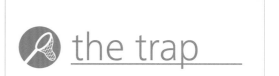

GUIDING PRINCIPLES FOR STATE LEADERS

Think design, not legislation

Too often, those drafting a bill are only thinking about what they can get passed. Lawmakers should also think about implementation and recognize that a "bill" is really a blueprint for a bureaucracy.

Involve implementers

Good implementation cannot save a poor design. Policy implementers who faithfully execute on a flawed design cannot create success. By the time a bill is passed, the bureaucrats who will have to actually implement your bill should be your new best friends.

Don't confuse good intentions with good design

No one cares about how high-minded your design is if it doesn't work in the real world. No Child Left Behind sounds nice, but it failed to produce the anticipated results. Use a variety of design techniques to obtain information about how your idea will work in the real world.

Probe for design weaknesses

Assign someone to shoot holes in the design at an early stage. If someone isn't looking for the weaknesses during the design phase, rest assured that people will be finding weaknesses in your policy after it is launched — with far more serious consequences. (Think Enron.) Design review makes sense at the building department, and it makes sense at the legislature.

Design-free design and California's electricity deregulation

One of the biggest policy fiascos in recent times was California's electricity deregulation. In 1996, Democrats and Republicans in the California legislature worked together to pass a major redesign of the state's electricity markets. The reforms were intended to introduce competition, spur innovation and reduce the cost of electricity.

That was the intent, anyway. But by 2000, California's electricity system was in shambles. The new law caused soaring prices, rolling blackouts and the recall of Governor Gray Davis. A government reform launched with high hopes turned into a total disaster. What went wrong?

The problem had its origins in the design. Some energy companies such as Enron exploited design flaws in the legislation, racking up profits and ripping off consumers. What looked good on paper turned into a fiasco when it was actually implemented.

TOOLS AND TECHNIQUES

Use Failure Modes and Effects Analysis (FMEA)

Charge a team with answering the question: "How is this going to fail?" Have someone other than the designers search for flaws.

Prototype, if possible

Fail fast, and fail small. Test and retest your design through multiple small-scale trials with real users. Use real-world, unanticipated feedback from prototyping to adjust your design in real time.

Put on your scammer hat

Role play how those affected by your new system might exploit potential design flaws to their benefit. Scammers can come from anywhere. New rules will generate new behaviors. Try to imagine how certain unscrupulous individuals within the affected population might try to exploit the new system for their benefit. Offer a modest prize for whoever can game your design.

Make a business case

Formal articulation of the intended goals, intended benefits and expected costs of any state initiative can help focus the design process and bill drafting. It also helps stiffle scope creep.

Do some "pre-engineering"

Show how the new system you have designed will work — or not work — in the real world, through flow charting. Use process mapping to uncover duplication, overlap and needless complexity in design. (It's just like reengineering, except it's done during the design phase.)

Change the psychic terrain

If you do all of your designing within the political stew of a state legislature — with the associated lobbyists, partisan politics and horse trading — your design is likely to reflect political imperatives, not design imperatives.

Source: Deloitte Research

Critical questions to ask of your initiative during the Design Phase

- Why is this the right approach?
- Is this an efficient use of government funds?
- Why will the program work?
- Do you understand the ways in which your program could fail?
- How will the program be implemented?
- How will you monitor success and rethink the approach down the line?

Getting through the political stargate

The democratic commitment point separates the political universe of policy development from the bureaucratic universe of implementation

In the journey from idea to results, there is a moment at which the democratic process commits to an action, transforming the possible into the real. The book *If We Can Put a Man on the Moon...* refers to this moment of democratic commitment as the "Stargate."

Stargate is the name of a sci-fi movie and long-running television series. The Stargate is the show's main prop, a big circular ring that creates a wormhole in space such that when you walk through it, you instantly travel from one part of the universe to another. By taking a single step, you wind up in a strange new world, where the people are different, the customs are different, and a new set of bad guys is waiting to mess with you. Walking through the Stargate represents a serious commitment, because you can't just turn around and walk back. Getting through isn't easy since the Stargate may be guarded by unsavory aliens, or it may be closed altogether.

the trap

Stargate Trap

The Stargate Trap isn't something you avoid; it's something you get through. The most unpredictable phase in the journey, the challenge is to get through with your integrity intact, your idea recognizable and a design that can be actually implemented. The biggest dangers are the distorting, and sometimes lethal, effects of the dangerous political terrain of the Stargate itself.

GUIDING PRINCIPLES FOR STATE LEADERS

Hold on to your integrity

The Stargate is the essence of democracy — both good and bad. The best and worst of democracy are right in front of the Stargate. It is where the statesmen prevent bad ideas from going through but also where all the unsavory characters hang out: the special interests, the log rollers, the horse traders. Avoid the temptation to sacrifice your principles to get something through.

Maintain the integrity of your idea

There is a temptation to water down an idea to get it through Stargate, but what is gained?

Be ready to champion change

Democracy is designed to limit big change. Work through all the things that could go wrong during the legislative process. Develop strategies to counteract each scenario and be prepared to make a public case.

Take it to the people

The Stargate is heavily guarded. Those in power are often beneficiaries of the status quo who will resist change. If you can win the hearts and minds of the people, legislators will take heed, and change will follow.

Don't rush or force an idea through Stargate before you've achieved consensus

If you force something through by executive order, it can often be harder to execute because if things get tough, you might be abandoned.

Don't stifle debate

See the Stargate not just as a barrier on the way to getting something done but as a part of the democratic process. In the long run, the civil debate that takes place is critical to being able to achieve what you really want done. It is much more difficult to execute on an unpopular exercise when there hasn't been a true democratic commitment.

TOOLS AND TECHNIQUES

Articulate your deal breakers

Every dog has fleas, and every law has flaws. What principles are essential? What aspects of reform are negotiable? What are the non-negotiables that will cause you to walk away from your own bill?

Get "sticky"

Those opposed to the 2005 comprehensive immigration bill had a short, simple message that resonated with voters: we don't reward lawbreakers in America. Proponents had position papers and economic statistics. Guess who won?

Public debate

From the Lincoln-Douglas debates to the less grand exchange between Al Gore and Ross Perot on Larry King Live, public discourse is the lifeblood of democracy.

Workability assessment

Require an "implementability" assessment before a bill passes out of the political world to the bureaucratic world. Are the timelines realistic? Is the funding sufficient? In Canada, departments coming forward to the Cabinet with new program proposals are required to detail the implementation implications of their proposals (as opposed to simply coming forward with a new program proposal — and funding request — with only a broad implementation plan).

The challenge is to get your idea through the state legislature with your integrity intact, your idea recognizable and an implementable design.

Policy implementation

Making desired results happen — on time and on budget

Confident, bold and optimistic. These are the traits that voters look for in a governor. They are wonderful characteristics. Then again, so are their complements. But who wants to vote for someone who is humble, cautious and realistic?

Voters tend to prefer leaders who exhibit self-confidence that borders on narcissism. Politicians give it to them. Unfortunately, sometimes the self-assured, successful men and women in position of public leadership devote insufficient attention to the details of implementation. Too often, champions underestimate the risks that accompany a new initiative. We call this the Overconfidence Trap. When they're overconfident, leaders sometimes don't take the sort of prudent steps they should to ensure successful execution.

Herein lies the paradox of political confidence. Governors and other state leaders have to be confident enough to take on big challenges, while at the same time being cognizant of the very real possibility of failure. Somewhere between timidity and foolhardiness exists a sweet spot of self-confidence that recognizes both the possibility and the peril of tackling a big challenge. A smart mountaineer is confident he can reach the summit, but he respects the hazards of the journey.

GUIDING PRINCIPLES FOR STATE LEADERS

Establish clear ownership

Who is the high-level political sponsor? Who is the day-to-day manager?

Make a great first impression

You only get one chance.

Be realistic

Don't downplay the resources, time and costs needed to execute the initiative. Fight the political pressure to produce unrealistically rosy projects and timelines. Assign a dedicated team. It is unrealistic to ask individuals who are already overwhelmed to do it.

Manage expectations

Set low expectations, and avoid making overly optimistic pronouncements.

Embrace the risk of failure

Understand that your initiative may fail, and take steps to avoid it.

Bring a design perspective to program design

To some extent, implementation requires a certain amount of discretion with respect to building a program based on a legislative blueprint.

Source: Deloitte Research

Make sure to introduce a design perspective when making implementation choices.

TOOLS AND TECHNIQUES

Embrace the project management mindset

Gantt charts, Microsoft Project, task lists — you need people with the skills to use the tools that manage implementation. Effective project management hinges on several key activities.

- **Task and milestone management:** Set your goals, timelines, key milestones/achievements.
- **Stakeholder management:** Accurately identify stakeholders and their needs. Set expectations appropriately.
- **Change management:** Develop transition strategy and change management to increase program support and adoption.
- **Technical management:** Almost all implementations involve technology. Use what you need, but avoid "gee-whiz" and "bleeding edge" technologies.
- **Risk mapping:** This is a tool used to identify, evaluate and prioritize a group of risks that could significantly influence the ability to successfully achieve a given initiative. By plotting the significance and likelihood of the risk occurring, the map allows you to visualize risks in relation to each other, gauge their extent, and plan what type of controls should be implemented to mitigate the risks.

Set up a war room

Take a cue from many successful state initiatives and set up a war room to manage your implementation. Avoid the box-checking tendency of many project management organizations (PMOs).

Scenario plan

Don't just plan, scenario plan. Expect the unexpected.

Use the crowd to detect potential failure

Catch risks before they doom a project. Use social media to take the pulse of an organization — to surface issues, doubts and problems in order to identify risks before they become obvious to leadership.

Segment your customers

Break up the universe of potential customers into manageable segments with similar characteristics. Done correctly, segmentation involves data-driven analysis that's based on surveys, focus groups and test marketing that cover almost all aspects of an initiative.

Chunk your projects

Government projects are often huge — much larger and more complex than their private sector equivalents. Chunking state initiatives and projects into bite-sized pieces that can deliver incremental, stand-alone value reduces risk by making projects smaller and less complex. It also encourages organizational learning because later chunks can learn from the earlier ones.

the trap

The Overconfidence Trap

Despite what you may hear from some politicians, failure is always an option. Those who fall into The Overconfidence Trap dismiss those who advise caution, consider only the best-case scenario, and plan with unrealistic budgets and impossible time lines. It can occur anywhere, but most often it arises during the implementation phase. The best way to avoid the overconfidence trap is to take the possibility of failure seriously — and take precautions to avoid it.

Generating results

Asking real people to do difficult things within a challenging environment

When the Greek gods decided to punish Sisyphus for his trickery, they assigned him the task of rolling a huge boulder up a really steep hill. Each time, before he could reach the top of the hill, the rock would roll back down again, forcing Sisyphus to repeat this fruitless task throughout eternity. Those who work in the public sector often feel like Sisyphus rolling and rerolling a rock up a hill.

The Sisyphus Trap is the unique set of challenges in the public sector facing the person rolling the rock up the hill. State leaders fall into The Sisyphus Trap when they fail to comprehend the special challenges of the public sector terrain. Too often, state policymakers believe that they can achieve results simply by devising the right strategy or passing the right law. They miss a critical ingredient for success because the problem of getting big things done in government isn't merely a systems problem. It isn't merely a policy problem. It's also a human problem.

One thing is abundantly clear: nothing is as vital to success as the attitude of the living, breathing human beings charged with getting the rock up the hill. Remember that even as Sisyphus is pushing on the rock, the rock is pushing back on Sisyphus. To make a difference in state government means operating within a rule-laden bureaucracy — some rules are sensible, many of them are not. It means working in an environment where the incentives are all wrong. It means swimming in the sometimes unsavory stew of politics. To succeed in large state undertakings, it is necessary to deeply understand the terrain that state government executives, managers, and frontline employees must contend with every day — the forces that make it so hard to push the rock up that hill.

GUIDING PRINCIPLES FOR STATE LEADERS

Understand the terrain

The public sector hill is steeper than its private sector counterpart. Making a difference in state government means operating within a bureaucratic system that's rife with rules that represent varying levels of sensibility.

Focus on the mission

Having an inspiring mission may be the most important competitive advantage in state government. Emphasize the importance of what you are doing. People want to make a difference. An undertaking of any significance requires an organization that's aligned to the mission.

Incentives matter

Self-interest is part of human nature. Performance incentives, award ceremonies, recognition — they make a difference. The lack of built-in incentives and feedback, however, makes results in government harder to come by.

Be cognizant of culture

Think twice before asking a state agency to work outside its cultural comfort zone. One mismatch, for example, is when social workers are asked to be "enforcers," in essence, turning in their clients.

Bridge the political-bureaucratic divide

This requires a leader who can act as an interface between distinctly different worlds — the rare person who can translate bureaucratic language to politicians and tell the political masters when they are off-course.

TOOLS AND TECHNIQUES

Know the people doing the work

Data are important, but getting to know the people in the trenches will foster a different understanding of the challenge ahead. Get out of the office and work the phones, work the line, work something. Attitude is everything.

Invest in your people, develop your people

Government is notorious for under-investing in the productive capacity of its workers. Training in the tools of process management and change management is a good start. Programs aimed at developing a deep competency can help groom the "bridgers" needed to bridge the political and bureaucratic realms over time. One example: the British Civil Service's Fast Stream program where the best and brightest are exposed to a series of intensive job placements designed to prepare them for senior management positions.

Cultural transformation toolkit

Systems you use to manage your state workforce have a huge influence on attitudes of employees. Civil service, union rules and retirement structures have a huge impact on the state workforce and on getting big things done. Several tools can help to transform an organization's culture.

- **Cultural assessment:** Survey an organization to identify its core beliefs and values — both those that are currently present and those that are desired.
- **Change readiness assessment:** Quickly assess organizational strengths and challenges to change with respect to leadership, workforce, structure and process.
- **Flexible retirement approaches:** Greater flexibility in retirement packages allows for workers to choose the point in time when it makes sense for them to stay or move on, and it helps organizations to attract young talent.
- **Project-based, flexible staffing:** Skills repositories provide information on the skills and capabilities of employees. These can help managers match skills to employees and manage project performance.

the trap

The Sisyphus Trap

The Sisyphus trap is the distinctive interaction between the uniquely challenging public sector operating system and the people who work in government. Though understanding the systems of government is critical to success, we also need to understand the people rolling the boulder up the hill, particularly how their behaviors are shaped by the culture in which they toil. The Sisyphus trap can arise anywhere, but problems most commonly arise at the results phase.

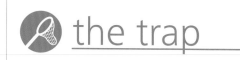

"I drop-in impromptu in a lot of DMV branches. I always ask how the numbers are, not just the branch manager but the assistant and sometimes the person at the counter."

~ Indiana Governor Mitch Daniels

Overcoming The Sisyphus Trap: Lessons from Wisconsin's welfare reform

Wisconsin is widely considered the father of welfare reform. The state reduced its welfare rolls by an astounding 82 percent in six years. Wisconsin overcame The Sisyphus Trap by changing the incentives (both for recipients and for providers), getting the culture right and closing the political-bureaucratic divide.

First, Wisconsin achieved bipartisan consensus about the goal of welfare reform. In fact, it was Democrats in the legislature who first proposed abolishing Aid to Families with Dependent Children (AFDC) and replacing it with another model by 1999. The shared commitment to the main goals of welfare reform removed what turned out to be a major stumbling block in other states: achieving goal alignment.

Second, the state built on earlier experiments and successes at the local level in counties like Kenosha. Rather than simply impose an untested, top-down solution, policy designers took their cue from implementers, and this eliminated much of the friction that typically exists between levels of government.

Third, Wisconsin got both the incentives and the cultural issues right. It did so by introducing a novel system of competition. It put the administration of the welfare to work programs out for bid, allowing public, private and nonprofit organizations to submit proposals for running the program in all ninety-two counties. This forced many of the organizations that would be delivering on the reforms — organizations with very different cultures that might previously have operated at cross-purposes — to team up and coordinate their efforts.

Last, the state agency in charge of implementing welfare reform was more than up to the task. Larry Mead, the author of *Government Matters*, an acclaimed book on Wisconsin's welfare reform, argues that "bureaucratic statecraft," the development of a strong, efficient and engaged administrative structure was — more than anything else — responsible for Wisconsin's success.[93] Wisconsin's welfare reformers skillfully navigated the interplay of people and systems.

Source: Eggers and O'Leary, *If We Can Put a Man on the Moon: Getting Big Things Done in Government*, Harvard Business Press, 2009.

Reevaluation

State governments must continually evaluate what they do and how they do it

Management guru Peter Drucker contends that successful business executives periodically reexamine the nature and purpose of everything their corporation does by asking two questions: "If we were not already doing this, would we now go into it?" If the answer is yes, they ask the follow-up question: "If we were to start doing this today, how would we do it?"[94] Drucker's questions get at a simple but profound truth: in some cases, what is being done no longer makes sense. In other cases, how it is being done no longer makes sense. In either case, change is called for.

Drucker referred to this as "sloughing off yesterday" and "purposeful abandonment." Innovation brings change, and while it introduces new and improved ways of creating wealth, it also means that old structures become obsolete. Economists sometimes refer to this as the process of "creative destruction," the removal of what exists to make room for what might be — the organizational equivalent of pruning a bush. Drucker notes that successful businesses tend to be fanatical at such pruning. This is not because businesspeople are so smart; it's because businesses that don't do this don't stay in business.

Not surprisingly, states typically haven't done a good job of "sloughing off yesterday." Most state governments lack the painful feedback mechanism of the market that drives this sort of change. Companies evolve or disappear, but all too often, government programs simply endure, operating as they have for decades with only incremental changes. One of the biggest challenges in government is that, unlike a business, no one "owns" that part of the journey. While the executive branch owns the launch of a program, in many cases, no one owns the task of reevaluation.

the trap

The Complacency Trap

In our modern world, conditions change fast, but democracy changes slowly. The result is that state programs and agencies need regular reevaluation. The Complacency Trap occurs when the status quo blocks our vision of what could be. Beating The Complacency Trap means embracing deep, systemic change to both the "what" and the "how" of state government.

Source: Deloitte Research

GUIDING PRINCIPLES FOR STATE LEADERS

Don't let "what is" prevent you from trying "things that never were." What exists today can be both a political and psychological barrier to what could be.

Improve your focus — do less, better

Constantly reevaluating what government does and pruning nonessential activities is essential to improving how government operates.

Change the default status

By changing the default from keep to eliminate, the sunset process provides an ongoing mechanism for government to rethink how agencies can best fulfill their obligations.

Wonder "what if?"

When things are going well, the tendency is to assume that they will continue to go well. To counter this tendency, you need a process and a team that actively creates "what if" scenarios. Such teams should produce a range of possible disaster scenarios. Don't wait for a tragedy to address risk.

Critical questions to ask during the reevaluation phase

- What is the goal of the state program? Is it still critical to the organization's mission?
- Are these goals being realized? How has actual overall performance differed from the original goals?
- What would you do with a clean slate?
- Would the state program look the same if you built it today? What are the alternatives?
- Have technological developments rendered any of the programs obsolete or less effective than they could be?
- Do stakeholders have the ability to "weigh-in" on the reevaluation process?

TOOLS AND TECHNIQUES

Idealized design

Try to imagine the ideal way to accomplish your policy goals, irrespective of how you do things today. Then, consider where you are today, and identify the obstacles to getting to your ideal state.

Sunset review

Establish an action-forcing mechanism to encourage elimination, reform and merger.

BRAC model

A variant of the sunset review, the Base Realignment and Closure model used an independent commission to recommend military base closures. Congress had to vote up or down on a package of proposals within 45 days. This process helped to overcome parochial political interests in Congress. Similar thinking could be applied to state government.

Look out for the black swans

Periodic risk analyses can help guard against complacency by identifying big consequences and rare or unforeseen events. Monitoring metrics for unexplained changes can help to uncover such "black swans" and other hidden risks.

Strategic options analysis

This tool identifies various strategies across a range of potential futures for the organization.

Texas Performance Review

When Texas was facing a massive state budget deficit in the early 1990s, then-governor Ann Richards, Comptroller John Sharp and the state legislature assembled over 100 of the best budget analysts, auditors and number crunchers in Texas government and gave them a single mission: Get us out of this budget crunch. In a few short months, the team came up with over 1,000 recommendations and identified over $2.4 billion in budget savings, ending the budget crisis and averting the need to impose a state income tax. The success of the review gave rise to the Texas Performance Review, a biennial evaluation of Texas government that has resulted in more than $15 billion in savings and gains to state funds since it was launched in 1991.[95]

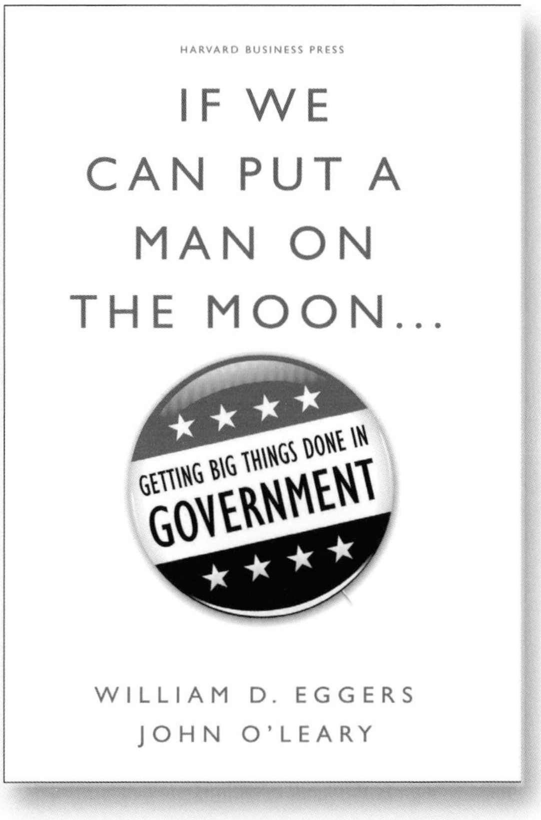

This chapter was adapted from material in *If We Can Put a Man on the Moon: Getting Big Things Done in Government* (Harvard Business Press, 2009) by William D. Eggers and John O'Leary.

Interview with **Chip Heath**

Author of ***Switch: How to Change Things When Change Is Hard***

Q... You compare the human mind to an elephant and a rider, two forces within ourselves that either obstruct change or make it happen. Can you describe that analogy?

It's not right to say that people "resist change." Typically, part of us embraces change, and part doesn't. One part of us wants a better beach body come summer. But another part wants that Oreo cookie. For years, psychologists have talked about the difference between the analytical brain that plans for a change and thinks through it, and the emotional side that's attracted to the Oreo cookie — to the comfort of the existing routine.

I love the analogy by Jonathan Haidt at the University of Virginia. He imagines the analytical side of the brain that decides we want to change something as a tiny human rider riding on top of a big, emotional elephant. I love this metaphor because it gets the relative weight classes right. If you think you're going to think your way into change, that's the tiny human rider on the big emotional elephant. In any direct contest of wills, the elephant is going to win. It's got a six-ton weight advantage.

Q...Change can't really happen until we're hungry for it. How can we foster the requisite appetite for change?

In this battle between the rider and the elephant, we typically approach change situations almost exclusively talking to the rider. Think about public health in the United States. We have warnings on cigarette packs saying "cigarette smoke contains carbon monoxide." Who is this appealing to in this battle between the rider and the elephant? It sounds like a purely logical appeal to the rider.

But Canada slaps a photo on the cigarette pack that takes up half the pack with a very vivid image of yellow teeth and says "smoking makes your teeth yellow." What's going to work better to change the behavior of a sixteen-year-old thinking of taking up the smoking?

Too often, we start off our change efforts with the thirty-five page Power Point deck filled with graphs and statistics. That's a great appeal to that analytical rider side of our brains. But it's not particularly effective at providing that motivation for change for the elephant, the emotional side.

Q...Is it always necessary to appeal to both the elephant and the rider, or can a sufficiently strong appeal to one overcome the barriers placed by the other?

You've got to do a little bit for both sides of the brain. Analytical appeals alone don't work without some emotion. But pure emotional appeals don't work either. A lot of the political discourse in this country is about anger, a feeling that we're going down the wrong path. But if there's not a clear direction for the analytical side of our brains, for that rider side, then you end up spinning your wheels and getting frustrated. Bad things happen when emotions are heightened but you don't have a clear path in front of you.

Q...You write "We seem wired to focus on the negative." How does this hamper our attempts to change something? Doesn't change begin with the identification of a problem?

There's a natural tendency in the analytical side of our brains to focus on problems. One of the points we make is, why don't we use the analytical side of our brains to focus on what's going right? Suppose a married couple shows up in a therapist's office. The classic therapy would be problem-focused. We go back into your childhood and figure out the source of the problems you're having in your relationship. The problem with that is a year into the analysis the couple says, now we understand why we're fighting, but how do we stop? Solutions-focused therapy says, "Let's think about the last time you as a couple had a discussion about a controversial issue and didn't devolve into an argument." The couple says, "Last Tuesday we talked for thirty minutes about finances without fighting." So the therapist will say, "Next week, get up in the morning, pour yourself a cup of coffee, and talk about child-rearing for thirty minutes. Can you use that success story to extrapolate for the future?" That's the goal of solutions-focused therapy.

We call this tendency to look for positive examples "looking for the bright spots." By focusing on the bright spots we can say, "What have you done successfully in the past, and can you do more of it the future?" Especially in the economic downturn we just lived through, there are lots of negative things to pay attention to, but often, we wind ourselves up spinning our minds in unproductive directions.

Q...What makes this focus on bright spots so effective?

You're aligning both sides of the brain there. For the analytical rider side, you're providing a clear direction, at least in the short term. This is not a long distance plan; we're not trying to account for every possible contingency; we're just trying to do one thing to move us a step in the right direction. The second thing you're doing is evoking that emotional elephant side because change is paralyzing when we think it's too big and pervasive. No one goes straight from the first date to marriage. It's a progression of first steps and you gradually experiment your way into that relationship. And yet, when we try to do public or corporate changes, we try to come up with the whole plan at once. That's paralyzing and scary to the elephant. And yet, by shrinking down that change and talking about the critical moves, you're providing direction to the rider analytically and motivation to that elephant.

In our book, my brother and I put it this way: "Trying to fight inertia with analytical arguments is like tossing a fire extinguisher to someone who's drowning. The solution doesn't match the problem."

Q...Along with the elephant and the rider, the framework in your book has a third component — the world outside the conflict in our brains. You call it the path.

One of my favorite examples is the one-click button on the Amazon site. What most people don't know is that Amazon has the patent on one-click ordering. That's a remarkable statement. You don't get patents if anyone else in the history of the universe has ever considered what you're trying to patent. But of all the firms doing e-commerce, only Amazon took the time to take away this obstacle. We spend a third of the book talking about techniques for shaping the path. The simpler the solution, and the more it's been prototyped and workshopped, the more likely you are to have taken away the bumps in the road that prevent change from happening, even for a motivated elephant or a directed rider.

APPENDIX

LETTING GO OF T

A CHECKLIST FOR TRANSFOR

TRANSFORMING HEALTH AND HUMAN SERVICES

5
responding to health care reform

Much of the action and implementation responsibilities of health reform will reside with the states. They will be responsible for many newly eligible citizens, as well as the technology and business process that support the reform programs — all during a period of unprecedented Medicaid growth.

KEY CHECKLIST ITEMS

- ☐ Have you identified all the requirements for which you are responsible under the Patient Protection and Affordable Care Act (PPACA) and determined a holistic approach to meet them?
- ☐ What unique requirements do you have in implementing a health benefit exchange? Are there regional, private or nonprofit partners whom you can partner with in implementation?
- ☐ How can you use PPACA to drive innovation in health care?
- ☐ Have you properly invested in the IT infrastructure required to support health reform?
- ☐ How well do you tie expenditures to outcomes? Are you incentivizing evidence-based, cost-effective health care?
- ☐ What options are available for treating long-term care patients in non-institutional settings? Are there options you've cut or underfunded for budgetary reasons?
- ☐ Does your delivery model allow you to address the unique needs of each citizen, including those with chronic care conditions?
- ☐ Do you encourage and enable care in community settings?
- ☐ Do you do enough to encourage preventative health care and healthy living for Medicaid enrollees?
- ☐ Are you utilizing a single point of entry system to coordinate health care? If not, how do you coordinate care teams, patients and caregivers?

6
improving human services

The long economic downturn has increased demand for anti-poverty programs, putting strong pressures on human services' budgets. With ARRA stimulus funding set to expire, cash-strapped states will need to find creative ways to reduce the costs associated with delivering human services programs while accommodating increased demand.

KEY CHECKLIST ITEMS

- ☐ Have you developed a comprehensive set of metrics for human services that focus on client outcomes?
- ☐ How can you make clients smarter consumers of your services?
- ☐ What tools can be used to reduce the administrative costs of human services programs?
- ☐ How can you reengineer business processes (e.g. removing duplicative or stovepipe areas) to create more efficient delivery of human services?
- ☐ Can you demonstrate that you are funding the programs that deliver results?
- ☐ Does your incentive structure encourage recipients to stay on programs, or move off them?
- ☐ Do your current models of financing human services sacrifice long-term effectiveness for short-term efficiencies?
- ☐ How can access to health and human services programs be made more client-centric?
- ☐ What is your vision for service integration? What will it take to realize that vision?

7
techno rebo

States have an opportunity to help address their most pressi challenges. These technologie positively disrupt cost, capabil and even the core operating

KEY CHECKLIST ITEMS

- ☐ Is there a thorough invento
- ☐ Has your IT infrastructure b consolidated? If not, why
- ☐ Have you examined consol application development a
- ☐ Is the impact of consolidat IT workforce well understo
- ☐ Do you have a thorough u of the transition and replac if IT assets are consolidate
- ☐ Have you identified a comp repeatable framework of c to deploy across the state
- ☐ Does your state chief infor officer have enterprise-leve
- ☐ What are your biggest cyb external and those of your Which are the most pressi How can you mitigate thes
- ☐ What opportunities are the leverage cloud computing?
- ☐ What type of cloud model
- ☐ Do you have advanced dat capabilities to support you not, how can you build the
- ☐ How can you enlist partne mashup and analyze your

[T]HE STATUS QUO

[...]MING STATE GOVERNMENT

OVERHAULING STATE OPERATIONS ▶ GETTING IT DONE

[...]logy [...]ot

[...]everage technology to [...]g policy and operational [...] have the potential to [...]ies, service provision [...]odel of government.

[...]y of the state's IT assets?

[...]en [...]ot?

[...]dating systems such as [...]d payment processing?

[...]n on the [...]d?

[...]derstanding [...]ment costs [...]

[...]ehensive and [...]persecurity standards [...]nterprise?

[...]ation security [...] authority?

[...] threats — internal, [...]hird party providers? [...]g to address? [...] threats?

[...]e to

[...]est fits your needs?

[...] analytics [...] core mission? If [...]n or buy them?

[...] to [...]ata?

8

innovation state

If ever state government needed to be daring and innovative, it's now. Without a mindset that prizes innovation, it will be next to impossible to address the daunting issues facing states today. State policymakers need to embrace innovation as a necessary discipline, much like strategic planning and budgeting.

KEY CHECKLIST ITEMS

- ☐ Do you have a system or process for fostering innovation? At what stage of the innovation process are you strongest? Weakest?
- ☐ Do you utilize a full array of innovative strategies, from cultivating innovation to using more of an open source model?
- ☐ What incentives are there to innovate? Are they powerful enough?
- ☐ Do you have an incentive structure that rewards intelligent risk taking and does not overly penalize failure?
- ☐ Are you using Gov 2.0 tools and technologies to engage citizens, academia and businesses to help develop solutions to problems?
- ☐ Can you use contests or prize systems to solicit and enact innovative ideas from outside government?
- ☐ Is data held as an enterprise asset at the state level or held narrowly by individual agencies?
- ☐ Do you make raw government data available to the public online? Can you go further?
- ☐ Do your "Open Gov" initiatives tie directly to your department missions?

9

from big ideas to big results

Translating big policy ideas and campaign promises is filled with perils and potholes. To succeed a public undertaking must have the following basic elements: a good idea, an implementable design, political support, strong implementation and then generate results. Success requires taking the process of getting big things done seriously.

KEY CHECKLIST ITEMS

- ☐ Do you fully understand the key factors that influence the achievement of your goal?
- ☐ Has your idea benefited from a wide range of views? How do people with different viewpoints think you could achieve your goal?
- ☐ How did your idea evolve as you examined different ways to achieve your goal?
- ☐ Have you consulted stakeholders? Do you have their agreement on your direction?
- ☐ What is the evidence that this is the best approach for addressing the issue?
- ☐ Why will the initiative work? Do you understand the ways in which it could fail?
- ☐ What were the results of scenario planning to identify the various ways in which the program could unfold?
- ☐ What aspects of the program are considered "deal breakers," and can you articulate them to opponents of the program?
- ☐ Are the people implementing the program ready to take on the task?
- ☐ Do you have the necessary resources and authority to achieve the task?
- ☐ What level of commitment is there among employees and stakeholders to achieving your vision?
- ☐ Who will hold you and the lead in each key partner organization to account for delivering the program?
- ☐ What will happen if key performance indicators are not met?
- ☐ How much failure — and what kind of failure — will you tolerate?
- ☐ How has actual overall performance differed from the original trajectory?
- ☐ How did your program's various components perform compared to their original planned trajectory?
- ☐ Based on the trajectory results, where is your program headed in the next five years?

Additional resources

Books, studies and Web sites

General

www.deloitte.com/us/stategovernment

www.deloitte.com/us/stategovplaybook.com

States of Transition: Tackling Government's Toughest Policy and Management Challenges
(Deloitte Research, 2006)

If We Can Put a Man on the Moon: Getting Big Things Done in Government
(Harvard Business Press, 2009)

Chapter 1

Red Ink Rising: The Journey to Sustainable Government, Deloitte Research
www.deloitte.com/redinkrising

Paying for Tomorrow: Practical Strategies for Tackling the Public Pension Crisis
Deloitte Research

The Pew Center on the States: www.pewcenteronthestates.org

National Association of State Budget Officers: www.nasbo.org

Better, Faster, Cheaper: www.governing.com/blogs/bfc

National Governors Association Center for Best Practices: www.nga.com

The Big Reset: State Government after the Great Recession
NGA Center for Best Practices

State Government Redesign Efforts 2009 and 2010
NGA Center for Best Practices

Chapter 2

Measuring the Forces of Long-Term Change: The 2009 Shift Index
Deloitte Center for the Edge

2010 Global Manufacturing Competitiveness Index
Deloitte Touche Tohmatsu and the Council on Competitiveness

Deloitte Center for the Edge
www.deloitte.com/centerforedge

The Manufacturing Institute
http://institute.nam.org

Council on Competitiveness
www.compete.org

Chapter 3

Deloitte 2009 Education Survey Overview: Redefining High School as a Launch Pad
http://www.deloitte.com/assets/Dcom-UnitedStates/Local%20Assets/Documents/us_leadership_EducationSurvey120109.pdf

States of Transition: Tackling Government's Toughest Policy and Management Challenges
(Deloitte Research, 2006, pp. 207-244.)
www.deloitte.com/statesoftransition

Increasing Student Engagement in Math and Science Education in America
Deloitte Research

US Department of Education Office of Innovation and Improvement
www2.ed.gov/about/offices/list/oii/index.html

Chapter 4

Partnering for Value: Structuring Effective Public-Private Partnerships for Infrastructure
Deloitte Research
www.deloitte.com/assets/Dcom-Global/Local%20Assets/Documents/Public%20Sector/dtt_ps_partneringforvalue_090710.pdf

The Changing Landscape for Infrastructure Funding and Finance
Deloitte Research
www.deloitte.com/assets/Dcom-Global/Local%20Assets/Documents/Public%20Sector/dtt_ps_infrastructurefunding_190810.pdf

Closing America's Infrastructure Gap: The Role of Public-Private Partnerships
Deloitte Research
www.deloitte.com/assets/Dcom-UnitedStates/Local%20Assets/Documents/us_ps_PPPUS_final(1).pdf

Chapter 5

Reducing Costs While Improving the U.S. Health Care System: The Health Reform Pyramid
Deloitte Center for Health Solutions
www.deloitte.com/us/healthreformpyramid

Medicaid Medical Management: A Complex Challenge for States
Deloitte Center for Health Solutions
www.deloitte.com/assets/Dcom-UnitedStates/Local%20Assets/Documents/us_chs_MedicaidMedicalManagement_0908w.pdf

Chapter 6

Are We There Yet? Vol. II – Service Integration 2.0: Using Collaborative Tools to Transform Human Service Delivery
Deloitte Development LLC
www.deloitte.com/assets/Dcom-UnitedStates/Local%20Assets/Documents/us_ps_AreWeThereYet_011209.pdf

Human Services Financing for the 21st Century: A Blueprint for Building Stronger Children and Families
Deloitte Development LLC
www.deloitte.com/assets/Dcom-UnitedStates/Local%20Assets/Documents/us_ps_FinancingHumanServicesReport_080709.pdf

Chapter 7

Cloud computing
Deloitte Center for the Edge
http://www.deloitte.com/centerforedge

Data analytics
Deloitte Analytics Institute
www.deloitte.com/view/en_US/us/Services/consulting/feature-offerings/deloitteanalytics/analytics-institute/index.htm

Technology trends
Depth Perception: A Dozen Technology Trends Shaping Business and IT in 2010
Deloitte
www.deloitte.com/us/2010technologytrends

Cybersecurity
Deloitte Center for Cyber Innovation
www.deloitte.com/view/en_US/us/Insights/centers/centers-center-for-cyber/index.htm

State Governments at Risk: A Call to Secure Citizen Data and Inspire Public Trust, 2010
Deloitte-NASCIO Cybersecurity Survey
www.deloitte.com/view/en_US/us/Industries/us-state-government/ae3572eefd25b210VgnVCM2000001b56f00aRCRD.htm

Chapter 8

Public Innovators Playbook: Nurturing Bold Ideas in Government
(Deloitte Research, 2009)
www.deloitte.com/innovatorsplaybook

Council of State Governments Innovations Award Program
www.csg.org/programs/innovations.aspx

Harvard Kennedy School Government Innovators Network
www.innovations.harvard.edu/

Capital Ideas: How to Generate Innovation in the Public Sector
Center for American Progress
www.americanprogress.org/issues/2010/07/dww_capitalideas.html

Scaling New Heights: How to Spot Small Successes in the Public Sector and Make Them Big
Center for American Progress
www.americanprogress.org/issues/2010/07/dww_scaling.html

Government 2.0: Using Technology to Improve Education, Cut Red Tape, Reduce Gridlock, and Enhance Democracy
(Rowman and Littlefield, 2005)
www.deloitte.com/view/en_GX/global/insights/deloitte-research/article/cfd25915531fb110VgnVCM100000ba42f00aRCRD.htm

Unlocking Government: How Data Transforms Democracy
Deloitte Research
www.deloitte.com/ca/government20

Chapter 9

If We Can Put a Man on the Moon: Getting Big Things Done in Government
(Harvard Business Press, 2009)
www.deloitte.com/us/manonthemoon

The Journey to Success interactive map
www.journeytosuccessmap.com

Getting Results in Government: A Checklist for Effective Policies and Programs
Deloitte GovLab

Center for American Progress "Doing What Works" Project
www.americanprogress.org/projects/doing_what_works

Endnotes

Introduction

1. Elizabeth McNichol, Phil Oliff and Nicholas Johnson, "States Continue to Feel Recession's Impact," Center on Budget and Policy Priorities, October 7, 2010, <http://www.cbpp.org/cms/?fa=view&id=711>.

2. Mitch Daniels, "The Coming Reset in State Government," *The Wall Street Journal*, September 3, 2009, <http://online.wsj.com/article/SB1000142405297020473180457439063114939642.html>.

3. "Facing Facts: Public Attitudes and Fiscal Realities in Five Stressed States," The Pew Center on the States and Public Policy Institute of California, October 2010, http://www.pewcenteronthestates.org/uploadedFiles/PCS_PPIC.pdf?n=4566>.

4. Ibid.

5. Members of the 2005 "Rising Above the Gathering Storm" Committee, *Rising Above the Gathering Storm, Revisited: Rapidly Approaching Category 5* (Washington, DC: The National Academies Press, 2010).

Chapter 1

6. "Overall State Tax Revenue Is Up, But Losers Still Outnumber Gainers: Income Taxes Decline Once Again in April," The Nelson A. Rockefeller Institute of Government, State Revenue Flash Report, June 3, 2010, <http://www.rockinst.org/pdf/government_finance/state_revenue_report/2010-06-03-State_Revenue_Flash.pdf>.

7. Elizabeth McNichol, Phil Oliff and Nicholas Johnson, "States Continue to Feel Recession's Impact," Center on Budget and Policy Priorities, October 7, 2010, <http://www.cbpp.org/cms/?fa=view&id=711>.

8. "The Trillion Dollar Gap: Underfunded State Retirement Systems and the Roads to Reform," Pew Center on the States, February 2010, <http://downloads.pewcenteronthestates.org/The_Trillion_Dollar_Gap_final.pdf>.

9. Claire Heininger and the Statehouse Bureau, "Gov. Chris Christie Tells N.J. Mayors to Expect State Aid Cuts in Upcoming Budget," NJ.com, February 25, 2010, <http://www.nj.com/news/index.ssf/2010/02/gov_chris_christie_tells_mayor.html>.

10. The Commission for a New Georgia, "A Best-Managed State: Government That Works Best and Costs Less," <http://newgeorgia.org/bestmanaged.html>.

11. Representative Carl Isett, Texas House of Representatives, interview with William D. Eggers and John O'Leary, June 2008.

12. Governor Martin O'Malley, interview with Jonathan Walters, August 25, 2009. For full text of interview, see "2009 Public Officials of the Year: Interview with Martin O'Malley," *Governing*, 2009, <http://governing.com/poy/Martin-OMalley.html?p=interview>.

13. Representative Diana S. Urban, Connecticut House of Representatives, interview with Jonathan Walters, September 15, 2010.

14. See for example: William D. Eggers, John O'Leary and Joel Bellman, "Red Ink Rising: The Road to Fiscal Sustainability," Deloitte Research, July 2010, <http://www.deloitte.com/redinkrising>.

15. The full Peter Drucker quote is: "Every agency, every policy, every program, every activity, should be confronted with these questions: 'What is your mission?' 'Is it still the right mission?' 'Is it still worth doing?' 'If we were not already doing this, would we now go into it?' This questioning has been done often enough in all kinds of organizations—businesses, hospitals, churches, and even local governments—that we know it works. The overall answer is almost never 'This is fine as it stands; let's keep on.' But in some—indeed, a good many—areas the answer to the last question is 'Yes, we would go into this again, but with some changes. We have learned a few things.'" See Peter F. Drucker, "Really Reinventing Government," *The Atlantic*, February 1995, <http://www.theatlantic.com/past/politics/polibig/reallyre.htm>.

16. Monica Davey, "Hard Times Spur Ideas for Change," *The New York Times*, May 24, 2010, <http://www.nytimes.com/2010/05/25/us/25remake.html?_r=1>.

17. "The Trillion Dollar Retirement Systems and the Road to Reform," Pew Center on the States, February 2010.

18. Alicia H. Munnell, Jean-Pierre Aubry and Laura Quinby, "The Funding of State and Local Pensions: 2009-2013," Center for Retirement Research at Boston College, April 2010, <http://crr.bc.edu/images/stories/Briefs/slp_10.pdf>.

19. Ibid.

20. Jeannette Neumann, "State Workers, Long Resistant, Accept Cuts in Pension Benefits," *The Wall Street Journal*, June 29, 2010, <http://online.wsj.com/article/NA_WSJ_PUB:SB10001424052748703279704575335153612628676.html>.

21. Ronald K. Snell, "Pensions and Retirement Plan Enactments in 2010 State Legislatures," National Conference of State Legislatures, September 1, 2010, <http://www.ncsl.org/documents/employ/PensionReportSept1-2010.pdf>.

22. Labor's view of defined contribution plans is that they put retirees in a particularly vulnerable position during economic downturns, something that SEIU's Grillo argues was painfully proved during the recent housing crisis and stock market crash. Meanwhile, AFSCME's Kreisberg argues that defined benefit plans have proved not only vastly more reliable, but much more efficient to run.

Chapter 2

23. John Hagel, John Seely Brown and Lang Davison, "Measuring the Forces of Long-Term Change: The 2009 Shift Index," Deloitte Center for the Edge; Aleda V. Roth, Craig A. Giffi, Atanu Chaudhuri and Hans Roehm, "2010 Global Manufacturing Competitiveness Index," Deloitte Touche Tohmatsu and the Council on Competitiveness.

24. Ibid.

25. Ibid.

26. Ibid.

27. Governor Mitch Daniels, phone interview with William D. Eggers, September 21, 2010.

28. Joseph Cortright and Heike Mayer, "High Tech Specialization: A Comparison of High Technology Centers," The Brookings Institution, January 2001, <http://www.brookings.edu/es/urban/cortright/specialization.pdf>.

29. Soumitra Dutta and Irene Mia, "The Global Information Technology Report 2009-2010," World Economic Forum, 2010, <http://www.weforum.org/documents/GITR10/index.html>.

30. "World Urbanization Prospects: The 2005 Revision," Working Paper No. ESA/P/WP/200, United Nations, Department of Economic and Social Affairs, Population Division (2006), <http://www.un.org/esa/population/publications/WUP2005/2005WUPHighlights_Final_Report.pdf>.

31. Greg Pellegrino, "Back from the Brink," Deloitte, September 2009, <http://www.deloitte.com/assets/Dcom-Global/Local%20Assets/Documents/Public%20Sector/dtt_ps_backfromthebrink_130110.pdf>.

32. C. Farrell, "Brighter Lights for Big Cities," *BusinessWeek*, May 4, 1998, pp. 88-95.

33. Craig Giffi and Emily Stover DeRocco, "Made in America? What the Public Thinks about Manufacturing Today," Deloitte and The Manufacturing Institute, September 2010, <www.deloitte.com/us/mfgimageindex>.

34. Declan McCullagh, "Intel CEO: U.S. Faces Looming Tech Decline," *CNET News*, August 24, 2010, <http://news.cnet.com/8301-13578_3-20014563-38.html>.

35. The New England Council and Deloitte Consulting LLP, "Reexamining Advanced Manufacturing in a Networked World: Prospects for a Resurgence in New England," December, 2009, p. 17, <http://newenglandcouncil.com/pdf/rep_webReports/rep_2010.01.14_AdvancedManufacturing.pdf>.

36. "2010 Global Manufacturing Competitiveness Index," Council on Competitiveness and Deloitte, June 2010, <http://www.compete.org/images/uploads/File/PDF%20Files/2010_Global_Manufacturing_Competitiveness_Index_FINAL.pdf>.

Chapter 3

37. Members of the 2005 "Rising Above the Gathering Storm" Committee, *Rising Above the Gathering Storm, Revisited: Rapidly Approaching Category 5* (Washington, DC: The National Academies Press, 2010).

38. UNECSO Institute for Statistics.

39. Liz Wolgemuth, "The 50 Best Careers of 2010," *U.S. News & World Report*, December 28, 2009, <http://money.usnews.com/money/careers/articles/2009/12/28/the-50-best-careers-of-2010.html>.

40. Nicholas Johnson, Phil Oliff and Erica Williams, "An Update on State Budget Cuts," Center on Budget and Policy Priorities, November 5, 2010, <http://www.cbpp.org/cms/?fa=view&id=1214>.

41. Chris Farrell, "Failing U.S. Education Will Dumb Down Economic Growth," *Bloomberg Businessweek*, June 24, 2010, <http://www.businessweek.com/investor/content/jun2010/pi20100624_409585_page_2.htm>. (The Center for Labor Market Studies at Northeastern University calculates that the average high school dropout has a lifetime negative net fiscal contribution to society of some $5,200.)

42. "Fast Facts," Institute of Education Sciences, National Center for Education Statistics, U.S. Department of Education, 2009, <http://nces.ed.gov/fastfacts/display.asp?id=171>.

43. Robert J. Samuelson, "School Reform's Meager Results," *The Washington Post*, September 6, 2010, <http://www.washingtonpost.com/wp-dyn/content/article/2010/09/05/AR2010090502817.html>.

44. David Leonhardt, "Colleges Are Failing in Graduation Rates," *The New York Times*, September 8, 2009, <http://www.nytimes.com/2009/09/09/business/economy/09leonhardt.html>.

45. "District-Wide Reform: Interview with Joel Klein, Chancellor (2002-2010), New York City Department of Education," Making Schools Work with Hedrick Smith, PBS, 2005, <http://www.pbs.org/makingschoolswork/dwr/ny/klein.html>.

46. Tom Vander Ark, The Case for Smaller Schools; Vol 59, No. 5, January 2002, pg 55-59.

47. The Wallace Foundation, "Education Leadership: An Agenda for School Improvement," The Wallace Foundation's National Conference, Washington, DC, October 14-16, 2009, pp. 6-17, <http://www.wallacefoundation.org/KnowledgeCenter/KnowledgeTopics/CurrentAreasofFocus/EducationLeadership/Documents/education-leadership-an-agenda-for-school-improvement.pdf>.

48. Harold Wenglinksky, "How Teaching Matters: Bringing the Classroom Back Into Discussions of Teacher Quality," Educational Testing Service, Policy Information Center, October 2000, pg 6-7, <http://www.ets.org/Media/Research/pdf/PICTEAMAT.pdf>.

49. Leslie Postal, "Florida One of 10 Winners for Race to the Top Grant," *Orlando Sentinel*, August 24, 2010, <http://articles.orlandosentinel.com/2010-08-24/news/os-race-to-top-florida-20100824_1_top-grant-teachers-minority-students>.

50. "Finishing the First Lap: The Cost of First-Year Student Attrition in America's Four-Year Colleges and Universities," American Institutes for Research, October 11, 2010, <http://www.air.org/news/index.cfm?fa=viewContent&content_id=989>.

51. Bob Herbert, "Clueless in America," *The New York Times*, April 22, 2008, <http://www.nytimes.com/2008/04/22/opinion/22herbert.html?em&ex=1209096000&en=4002a301cbe9d193&ei=5087%0A>.

52. J.B. Schramm and E. Kinney Zalesne, "The Promise of Proficiency: How College Proficiency Information Can Help High Schools Drive Student Success," Center for American Progress and College Summit, December 2009, <http://www.collegesummit.org/images/uploads/whotepaper09.pdf>.

53. Sam Dillon, "School Is Turned Around, but Cost Gives Pause," *The New York Times*, June 24, 2010, <http://www.nytimes.com/2010/06/25/education/25school.html?_r=2> and Green Dot Public Schools, <http://www.greendot.org/about_us/about_us>.

54. Stacy Teicher Khadaroo, "After Katrina, How Charter Schools Helped Recast New Orleans Education," *The Christian Science Monitor*, August 29, 2010, <http://www.csmonitor.com/USA/Education/2010/0829/After-Katrina-how-charter-schools-helped-recast-New-Orleans-education>.

55. Ibid.

56. Michael S. Holstead, Terry E. Spradlin and Jonathan A. Plucker, "Promises and Pitfalls of Virtual Education in the United States and Indiana," Education Policy Brief, Center for Evaluation & Education Policy, Spring 2008, <http://www.ceep.indiana.edu/projects/PDF/PB_V6N6_Spring_2008_EPB.pdf>.

57. Governor Arnold Schwarzenegger, "Leading the Nation into a Digital Textbook Future," Office of the Governor, June 8, 2009, <http://gov.ca.gov/index.php?/fact-sheet/12455/>.

58. Barry Salzberg, "Where Are America's High-Performing Students?" *Forbes.com*, September 6, 2007, <http://www.forbes.com/2007/09/06/skills-college-nonprofit-lead-careers-cz_bs_0906salzberg.html>.

59. Peter J. Landis, "How U.S. Immigration Policy Hurts the U.S. Economy," *LAWFIRMS.com*, December 2008, <http://www.lawfirms.com/news/immigration-law/immigration-policy-hurts-us-economoy.htm>.

60. Louis Uchitelle, "Despite Recession, High Demand for Skilled Labor," *The New York Times*, June 23, 2009, <http://www.nytimes.com/2009/06/24/business/24jobs.html> and Nell Henderson, "Skilled Labor in High Demand," *The Washington Post*, August 25, 2004, <http://www.washingtonpost.com/wp-dyn/articles/A30139-2004Aug24.html>.

61. William G. Bowen, Martin A. Kurzweil and Eugene M. Tobin, "A Thumb on the Scale: The Case for Socioeconomic Affirmative Action," *Harvard Magazine*, May-June 2005, <http://harvardmagazine.com/2005/05/a-thumb-on-the-scale.html>.

62. Constance Steinkuehler, "MMOs, Learning & The New Pop Cosmopolitanism," Games + Learning + Society Initiative, University of Wisconsin–Madison, March 25, 2010, <http://web.nmc.org/files/2010-nml-symposium/constance-steinkuehler-slides.pdf>.

63. Rapid Intake, "Collaborative e-Learning Software Helps Improve Student Test Scores," *Online PR News*, January 21, 2010, <http://www.onlineprnews.com/news/18614-1264115111-collaborative-elearning-software-helps-improve-student-test-scores.html>.

Chapter 4

64. Building America's Future, "Building America's Future Releases New Poll: Majority of Americans Ready to Pay for Better Infrastructure but Demand Accountability," press release issued on January 8, 2009, <http://bafuture.org/poll-majority-of-americans-ready-to-pay-for-better-infrastructure-but-demand-accountability>.

65. "Top Executives Say Current Infrastructure Investment Won't Support Business Growth, Says KPMG Study," *PRNewswire*, January 14, 2009, <http://news.prnewswire.com/DisplayReleaseContent.aspx?ACCT=ind_focus.story&STORY=/www/story/01-14-2009/0004954443&EDATE>.

66. American Society of Civil Engineers, "2009 Report Card for America's Infrastructure," January 2009, <http://www.asce.org/reportcard/2009/index.cfm>.

67. "The Benefits of Private Investment in Infrastructure," Sphere Consulting in coordination with Abertis, Allen & Overy LLP, Barclays Capital, Castalia LLC, Carlyle Infrastructure Partners, CH2M Hill, Chadbourne & Parke LLP, Clifford Chance, Credit Suisse, Debevoise & Plimpton, Freshfields Bruckhaus Deringer, Fulbright & Jaworski, Greenhill & Co., Kirkland & Ellis, Mayer Brown, McKenna Long & Aldridge LLP, Merrill Lynch, Morgan Stanley, RBC Capital Markets, Scotia Capital, Skanska, and UBS, March 2010, <http://www.castalia-advisors.com/files/Private_Investment_in_Infrastructure_Presentation.pdf>.

68. Peter Samuel, "Abertis/Citi Selected in $12.8 Billion Bid for Pennsylvania Turnpike Lease," *TOLLROADnews*, May 19, 2008, <http://www.tollroadsnews.com/node/3547>.

Chapter 5

69. Surescripts, "Advancing Healthcare in America: 2009 National Progress Report on e-Prescribing, Plus What's Ahead in 2010 and Beyond," <http://www.surescripts.com/media/515306/2009_national-progress-report.pdf>.

70. Ibid.

71. Ibid.

72. These include: Colorado Medical Homes for Children, Community Care of North Carolina, Geisinger Health System, Group Health Cooperative, Intermountain Health Care, MeritCare Health System and Blue Cross Blue Shield of North Dakota, and Vermont's Blueprint for Health.

73. Fields D, Leshen E and Patel K. "Driving Quality Gains and Cost Savings through Adoption of Medical Homes," *Health Affairs*, May 2010; 29(5): 819-826 doi: 10.1377/hlthaff.2010.0009.

74. For further information, please see "Healthcare Consumerism — For Sustained Cost Reduction," Deloitte Development LLC, July 2010, <http://www.deloitte.com/assets/Dcom-UnitedStates/Local%20Assets/Documents/Consulting%20MOs/us_consulting_mo_HealthCareConsumerism_070510.pdf>.

75. "2008 Actuarial Report on the Financial Outlook for Medicaid," Office of the Actuary, Center for Medicare & Medicaid Services, U.S. Department of Health & Human Services, October 17, 2008, <http://www.cms.hhs.gov/ActuarialStudies/downloads/MedicaidReport2008.pdf>.

Chapter 6

76. Erik Eckholm, "Recession Raises Poverty Rate to a 15-Year High," *The New York Times*, September 16, 2010, <http://www.nytimes.com/2010/09/17/us/17poverty.html?th&emc=th>.

77. Richard Wolf, "Record Number in Government Anti-Poverty Programs," *USA Today*, August 30, 2010, <http://www.usatoday.com/news/washington/2010-08-30-1Asafetynet30_ST_N.htm>.

78. This is the intent of the horizontal integration in the bill but some state officials have concerns about its effectiveness or implementation abilities. The actual "teeth" in this part of the bill are pretty unclear to states since it requires integration, but doesn't actually clear any of the current hurdles that are stopping states from integrating these services further today.

Chapter 7

79. "The 2010 State CIO Survey," National Association of State Chief Information Officers, Tech America and Grant Thornton, Washington, DC, 2010, <http://www.nascio.org/publications/documents/NASCIO-2010StateCIOSurvey.pdf>.

80. "State CIO Priorities," National Association of State Chief Information Officers, November 18, 2009, <http://www.nascio.org/publications/documents/NASCIO-CIO%20Priorities2010.pdf>.

81. "State CIO Priorities," 2009.

82. "The 2010 State CIO Survey," 2010.

83. Ibid.

84. "Emerging Cyber Threats Report 2011," Security Summit 2010, Georgia Tech Information Security Center, <http://www.gtisc.gatech.edu/pdf/cyberThreatReport2011.pdf>.

85. Andy Opsahl, "Michigan Announces Unique Cyber-Security Partnership with Feds," *Government Technology*, December 15, 2009, <http://www.govtech.com/security/Michigan-Announces-Unique-Cyber-Security-Partnership-With.html>.

86. Russell Nichols, "Oregon Brings Google Apps to Public Schools," *Government Technology*, April 28, 2010, <http://www.govtech.com/education/Oregon-Brings-Google-Apps-to-Public.html>.

87. "Ohio to Lead Country in Statewide Cloud Computing Initiative," Ohio.gov and OARnet, June 10, 2009, <http://www.oar.net/press/releases/2009/cloud_computing.shtml>.

88. Justin Lee, "Michigan Seeks to Build Massive Shared Data Center," *Web Host Industry Review*, January 12, 2010, <http://www.thewhir.com/web-hosting-news/011210_Michigan_Seeks_to_Build_Massive_Shared_Data_Center>.

Chapter 8

89. Frank DiGiammarino, vice president for strategic initiatives, National Academy of Public Administration, speaking at Web 2.0: The Future of Collaborative Government, Washington, DC, June 3, 2008.

90. "Friends, Followers, and Feeds: A National Survey of Social Media Use in State Government," NASCIO, September 2010, <http://www.nascio.org/publications/documents/NASCIO-SocialMedia.pdf>.

91. Patrick Marshall, "Alabama's Layered Approach," *Government Computer News*, October 17, 2008, <http://gcn.com/Articles/2008/10/17/Alabamas-layered-approach.aspx>.

Chapter 9

92. "Welcome to Virtual Alabama," Alabama Department of Homeland Security, <http://www.virtual.alabama.gov/>.

93. Larry Mead, *Government Matters: Welfare Reform in Wisconsin* (Princeton University Press, 2004).

94. See Peter F. Drucker, "Really Reinventing Government," *The Atlantic*, February 1995.

95. Texas Legislative Budget Board.

Acknowledgements

This is the second book we have produced for incoming governors and state legislators. The first, *States of Transition*, was published in 2006 amidst a period of relative prosperity. The conditions today could not be more different. Though this means that the state fiscal challenge towers over all other issues, governors and legislators still don't have the luxury of ignoring many other pressing needs.

It is a cliché, but this book truly was a team effort. We express our gratitude to all those who assisted in the research, editing and manuscript review. This book is far better for their input. Any errors, omissions or faulty reasoning, however, are all ours.

First, we would like to thank our Deloitte Services LP colleagues who played a critical role in the book. Ryan Alvanos, an extremely talented writer and editor, put in dozens of hours helping us to improve the book's language. Teresa Loney helped to manage the production process and keep the project on track. Troy Bishop, Elizabeth Adams, Erin McAdams and Joey Suing worked for weeks to design the book's striking layout. Julia Richman of Deloitte Consulting LLP wrote the first draft of the section on IT consolidation. Steve Dahl, Christina Dorfhuber, and Kara Harris of Deloitte Consulting LLP, three top-notch strategic thinkers, reviewed multiple chapters of the book and offered dozens of thoughtful comments. The research of Aaron Young, our summer intern, helped to get us smarter about several subjects.

Other Deloitte colleagues who generously offered their time and insights to improve the book manuscript include: Governor Tom Ridge of Deloitte LLP; The Honorable Thomas M. Davis and Bill Ezzell of Deloitte & Touche LLP; Phil Benowitz, Peter Blatman, William Briggs, William Carroll, Stephen Cottle, Greg Dost, Devon Halley, Lindsey Hitchcock, Wade Horn, Pat Howard, Katie Jorgenson, Paul Keckley, Doug Laney, Mike Phelan, General Harry Raduege, Shrupti Shah, David Steier, Charles Tierney, Mark White and Tim Wiest of Deloitte Consulting LLP; Mark Davidoff, Greg Pellegrino, Irene Walsh and Jim Ziglar of Deloitte Financial Services LLP; and Dawn Desantis, Claire England, Craig Giffi and Tom Walker of Deloitte Services LP.

Deloitte Services LP colleagues Kim Andreotta, Katie Boals, Justine Brown, Shelly Metschan, Tourang Nazari and Karen Walsh assisted in the marketing and promotion of the book.

In addition, the manuscript benefited immensely from the writing talents of Merrill Douglass, Rob Gurwitt, John O'Leary and Jonathan Walters.

Lastly, we would like to thank all the state innovators, thinkers and doers we interviewed for the book, in particular, Governor Mitch Daniels, Governor Jennifer Granholm, Sean Connaughton, Dave Fletcher, Gopal Khanna, Alice Rivlin, Emily Stover DeRocco, Deborah Wince-Smith and Commissioner B.J. Walker.

Recent Deloitte Research public sector thought leadership

Red Ink Rising: The Journey to Fiscally Sustainable Government

Unlocking Government: How Data Transforms Democracy

If We Can Put a Man on the Moon ... Getting Big Things Done in Government (Harvard Business Press, 2009)

Partnering for Value: Structuring Effective Public-Private Partnerships for Infrastructure

The Changing Landscape for Infrastructure Funding and Finance

The Public Innovator's Playbook: Nurturing Bold Ideas in Government (Deloitte Research, 2008)

Changing the Game: The Role of the Private and Public Sectors in Protecting Data

Government Reform's Next Wave: Redesigning Government to Meet the Challenges of the 21st Century

Web 2.0: The Future of Collaborative Government

Changing Lanes: Addressing America's Congestion Problems Through Road User Pricing

Mastering Finance in Government: Transforming the Government Enterprise Through Better Financial Management

One Size Fits Few: Using Customer Insight to Transform Government

Bolstering Human Capital: How the Public Sector Can Beat the Coming Talent Crisis

Serving the Aging Citizen

Closing America's Infrastructure Gap: The Role of Public-Private Partnerships

Closing the Infrastructure Gap: The Role of Public-Private Partnerships

States of Transition: Tackling Government's Toughest Policy and Management Challenges

Building Flexibility: New Models for Public Infrastructure Projects

Pushing the Boundaries: Making a Success of Local Government Reorganization

Governing Forward: New Directions for Public Leadership

Paying for Tomorrow: Practical Strategies for Tackling the Public Pension Crisis

Medicaid Makeover: Six Tough (and Unavoidable) Choices on the Road to Reform

Driving More Money into the Classroom: The Promise of Shared Services

Are We There Yet: A Roadmap for Integrating Health and Human Services

Government 2.0: Using Technology to Improve Education, Cut Red Tape, Reduce Gridlock, and Enhance Democracy (Rowman and Littlefield, 2005)

Governing by Network: The New Shape of the Public Sector (Brookings, 2004)

Prospering in the Secure Economy

Combating Gridlock: How Pricing Road Use Can Ease Congestion

Citizen Advantage: Enhancing Economic Competitiveness through E-Government

Cutting Fat, Adding Muscle: The Power of Information in Addressing Budget Shortfalls

Show Me the Money: Cost-Cutting Solutions for Cash-Strapped States

Contacts

Robert N. Campbell III
U.S. State Government Leader
Deloitte LLP
Tel: +1 512 226 4210
E-mail: bcampbell@deloitte.com

John Skowron
Deloitte Consulting LLP
Tel: +1 412 402 5228
E-mail: jskowron@deloitte.com

Mark Davidoff
Deloitte Financial Advisory Services LLP
Tel: +1 313 396 3317
E-mail: mdavidoff@deloitte.com

Rene Hoffman
Deloitte & Touche LLP
Tel: +1 412 338 7302
E-mail: rehoffman@deloitte.com

Vincent Ferraro
Deloitte Tax LLP
Tel: +1 703 251 3450
E-mail: vferraro@deloitte.com

Commonwealth of Kentucky
John Hawkins
Tel: +1 502 562 2013
E-mail: jhawkins@deloitte.com

Commonwealth of Massachusetts
Michael J. Marino
Tel: +1 617 437 2310
E-mail: mmarino@deloitte.com

Commonwealth of Pennsylvania
Timothy A. Wiest
Tel: +1 717 651 6300
E-mail: twiest@deloitte.com

Commonwealth of Virginia
Eric D. Friedman
Tel: +1 216 589 5420
E-mail: efriedman@deloitte.com

State of California
Stephani Long
Tel: +1 916 288 3156
E-mail: stlong@deloitte.com

State of Colorado
Timothy A. Davis
Tel: +1 303 312 4062
E-mail: tidavis@deloitte.com

State of Florida
Thomas W. Walker
Tel: +1 404 631 3300
E-mail: tomwwalker@deloitte.com

State of Georgia
Thomas W. Walker
Tel: +1 404 631 3300
E-mail: tomwwalker@deloitte.com

State of Illinois
Ken Porrello
Tel: +1 312 486 3076
E-mail: kporrello@deloitte.com

State of Indiana
Mike Becher
Tel: +1 317 656 4300
E-mail: mbecher@deloitte.com

State of Louisiana
George A. Scott
Tel: +1 512 691 2397
E-mail: gscott@deloitte.com

State of Maine
Michael J. Marino
Tel: +1 617 437 2310
E-mail: mmarino@deloitte.com

State of Maryland
Mark Wiggins
Tel: +1 410 843 3222
E-mail: mawiggins@deloitte.com

State of Michigan
Mark Davidoff
Tel: +1 313 396 3317
E-mail: mdavidoff@deloitte.com

State of Minnesota
Steven D. Dahl
Tel: +1 612 397 4267
E-mail: stdahl@deloitte.com

State of New Mexico
Michael D. Phelan
Tel: +1 469 417 3585
E-mail: miphelan@deloitte.com

State of New York
Stewart Rog
Tel: +1 973 602 5275
E-mail: srog@deloitte.com

State of North Carolina
Winfield Shearin Jr.
Tel: +1 919 546 8029
E-mail: wshearin@deloitte.com

State of Texas
George A. Scott
Tel: +1 512 691 2397
E-mail: gscott@deloitte.com

State of Wisconsin
Jeffrey Bradfield
Tel: +1 312 486 5230
E-mail: jbradfield@deloitte.com

About the authors

William D. Eggers
Deloitte Services LP
Tel: 571-882-6585
Email: weggers@deloitte.com

An author, columnist, and popular speaker for two decades, **William Eggers** is a leading authority on government reform. As a global director for Deloitte Research, he is responsible for research and thought leadership for Deloitte's Public Sector industry practice. His new book (with John O'Leary) is *If We Can Put a Man on the Moon: Getting Big Things Done in Government* (Harvard Business Press, 2009).

His other books include *Governing by Network* (Brookings, 2004), *Government 2.0* (Rowman and Littlefield, 2005), and *The Public Innovator's Playbook* (Deloitte Research 2009). His writings have won numerous awards including the Louis Brownlow award for best book on public management, the Sir Antony Fisher award for best book promoting an understanding of the free economy, and the Roe Award for leadership and innovation in public policy research.

A former manager of the Texas Performance Review, he has advised governments around the world. His commentary has appeared in dozens of major media outlets including the *New York Times*, *Wall Street Journal*, *The Washington Post*, and the *Chicago Tribune*.

Robert N. Campbell III
Deloitte LLP
Tel: 512-226-4210
Email: bcampbell@deloitte.com

Robert N. Campbell III serves as vice chairman and U.S. State Government leader, Deloitte LLP, which includes audit, consulting, financial advisory services and tax services to the states. Bob oversees our services to state, local, education, public health care and nonprofit clients. He also works closely with Deloitte Research, the Deloitte Center for Health Solutions and the Deloitte Center for Network Innovation. Throughout his 37-year career with Deloitte, Bob has assisted government leaders at all levels with program planning and analysis, technology planning, business process transformation, performance improvement and reorganizational engagements.

Bob has worked closely with government leaders to address and resolve their critical policy, financing and operational issues at all levels of government. He has worked extensively with leaders of major federal agencies and more than 40 states on projects spanning central finance and administration, developmental disabilities, economic development, employment, higher education, human services, K-12 education, Medicaid, mental health, public health care, revenue and taxation, and student loan finance.

Tiffany Dovey Fishman
Deloitte Services LP
Tel: 571-882-6247
Email: tfishman@deloitte.com

Tiffany Dovey Fishman is a Research Manager with Deloitte Research where she has responsibility for public sector research and thought leadership. She has written extensively on a wide range of public policy and management issues and is the co-author of *States of Transition* (Deloitte Research, 2006). Tiffany's work has appeared in a number of publications, including *Public CIO*, *Governing* and *EducationWeek*. Tiffany holds a BA in philosophy and public health and community medicine from University of Washington and a Masters in Public Policy from The George Washington University.